10

Sir Philip Sidney and
the Poetics of Protestantism

Sir Philip Sidney and the Poetics of Protestantism

A Study of Contexts

Andrew D. Weiner
Associate Professor of English
University of Wisconsin, Madison

UNIVERSITY OF MINNESOTA PRESS • MINNEAPOLIS

Publication of this book was assisted by a grant
from the publications program of the National Endowment
for the Humanities, an independent federal agency.

The University of Minnesota Press
also acknowledges the support for its
program of the Andrew W. Mellon Foundation.
This book is one of those in whose financing
the Foundation's grant played a part.

Published by the University of Minnesota Press,
2037 University Avenue Southeast, Minneapolis, Minnesota 55414
Printed in the United States of America.

Second printing 1980.

The University of Minnesota is an equal-opportunity
educator and employer.

The University of Minnesota is an equal-opportunity
educator and employer.

Library of Congress Cataloging in Publication Data

Weiner, Andrew D
        Sir Philip Sidney and the poetics of Prot-
estantism.

        Includes bibliographical references and index.
        1. Sidney, Philip, Sir, 1554-1586. Countess of
Pembroke's Arcadia. 2. Sidney, Philip, Sir,
1554-1586. Apologie for poetrie. 3. Poetry.
4. Protestantism and literature. I. Title.
PR2342.A6W4   808.1   78-25559
ISBN 0-8166-0873-3

PREFACE

Learn aright why and how that maker made—Sidney's injunction to those who would read poetry—is still honored more in the breach than the observance. The more we learn about the culture of the Renaissance, the more we learn we must talk instead about its cultures, existing side by side more or less uneasily and relating to each other with greater or lesser degrees of hostility. There is no guarantee that an intellectual movement fashionable in one circle was not ignored, misunderstood, or attacked in another. From country to country, court to court, even faction to faction, vociferous—if not murderous—philosophical, theological, intellectual, ethical, aesthetic disagreement flourished. Catholic humanists attacked the methodology of scholasticism and were in turn reproached by the Protestants for intellectual cowardice and theological blindness. Lutherans and Reformed Protestants quarreled bitterly over basic assumptions about the nature of the sacraments reflecting what seemed to be fundamental differences in their conceptions of man's relationship to God. Neoplatonists, neo-Aristotelians, and neo-Stoics agreed to disagree and skeptics tried to rise above it all. If we are to follow Sidney's dictum, we shall have to depend less upon some monolithic conception of the Renaissance and pay more attention to the particular beliefs of each "maker," trying to identify the concerns and biases of the audience he hoped to reach.

What follows undertakes just that. If "every man's vision is directed by the metaphors which rule his mind,"[1] then without knowing something both about the way in which those metaphors create relationships between otherwise unrelatable things and about the way different relationships create new metaphors, we shall hardly be able to see the same kinds of things as the makers of those metaphors. One has only to compare two very different metaphors—say those of Erasmus and Luther—on the relationship between man and God to realize that with the Reformation some very basic and very drastic changes occurred in the way men saw their universe and themselves. For Erasmus, man's relationship to God is that of child to father:

A father raises his child, which is yet unable to walk, which has fallen and which exerts himself, and shows him an apple, placed in front of him. The boy likes to go and get it, but due to his weak bones would soon have fallen again, if the father had not supported him by his hand and guided his steps. Thus the child comes, led by the father, to the apple which the father places willingly into his hand, like a reward for walking. The child could not have raised itself without the father's help; would not have seen the apple without the father's showing; would not have stepped forward without the father's helping his little weak steps; would not have reached the apple without the father's placing it into his hand. What can the child claim for himself? Yet, he did do something, but he must not glory in his own strength, since he owes everything to the father.[2]

Luther's vision of the relationship between man's will and God involves a different, if equally traditional, metaphor: "Thus the human will is like a beast of burden. If God rides it, it wills and goes whence God wills. . . . If Satan rides, it wills and goes where Satan wills. Nor may it choose to which rider it will run, nor which it will seek. But the riders themselves contend who shall have it and hold it" (p. 112).

From Erasmus' metaphor, one can take heart at the thought that a child, sooner or later, after a sufficient amount of help from his father, does grow up. Erasmus' conclusion, "Man is able to accomplish all things, if God's grace aids him. Therefore it is possible that all works of man be good" (p. 78), follows from his metaphor. From it also follows the prayer Erasmus makes in the *Paraclesis*, the preface to his Greek and Latin edition of the *New Testament* (1516), a prayer for eloquence:

I indeed might heartily wish, if anything is to be gained by wishes of this kind, so long as I exhort all men to the most holy and wholesome study of Christian philosophy and summon them as if with the blast of a trumpet, that an eloquence far different from Cicero's be given me: an eloquence certainly more efficacious, if less ornate than his. . . . an eloquence which not only captivates the ear with its fleeting delight but leaves a lasting sting in the minds of its hearers, which grips, which transforms, which sends away a far different listener than it had received.[3]

In Erasmus' conception of his role as helper and educator, he will "exhort" and "summon" his reader, hoping to present what he would have him learn so persuasively that the wisdom thus gained will "transform" the mind of his reader, enabling him to "walk" a little better than he could before. Literature, then, may function to help man put aside his childishness, to grow up a little faster than he would otherwise be able.

The aesthetic difference between Erasmus' Catholicism and Luther's Protestantism is as great as the distinction between their views of man's ability to choose good freely. As Luther rejects Erasmus' "moderate middle way" of allowing "a certain little to free will" (*Discourse*, p. 132), so he also rejects the possibility of eloquence being efficacious. Where Erasmus created his argument by comparing passages and interpretations, interweaving a commentary urging one set of conclusions on the grounds they were more probable than another, Luther feels flat statement is sufficient: "That you have failed is quite clear from this: 'you assert nothing, but have made comparisons.' One who is fully acquainted with the matter and understands it, does not write like that. On the contrary . . . I have not made comparisons, but have asserted and still do assert. I wish none to become judges, but urge all men to submit!" (p. 138). Behind this notion lies Luther's conviction that not he but God must be efficacious if conversion — not persuasion — is to occur; that of himself he can do nothing to make the truth more attractive. Either his readers will see the truth or they will not. If they do, it is neither their doing nor his but God's; if they do not, again, it is not because he has failed but because God has so willed. All he need do is state his truth — itself the gift of the Holy Spirit — and let God do the rest:

And who knows but that God may even condescend to visit you, dearest

Erasmus, through me, His poor weak vessel, and that I may . . . come to you in this book in a happy hour and gain a dearest brother. . . . I shall be even more grateful if you gain greater certainty through me, just as I have gained in assurance through you [i.e., by remaining unmoved by any of Erasmus' arguments]. But both are the gift of the Spirit, and not the work of our own endeavours. So we should pray to God that He will open my mouth, and your and all men's hearts: that He may be the teacher in the midst of us, who may in us speak and hear. [Pp. 98-99]

If literature cannot persuade man to put aside his childishness, what function is left for literature? If all that is needed is a voice crying out in the wilderness for those whose ears have been opened, what need is there for eloquence? None at all, if the speaker of Wyatt's second satire is to be trusted:

> Alas, my Poynz, how men do seke the best
> > And fynde the wourst by errour as they stray!
> > And no marvaill, when sight is so opprest,
> > And blynde the gyde; anon owte of the way
> > Goeth gyde and all in seking quyete liff.
> . . . .
> Then seke no more owte of thy self to fynde
> > The thing that thou haist sought so long before,
> > For thou shalt fele it sitting in thy mynde.
> Madde, if ye list to continue your sore,
> > Let present passe and gape on time to com
> > And diepe your self in travaill more and more.
> Hens fourth, my Poyngz, this shalbe all and some:
> > These wretched fooles shall have nought els of me
> > But to the great god and to his high dome
> None othre pain pray I for theim to be
> > But when the rage doeth led them from the right
> > That lowking backward vertue they may se
> Evyn as she is so goodly fayre and bright;
> > And while they claspe their lustes in armes a-crosse,
> > Graunt theim, goode lorde, as thou maist of thy myght,
> To frete inward for losing suche a losse.[4]

If the reader of the poem must "make playn" (line 92) his heart, the poet must make plain his poem so that even those who read, and know, and cannot do may know what it is they cannot do. The speaker's final prayer, it seems to me, is less pettish than pitying, for only if God takes pity on them and shows them what they have turned from, making them feel "inwards" their loss, will they ever know their own insufficiency and turn elsewhere for help.

If most men are indeed, as Sidney suggests, "childish in the best things, till they be cradled in their graves,"[5] poetry would seem to be able to do very little more than plainly tell them so, and the Protestant poets of the middle third of the century are notably plain in doing so. The Wyatt of the Psalms and the Satires, Barnaby Googe, and George Gascoigne exemplify the plain style of English Renaissance verse and all are notably Protestant.[6] It is, one might say, their very plainness that gives to their poems whatever power they may have. "Gascoignes Lullabie" may stand as a case in point. A six-stanza poem, it begins by announcing that the speaker has "full many wanton babes . . . / which must be stilld with lullabie" and proceeds to sing to rest his "youthfull yeares," his "gazing eyes," his "wanton will," and "Robyn," his sexual appetite. As the metaphor suggests, however, singing them to sleep will only still them for a while:

> *With Lullabye nowe take your leaue,*
> *With Lullabye youre dreames deceyue,*
> *And when you rise with waking eye,*
> *Remembre Gascoignes Lullabye.*[7]

Whether the "you" of the penultimate line is Gascoigne's "wanton babes" or the reader, it is clear that nothing will have changed save that we have been invited, once again, to see ourselves plainly for what we are and cannot help being. Erasmus' growing child has been replaced by a Protestant "old babe," as Gascoigne puts it in "Gascoigne's Woodsmanship." The poem, then, exists to accomplish nothing except to state that it cannot accomplish anything and to ask us to remember that. With this recognition, the poetry of the first generation of English Protestant poets has, in a sense, summed up its existential uncertainty. If for no other reason than the psychological health of poets, a new justification for the existence of poetry had to be found lest it perish under the attacks of those like Stephen Gosson, whose *Schoole of Abuse* (1579), dedicated to Philip Sidney, begins by condemning those plays that seem immoral to Gosson but ends by concluding, somewhat reluctantly, that even "moral" plays must be suppressed.

It is precisely this renewal of purpose that Sidney attempts in his *Defence of Poesie*, the focus of my first chapter. In it I attempt to sketch the ethical and political contexts that shed light on the aesthetic he created through his new synthesis of some fairly traditional ideas, ideas which were transformed in the process. In so doing, some basic perspectives emerge for the study not simply of Sidney's works, but also for those of poets with whom he associated (like Greville), or who shared many of his concerns (like Spenser), or who tried to follow his example (like Daniel), or who had to decide at some point in their poetic careers how useful to them Sidney's poetics was (like Shakespeare or Milton).[8] I have tried to show how firmly Sidney's poetics is rooted in the ideas and emotions that shaped his time as he perceived it by considering the psychological impact on Sidney and his circle both of Reformed Protestantism's basic theological conceptions about man's nature and of the political crisis of the late 1570s precipitated by Elizabeth's French flirtation. Sidney was very much a man whose vision was limited by his ideas and whose relationship to his age was shaped in large part by his impatience with its failure to conform to his ideals of what it should be.

In the succeeding chapters I turn to Sidney's *Old Arcadia* as a test case. Paul Alpers has suggested that Sidney's "decisive analytic intelligence . . . is his greatest strength as a writer,"[9] and that intelligence may be seen at work most clearly in the *Old Arcadia*. Although the *Old Arcadia* is very much a young man's book in the severity and absoluteness of its moral judgments, it is less because Sidney "identifies intelligence with judging" (see Alpers, p. 293) than because he perceives man himself as always being weighed against absolute moral standards and as always being doomed to fail to measure up to them so long as he stands for justice, a Shylock in a court more universal than Venice.

Critical discussion of the *Old Arcadia* has often gone astray by failing to recognize the generic clues Sidney provides; I have therefore devoted a chapter each to analyses of the characters and the eclogues according to Sidney's conception of genre in the *Defence*. My discussion of the characters intends to show that they are clearly shaped to fit Sidney's definition of comedy. The chapter on the eclogues likewise attempts to define their choral relationship to the five prose "books or acts" in which they are placed. In the final chapter I argue that to understand what Sidney means we must first understand how he makes us feel about his work as we experience it. My discussion of the *Old Arcadia*'s structure is also an exploration of Sidney's ability to give to the "airy nothing" of his theory a "local habitation and a name" or, as he put it, to show that his "delivering forth" of his "*idea* or fore-conceit" is not "wholly imaginative, as we are wont to say by them that build castles in air" but something rather more substantial (*MP*, 79).

An examination of Sidney's theory and practice within the framework I have described seems to me to suggest an alternative to the theories of Paul Alpers and Stanley Fish, each of whom, in the course of arguing the case for the importance of the reader — a case in which I should like to join — has tended to dissolve the structures of the works they discuss so that

> *That which is now a horse, even with a thought*
> *The rack dislimns, and makes it indistinct*
> *As water is in water.*
> [*Antony and Cleopatra*, 4.14.9-11]

I suggest instead that Sidney anticipates a mutually transforming relationship in which the work, always there in memory and on paper (growing more and more distinct as we return to it on repeated reading), offers itself as a means whereby we may journey imaginatively, intellectually, and emotionally to that "*idea* or fore-conceit" which was the poet's starting point and use it as a foundation upon which we may build a castle "not wholly imaginative" in which to dwell.

It may be said by some that this reading of the *Old Arcadia* reduces it from a work of literature to a Protestant (or, for those who are given to pejoratives, Calvinist) tractate and simultaneously turns the *Defence* into little more than a handbook for propaganda writers. From this view I should like to dissent in advance. De Mornay's *A Woorke concerning the trewnesse of the Christian Religion* is a Protestant tractate, and Sidney's motives in translating it (since neither compensation nor mere friendship will suffice as grounds for engaging upon such an extensive project) may be assumed to agree with those of its creator. The *Old Arcadia*, though it arises out of a similar view of life, has a different form. It is a poem, not a polemic; its aim is not merely to teach but to delight and teach that it may move. It is not a presentation but an embodiment of a world view within the form of a fiction, not a statement of dogma but a reflection of a world as seen through the deeply held beliefs of its maker. If I am correct, its hope was not to convert its readers to that view but to console them with it, and the nature of that consolation grows primarily not from the ideational content of the fore-conceit but from the emotional response the work arouses in its readers.

This book intends to provoke rethinking the way in which we approach the literature of the English Renaissance generally by examining the poetic which may have helped to call much of that literature into being and to reappraise one of the period's most impressive literary achievements. If it succeeds, thanks will be due to a great many of my friends and colleagues. Tom Roche endured an earlier version of chapters 2 and 3 long ago and with graciousness, but many others have since been enlisted, willingly or not, into the cause. Richard Lanham, S. K. Heninger, Ray Waddington, Bob Kimbrough, Joe Wittreich, and Madeleine Doran have read various parts of this book and offered many useful suggestions; whatever faults it may contain are to be laid not at their feet but at my own. John Shawcross and Norman Farmer have forced much clarity into my conceptions through their patient attendance at my monologues, for without them to provoke me to particularity I might never have been able to come up with any generalizations that could stand. Earlier versions of chapter 1, part III appeared in *Journal of Medieval and Renaissance Studies* 2 (1972): 259-78 (Copyright 1972 by Duke University Press), and in *Texas Studies in Language and Literature* 18 (1976): 341-61, esp. 341-44 (Copyright 1976 by the University of Texas Press); I thank the editors for permission to reprint them here. Research grants from the University of Wisconsin Graduate School and the National Endowment for the Humanities helped get this book written. My greatest debt is to my wife, Sonja, who is at once my harshest critic and my greatest encouragement. It is to her and to my children, Heather, Adam, and Holly, that I dedicate this book.

A. D. W.
Madison, Wisconsin
January 1978

CONTENTS

*Sir Philip Sidney and
the Poetics of Protestantism*

CHAPTER 1

"The knowledge of a man's self, in the ethic and politic consideration": The Sidney Milieu

The knowledge of our selves no doubte ought to be most pretious vnto us; and therein the holy scriptures, if not the only, are certainly the incomperable lanterne in this fleshly darkness of ours: For (alas) what is all knowledge? if in the end of this litle and weerisome pilgrimage, Hell become our scoolmaster.

Philip Sidney to Edward Denny,
May 22, 1580[1]

Although recent studies of Sidney and his works have begun to dispel the romantic image of the courtier-lover-poet that was for so long an obstacle to the understanding of his works, no clear and consistent portrait of the man in the context of his times has yet fully emerged to take its place.[2] Sidney, as James M. Osborn's recent biography of his formative years confirms, was not raised to be a poet, but a statesman; and his conception of statecraft was dependent upon his conception of man's purpose in life, a conception which was in turn informed by his adherence to the "true religion." When, through his overzealous advocacy of a league of Protestant states and his overblunt discussion of her proposed French marriage, he overstepped the bounds of Elizabeth's tolerance and she no longer found him useful as a diplomat, he turned to poetry. He did not forget those ideas, however, but rather tried to achieve them through another mode of endeavor. When, finally, the obstacles to his political career began to fall away, he apparently ceased writing poetry and attempted instead to achieve his goals through action, in the course of which

3

he met his death. Without an understanding of the manner in which Sidney's thought was shaped and of the political situation in which he found his theater for action, no comprehensive assessment of Sidney's literary achievement is possible.

To understand Sidney's poetic career, then, we must consider, at least briefly, the forces that shaped the Sidney his associates knew. Fulke Greville, Sidney's closest friend throughout his life and his memorialist afterwards, insists that Sidney's "chief ends" were not "Friends, Wife, Children, or himself; but above all things the honour of his Maker, and service of his Prince, or Country."[3] This dual concern is everywhere manifested in Sidney's letters, especially those to Languet, where the most commonplace thought is likely at any time to set off a chain of reflections leading to either religion or politics (or both, since for Sidney politics is ultimately an appendage of religion whose concern is to further God's cause in the world).[4] Thus, in the course of telling Languet that he will follow his advice for improving his style in Latin and Italian, Sidney comments "there are some things also which I wish to learn of the Greeks, which hitherto I have but skimmed on the surface. But the chief object of my life, next to the everlasting blessedness of heaven, will always be the enjoyment of true friendship, and there you shall have the chiefest place."[5] Similarly, in response to a rather doleful catalog of recent continental political setbacks from Languet, Sidney offers consolation to his mentor in an interesting analysis of contemporary affairs:

I entreat you to look at the wounds from which the Church of God is now suffering, singly and separately, that you may not by an accumulation of ills be tempted to despair. I mean, for example, that you should consider the troubles of France by themselves, and not crowd into the same picture, your own misfortunes and those of Flanders too. . . . The last part of your lamentation, is upon the danger which seems to threaten Italy from the Turk; and yet, if this should come to pass, what could be more desirable. First of all that rotten member will be removed, which has now so long infected the whole Christian body; and the forge in which, as you observe, are wrought the moving springs of all these ills will be swept away: and then will the Princes of Christendom be forced to wake up from their deep sleep; and your countrymen, who are now cutting each other's throats, will be driven to join forces.[6]

Sidney's conclusion, like the one Languet drew from events four years later, is clearly that "all this has proceeded directly from the Providence of God, and contrary to our calculations."[7]

Sidney's faith in the providence of God and his desire to heed the call he felt he heard to contribute to the working out of its designs are essential to any understanding of "why and how that maker made," and consequently must direct the beginning steps of this study. I shall turn first to a consideration of how Sidney's Protestantism shaped his assumptions about the nature of man's life and next to an examination of the stage upon which Sidney's life was played before concluding this introductory chapter by considering Sidney's poetic as expressed in the *Defence of Poesie*.

I. "There is a hyer power that must uphold me"
(*Prose Works*, 3:167)

To determine the exact point along the religious spectrum where Sidney's religious beliefs lay would be a difficult and largely fruitless task.[8] The lines, later to be more clearly drawn between Puritan and Anglican, had not yet solidified in the 1560s and 1570s, the years of Sidney's schooling and travels, the years too of Languet's mentorship and Sidney's first entry into court and diplomatic service, and his first efforts as a poet. Geoffrey Shepherd has suggested that Sidney "can be termed a Puritan, but a first generation Puritan, of the years before Cartwright gave English Puritanism its later doctrinaire complexion."[9] Although this seems to be a sensible conclusion, there are several difficulties to be taken into account. Sidney's uncle, the Earl of Leicester, was Cartwright's patron,[10] and Sidney himself patronized "doctrinaire" Puritans. James Stiles, a Puritan lecturer in London whose license to preach was suspended in 1574, became Sidney's chaplain in 1582 and held that post until Sidney's death in 1586.[11] Another of Sidney's chaplains—and one of the two who were present at his deathbed—was George Gifford, a nonconforming minister who was suspended in London in 1584 for publicly refusing to subscribe to Whitgift's *ex officio* oath.[12] Before we conclude that

Shepherd's qualification should be ignored, however, we must consider that when Leicester was accused by Thomas Wood, formerly one of the elders of the Marian congregation at Geneva, of being chiefly responsible for the suppression of the Southam prophesying, his defence (which consists for the most part of a mixture of denial and self-praise for all he has done for the cause) concluded with the statement that he found "the substance" of the true religion to be "soundely and godly set forth in this Universall Church of England . . . which doctrine and religion I wish to be obeyed dewly as it ought of all subjects in this land, and that men seek not so farr to perswade the mislyking thereof for some particular respects that they doe more hurt to the generall then ever it may lye in them to repay agayne. . . . If these divisions or discentions shold continue awhile as it hath done of late yeares . . . such inconveniences must follow to the Church as all true gospellers in deed shalbe sory for."[13] Evidently, one could support Puritans fervently in the 1570s without accepting their definition of discipline, yet it is precisely the issue of discipline that has come to define Puritanism for most modern scholars.

The difficulty, I think, is one of terminology and chronology. One cannot apply a term which later in its history comes to acquire certain meanings to a period before those meanings were clearly developed without doing a certain amount of damage to the clarity of his argument. In talking of the 1560s, 1570s, and 1580s, it might be better to adopt contemporary terminology and refer to those who might later have been Puritans by the term which they most frequently use to describe themselves, the "godly." The defining mark of the godly, I suggest, is to be found not in adherence to any one particular set of doctrines or any one particular definition of discipline, but in the zeal with which they applied their religious convictions to their daily life. Thus, despite Leicester's possible role in the suppressing of the Southam exercise, Wood can still speak of the earl in a letter to his brother Ambrose Dudley, Earl of Warwick, as one of the "zealous mayntainers of his [God's] glory and of the true professors thereof, I meane specially of those faithfull ministers whom none can justly reprove either in doctrine or in life, and yet of the wicked worldlings and vaine courtiers falsly termed Puritanes."[14] While questions of discipline and vestments may have been burning issues to ministers about to be deprived for nonconformity and to flocks facing the loss of their preacher, to those godly Protestants rich enough to have their own chaplains and zealous enough to want to reform the Church by patronizing a learned preaching ministry the various controversies must have seemed like so many annoyances, caused by the stiffness of both bishops and ministers.

Godly aristocrats like the Earls of Leicester, Warwick, and Huntington (all Sidney's uncles), Bedford (Warwick's father-in-law), Pembroke (the second earl was Sidney's brother-in-law) or godly (but non-noble) privy councillors like Sir Henry Sidney, Sir Francis Walsingham (Sidney's father-in-law as of 1583), and Sir Walter Mildmay (Walsingham's brother-in-law)[15] would have seen their calling as providing them with the obligation of promoting and supporting a godly ministry as a means of advancing Protestantism.[16] As Patrick Collinson remarks, "Lively, rather than formal faith was generated by preaching, regarded by protestants as 'the ordinary means of faith,' and by the printing presses,"[17] and these godly members of what I shall call the Sidney circle patronized both. So long as a minister was zealous in preaching, godly in life, and Protestant in doctrine, he could probably expect one of them to come to his aid should need arise. Increasingly, throughout the late seventies and the eighties, need did arise as more and more preachers were called before ecclesiastical commissions on charges of nonconformity. As Collinson says of the Protestant noblemen and gentlemen of whom we have been speaking, "The formularies of the Elizabethan settlement were no delineation of their religion, and like the preachers whose interest they advanced, they must have regarded that settlement as imperfect and provisional. Their outlook was international, and increasingly so as the ideological struggle of the later sixteenth century intensified. Consequently only two religions were recognized in most places in Elizabethan England and 'Anglicanism' was not one of them."[18] To the godly, their less zealous fellows were not members of some other religious sect, they were merely "cold statute protestants";[19] the two religions in England were Reformed Protestantism and Roman Catholicism, and the role of the godly preacher was to eradicate the latter by inflaming them with the transforming zeal born of conversion.[20] On occasion this effort brought them into conflict with Elizabeth's policies and thus created a need for the aid and protection of those of the godly in a position to offer it.

When one turns to the "substance" of the religion of the godly, difficulties again appear in the way of an exact description. One can say with some confidence that Sidney and his circle would have seen Calvin as a definitive interpreter of their faith. Sidney's maternal grandfather, the Duke of Northumberland, brought England to its closest point of contact with Geneva during his tenure as head of Edward VI's council, and Leicester and Warwick were apparently raised as "Calvinists."[21] Sidney's education at Shrewsbury School took place under the direction of Thomas Ashton, the headmaster, who was well known for his zeal, and one of Sidney's first purchases upon coming to Shrewsbury was a copy of Calvin's catechism.[22] His closest friends, Fulke Greville, Hubert Languet, John Casimir, and Philip de Mornay, have likewise all been called Calvinists.[23] Yet the term "Calvinist" is as temporally confusing as its English equivalent, "Puritan." To say that someone is a Calvinist in the middle of the sixteenth century does not necessarily mean the same thing as it would in the years after Calvin's death when his successors began the process of "canonizing" Calvin and his works. Calvin's theology at Geneva had not yet become an enshrined dogmatic system totally distinct from the doctrines of the other founders of the reformed church. In the 1570s, the reformed Swiss, French, German, and English churches had to defend themselves from the attacks of both the Roman Catholics and the Lutherans; Bullinger's *Second Helvetic Confession* (1566), issued in the name of the Swiss Cantons (including Geneva) and the German Palatinate in defense of reformed Protestantism, could be subscribed to by the reformed churches of Scotland (1566), Hungary (1567), Neufchâtel (1568), Basle, France (1571), and Poland (1571 and 1578).[24] Since the *Second Helvetic Confession* stands as the most generally accepted sixteenth-century statement of the reformed faith, I shall use it along with Philip de Mornay's *A Woorke concerning the trewnesse of the Christian Religion* (which Sidney translated) as the basis of my discussion of the religious ideas that shaped the way Sidney saw his world.[25]

And yet, one must pause for a moment at the thought of such

an enterprise. Theology, particularly, it seems, the formal doctrinal theology of the late sixteenth century, is no longer a subject capable of arousing much interest in most readers. Yet, as H. C. Porter has commented, "the doctrines of grace and predestination, reflecting, in their immense complication, simple convictions about the sort of being God is and the kind of creature man is, concern not merely theology but all aspects of the human condition: literature, psychology, politics, to mention no others."[26] Of necessity, then, it is to those "simple convictions" that we must now turn.

Although it might fittingly be said that the doctrine of Reformed Protestantism begins and ends with God, we will do well to begin our exposition of it instead with man. Hamlet offers us one view in his comments to Rosencrantz and Guildenstern: "What a piece of work is man, how noble in reason, how infinite in faculties; in form and moving how express and admirable, in action how like an angel, in apprehension how like a god: the beauty of the world, the paragon of animals!"[27] This image corresponds to the *Confession*'s picture of man at his creation: "Man was in the beginning created of God, after his Image, in righteousness, and true holines, good, and vertuous" (sig. C). After his fall, however, this image was defaced by sin, "That naturall corruption of man, derived or spronge from those our first parentes to us all, wherwith we being drowned in wicked concupiscence, geven to no good, but prone to all mischiefe, ful of naughtinesse, distrust, contempte, and hatred of God, are able of our selves to doo, no not so muche as to thinke any good" (sig. C).[28]

In this state man stands. His reason, the "inward light" (*MP*, 91) God gave man to rule his passion, is "both weak and immersed in darkness."[29] With his "noble" and "god"-like reason so debased, it is hardly surprising to find that man's "action" is no longer angelic. According to the *Confession*, after the fall, man "was not bereft of his understandyng, his will was not taken from him, & he cleane chaunged into a stone or a blocke, yet those giftes were so altered & diminished in him, that they were not so excellent, or able to doo so much, as they were before his fall. For his knowledge was darkned, his will was made bonde, whereas before it was free: for nowe it serueth sinne not unwillingly, but willingly, for it is called Will . . . therefore as touching wickednesse or sinne, man

not compelled either of God, or the Diuell, but of his owne motion, doth euell, and in this behalfe hath freewill, to doo mischiefe"
(sigs. C₃v-C₄).³⁰ Fallen man, then, rather than being "the beauty
of the world, the paragon of animals," has instead been reduced to
the "quintessence of dust."

Hence Calvin argues that, "since reason, by which man discerns
between good and evil, and by which he understands and judges, is
a natural gift, it could not be entirely destroyed; but being partly
weakened and partly corrupted, a shapeless ruin is all that remains"
(*Institutes*, 2.2.12). It is in acknowledgement of that "first accursed fall of Adam" (*MP*, 79) that Sidney qualifies the function
of "learning" as he does: "the final end is to lead and draw us to
as high a perfection as our degenerate souls, made worse by their
clayey lodgings, can be capable of" (*MP*, 82). Thus, too, although
he acknowledges that "learned men have learnedly thought that
where once reason hath so much overmastered passion as that the
mind hath a free desire to do well, the inward light each mind hath
in itself is as good as a philosopher's book" (*MP*, 91), he insists
that even if our "erected wit"—a term we must return to shortly—
"maketh us know what perfection is . . . yet our infected will
keepeth us from reaching unto it" (*MP*, 79).

Man, whether "regenerate . . . [or] not regenerate," may have a
truly free will in "outwarde things: for man hath his constitution
as other liuing creatures haue, that he will doo one thing and will
not doo an other thinge" (sig. C₆ᵛ), but he is still dependent upon
God's mercy for leaving him this remnant of his wit, for "It is
manifest how litell or nothing we profite in any arte, without the
blessing of God. Truely . . . all sciences come of him" (sig. C₅).
Yet if man is thus dependent where his will is free, what is his case
in spiritual matters, where his freedom is merely freedom to be the
slave of sin? As de Mornay says, "We be free to followe our owne
Nature; and our Nature is becomme euill through sinne. O wretched
freedome, which bringeth vs vnder such bondage! And a fore this
nature of ours, we can neither shun it nor drive it from vs: for we
be bondslaves to it, and it to sinne, and there behoueth a stronger
than ourselves to rid vs thereof. Therefore let vs pray God to bring
the freedome of our wills in bondage to his will, and free our soules
from this hard and damnable kind of freedome" (sig. O₈ᵛ).

Although man has cut himself off from God, God has not abandoned man. Despite man's leap into the bondage of sin when he turned away from God and fell, God has given him His law, in which is "declared to vs his will, what he would, and what he would not haue vs to doe, what is good and iuste, what is euill and vniuste. . . . This lawe was bothe written with the finger of God, in the hartes of men, and is called the lawe of nature: and also . . . it was grauen with the finger of God, in the twoo Tables of Moises" (*Confession*, sig. D$_7$^{v}). Because of the transformation of man's nature, because his will is now free only to do evil, God's law can serve not as a guide to be followed but only as an indictment of man's evil. As the *Confession* says, "This Lawe is not geuen to man, to the ende he should be iustified, by the keepyng and obseruyng it, but rather, that by the knowledge of the lawe, he might acknowledge his infirmitie, sinne and condemnacion, and dispaire of any helpe by his owne strength" (sig. D$_8$). Man's heart is thus left only the power to feel its own deformity as it looks into the mirror of the Law.

Through the law written both in his heart and in stone, then, man knows that God exists, that He created everything including man, and that God is good; he knows also how far from God he is. The law teaches him that the way to God is by righteousness, for God is righteousness; yet the law also teaches him how far from righteousness he is, and his heart convicts him of his own unrighteousness and bids him fear God's wrath. God, however, has offered man more than a reason for despair, for He has given him a way to return to Him through religion. As de Mornay says in his dedicatory epistle to Henry of Navarre, "Religion (to speake properlie) is nothing else but the schoole wherin we learne mans dutie towards God, and the way to be linked most straightly vnto him. . . . The duty therfore of trew Religion, is to conuict vs by the Law, and to iustifie vs by grace, to make vs feele our disease, and therewithall to offer vs remedy" (*A Woorke*, sigs. **-**^{v}). "Trew" religion does this by teaching us that God Himself has devised the way to satisfy His wrath, to bring us to Himself, and to link us "most straightly" to Him.

Man's part in this operation of salvation is nil, according to the *Confession*, for his sin bars him from any useful participation: "By the law cometh knowledge of our synnes: For if there had been a lawe giuen, which could haue giuen life, surely rightuousnes should a been by the lawe: but the scripture concludeth all vnder synne, that the promes thorowe faithe in Jesus Christe, would be giuen to theim that beleue: wherefore the lawe was a schole master, to bring vs to Christe, that wee maie bee made rightuous by faithe. Neither could, nor yet any flesh is able, to satisfie the law of God, and to fulfill it, for the weakenes that is in our fleshe, and still remaineth in vs, euen to our laste gaspe" (sigs. D$_8$ -D$_8$^{v}). *Because* man could not and cannot satisfy the Law, God must do so if religion is not to be merely "a definitive sentence of death, and an expresse condemning of vs" (*A Woorke*, sig. Z^v). This "God performed, by sendyng his owne soonne, in the forme of fleshe, subiecte to synne. Therefore Christe is the perfection of the Lawe, and hath fulfilled it for vs:who, as he did beare the cursse of the lawe, while he was made accursed for our sakes, so he maketh vs by faithe, partakers of his fulfillyng of the Lawe, his rightuousnes and obedience beying accepted, as though it were ours" (*Confession*, sig. D$_8$^{v}).

Man's inability to satisfy God's law, his inability to achieve righteousness, thus redounds to his benefit, for by making God perforce the author of his salvation he makes his salvation sure. As de Mornay says, "if neither ye world nor man can dischardge man against God, what remayneth to doe it, but God himselfe, whom Religion must offer to man for his discharge; even God mercifull, to God iust; God a paymaster, to God the creator. . . . For it is only God that both doth and can satisfie himself" (*A Woorke*, sig. Z^v).[31] This realization lies at the heart of reformed Protestantism and, in a sense, defines and shapes all of its other conceptions of man, his duties and responsibilities, and of God. In place of the traditional Catholic view of man working out his salvation in fear and trembling, through "prayers, tears, fasting, sackcloth, and ashes," but especially through the works of charity, since "kindness to our neighbor actually, if I may use the expression, wrests it [i.e., mercy] from Him,"[32] the reformers offered man a new view of his relationship to God.

This new relationship can be seen emerging from the older conception in Sir Thomas Wyatt's version of the Penitential Psalms. His David, like Calvin's, is a "mirror" in which we can see "both the commencement of [our] . . . calling, and the continued course of . . . [our] function.''[33] David, in fact, becomes the prototypical Reformed Protestant and the Psalms (which Sidney began to translate with his sister) "An Anatomy of all the Parts of the Soul" because, as Calvin suggests, "there is not an emotion of which any one can be conscious that is not here represented as in a mirror. Or rather, the Holy Spirit has here drawn to the life all the griefs, sorrows, fears, doubts, hopes, cares, perplexities, in short all the distracting emotions with which the minds of men are wont to be agitated."[34] David's qualifications for "mirror" are obvious: the man chosen by God, he nevertheless falls into sin yet repents and is vouchsafed a prophetic vision of Christ.

Wyatt's David discovers, painfully, that his own virtues, no matter how great, are not sufficient to let him stand without falling:

> *And when myn enmys did me most assayle,*
> *My frendes most sure, wherein I sett most trust,*
> *Myn own vertues, sonest then did ffaile,*
> *And stond apart, reason and witt vniust,*
> *As kyn vnkynd were fardest gone at nede.*
>
> [Psalm 38, poem 108. 364-68]

To the reformers, the old formulations of man's duty to God must be dismissed because they are untrue. If man seeks mercy, it must be as a freely given gift, not something "wrested" from a God who must fulfill a contract. If man is to be justified, it must be by God, not by his own works. As Wyatt's David proclaims,

> *But off thi sellff, o god, this operation*
> *It must proced, by purging me from blood,*
> *Among the just that I may have relation;*
> *And off thy lawdes for to let owt the flood;*
> *Thow must, o lord, my lypps furst vnlose:*
> *Ffor if thou hadst estemid plesant good*
> *The ovttward dedes that owtward men disclose,*
> *I wold have offerd vnto the sacryfice.*
> *But thou delyghtes not in no such glose*
> *Off owtward dede, as men dreme and devyse.*
>
> [Psalm 51, 108. 490-99]

God does not demand that man "work" for salvation; he offers it freely through faith given by grace.[35] In return man can only try to offer his love and his reverence. As David says,

> Ffor, lord, if thou do observe what men offend
> And putt thi natyf mercy in restraint,
>   If just exaction demaund recompense,
>   Who may endure o lord, who shall not faynt
> At such acompt? dred, and not reuerence,
>   Shold so raine large. But thou sekes rather love,
>   Ffor in this hand is mercys resedence,
> By hope wheroff thou dost our hertes move.
>
> [Psalm 130, 108. 675-82]

By changing the relationship between God and man, the reformers also changed the rhythms of man's life. No longer striving to do good works in order to win salvation,[36] those men who have been called to God ("by the meane of preachyng the Gospel and faithfull praier" [*Confession*, sig. F₃ᵛ]), who have been given the faith to see that the law has been fulfilled by Christ and have thus felt its burden lifted from themselves,[37] are now "free" to respond in kind. As the *Confession* insists, those who have been regenerated and have turned to God receive the Holy Spirit as a gift: "In regeneration the mind is inspired with the holy spirite, to vnderstand and know the secretes & will of God. And the will is not onely chaunged by Gods Spirite, but is made of habilitie also of her owne accorde to be willing, and able to doo good. Except we graunt this, we shall denie Christian libertie, and shal bring in, the bondage of the lawe" (sig. C₅). But while man is "free" to be "willing" to do good, he is not always able to achieve that goodness he seeks to perform: "we must note that an infirmitie and feblenes remayneth in them which be regenerated. For seeinge that sinne dwelleth in them, and the flesh (although thei be borne a new) striueth against the spirite, as longe as they live, thei doo not altogether without comberaunce bringe that to passe, which they determined" (*Confession*, sigs. C₅ᵛ-C₆).

Christian liberty then consists not in a will capable of achieving what it knows it should desire, but in desiring to will what it cannot always bring to pass. As Bullinger insists, "weake is our freewill by reason of the dregges of old Adam, and the naturall corruption of maner, stickinge faste in vs to our liues ende. Howbeit, seinge that the stre*n*gth of the fleshe & reliques of the olde man be not so stronge, & of such puisance as vtterly to suppresse & conquere the woorking of the spirit, therfore the faithful are said to be free, yet so that they acknowledge their infirmitie & weakenesse, without bostinge & bragginge of their freewill" (sig. C₆).[38] Christian life, by the same token, consists not in the achievement of perfection but in the attempt to desire to reach perfection and the awareness that our failure in the attempt is the mark of our constant dependence upon God.

Even for regenerate man — in fact especially for regenerate man — constant gazing in the glass of man's own incapacity is necessary to keep him faithful to God. As de Mornay observes, "If God should hold vs always by the hand, it is certeyne that we could neuer trippe. And it is not to be doubted also, but that we would think at the length, that it was of our owne steadynesse, and not of Gods vpholding of vs, not only that we tripped not, but also that wee tumbled not downe. For what made vs fall but pride: and what maner of pride, but that we thought we would be Gods without God, yea even of our selves? Now, to make vs to knowe our infirmitie, wherin it is his pleasure to shew his strength: sometymes he letteth vs goe alone by our selves for a while, and then stumble we at the next job that we meete with. Neverthelesse, this tripping and stumbling saueth vs from a greater fall: for it maketh vs to call for his hand to hold vs up" (*A Woorke*, sigs. O-Oᵛ). In the rhythm of life thus seen, failure is the cause of "success," for "the falles of the vertuous . . . [are] but quickenings vp vnto vertue" (*A Woorke*, sig. Oᵛ).

In a sense, then, we might say that at the heart of the Reformed Protestant's notion about what makes a life "holy" is the perhaps paradoxical formulation that the godly life is one of "daiely" repentance (*Confession*, sig. G₄ᵛ). Bullinger defines repentance as "the amendement of the mynde, in the sinfull man, provoked therevnto by the preaching of the Gospell, and inward woorking of the holie ghost, and receiued with true faithe, wherby the synner doth straite waie acknowledge his naturall corruption: and all his synnes reproued by the woorde of God" (*Confession*, sig. E₄).

The consequences of this self-recognition follow inevitably: "bee-yng hartely sorie for the same, [the sinner] doth not onely be-waile his iniquities, but beeyng ashamed thereof, confesse theim, but also with disdaine deteste them, mynding earnestlie to amende, and alwaies indeuouryng to leade an innocent and vertuous life, as long as he liueth" (*Confession*, sig. E$_4$). Although, as we have seen, this "indeuour" will fail in its turn, the consequence will be an-other repentance, another turning—or returning—to God: "And this assuredly is unfeined repentaunce, to wit, a true conversion to God and all goodnesse, with a spedie departure from satan, and all euill. We also plainly affirme, that this repentaunce is the mere gifte of God, and not the worke of our strengthe" (*Confession*, sig. E$_4$). To carry out the paradox to its end, we might say that for the Reformed Protestant, as for Saint Paul, man's weakness *is* his strength.[39]

As a consequence of his perception of this ever repeating pat-tern, the emotional life of the Reformed Protestant must have been extraordinarily rich and varied, as gratitude at being saved gave rise to determination to lead an "innocent and vertuous" life only to rediscover the weakness of his flesh as it overruled his spir-it's desires and brought him once again to stare at himself in the mirror of God's law. From this despair, however, he was quickly raised to joy and exaltation by turning to God and finding renewed comfort in His promise of salvation through faith alone (see *Con-fession*, sigs. F-F$_v$). Whereupon the cycle began again.

In addition to the emotional security supplied by the knowl-edge that "man is iustified by faithe onely in Christe, not by the Lawe, or by any woorkes" (*Confession*, sig. F$_v$), is the comfort that comes from knowing that "all thinges in Heaven, in Earth, and all his creatures are preserued, and gouerned by the Proui-dence of this wise, eternall, and omnipotent God (*Confession*, sig. B$_5$^{v}). Consequently, nothing that we do (or fail to do) can frus-trate God's will and impede the fulfillment of his providential plan.[40] While we may not be able to contribute as much as we would or to do so much as we feel we should, our failures are, in a sense, irrelevant since God will convert them into His successes as He sees fit. Rather than grieving for our failures then and falling into despair, we are free, as de Mornay suggests, to "glorifie God, which maketh the euill good whether it will or no, which causeth vyce to doe seruice vnto vertue, and which guydeth euen the most sinfull deedes, to his glorie; the most vniust, to the executing of his iustice; and the most vncerteyne, to the hitting of his marke" (*A Woorke*, sig. O^v). In the unstable world of the godly, such glorifying, one suspects, is a considerable comfort indeed.

Perhaps the chief comfort, however, was the memory of the central experience of one's life, the discovery of, in Sidney's words, "the knowledge of a man's self" (*MP*, 83). Although all enter the church of God through baptism, "called of many, the first signe of gods people, because by it his electe begin, to retaine to the liuyng Lorde" (*Confession*, sig. I$_8$^{v}), always before the eyes of the godly was Paul's injunction (1 Cor. 13), "Prove your selues, whether ye are in the faithe, knowe you not your ownselues?" (*Confession*, sig. C$_7$^{v}). All those called to God have been chosen by God, "of his mere grace, for no respecte that is in men . . . before the foundation of the worlde" (sig. C$_7$), yet neither predestination, occurring before the creation of the world, nor baptism, occurring once and for all during infancy, provides the individual the opportunity to "prove" whether he is in the faith. The Church of God, after all, is not a visible but an "invisible" Church, "Onely known to God," (*Confession*, sig. G$_6$), and attendance at the visible one proves nothing. As Bullinger cautions, "not all that are nombred in the Churche are saintes, and the liuely or true members of the Churche. For there are many Hippocrites, which to the outwarde shewe, heareth the worde of God, and openlie receiueth the Sacraments . . . but inwardly thei are destitute of the lighte of the spirite, of faithe" (*Confession*, sigs. G$_6$-G$_6$^{v}).

At issue, in a sense, is the dual nature of faith. It is, first of all, "the free gifte of God, whiche onely he geueth of his grace to his electe, accordyng to measure, when, to whom, and as muche as he liste, and that by his holie spirite by the meane of preachyng the Gospel and faithfull praier" (*Confession*, sig. F$_3$^{v}). This is the "liuely and iustifiyng faithe" (sig. F$_3$) that saves us. The same faith, however, is also the means of our psychological "salvation" when we feel it not as "bare opinion, or persuasion of men," but as a "moste sure confidence, an euidente and constaunte assente of the mynde: to bee shorte, a moste certaine comprehendyng of God his truthe, set forthe in the Scriptures, conteined in the Apostles Crede, yea, and commaunded of God himself. . . . But chieflie, faith is a confidence in God, and his soonne Christ his promises, which Christ is thende of all promises" (*Confession*, sigs. F_3-F_3^v). At that moment, whenever and however it occurs—although Bullinger suggests that the "ordinary waye" is through the "woorde of God . . . preached in the Church by preachers lawfully therto called" (sig. A_5), for "faith is by hearinge, & hearinge by the woorde of God" (sig. A_5^v)—a "counterfet vaine, idle, or dedde faithe" (sig. F_2^v) consisting in a merely intellectual assent to the general truth that Christ died for all men is transformed into the "lively and quickenyng faithe . . . through Christ (who is life, and quickeneth hym, whom faith ketcheth hold on)" (sig. F_2^v) that Christ's sacrifice is "particulerly" (sig. K_6) for the individual. At that moment we exchange a "rational" belief for an emotional fervor and begin to count ourselves as God's. At that moment, fear is transformed into love, for, as "the Apostle plainly sheweth, that loue cometh of faithe: The ende of the Lawe is Loue, issuyng out of a pure hart, a good conscience, and an vnfained faithe" (sig. F_2^v). The emotional life of the godly begins at that moment and always centers itself on that moment, returning to it for consolation and proceeding from it to action "to the glory of God, to commende our vocacion, to shewe our thankfulnesse to God, and to profite our neighboure" (sig. F_5).

II. "Matters of love and affection be not guided by wisdom"
(Walsingham to Burghley, August 1579)[41]

This I thinke in haste a story [history] is either to be considered as a storie, or as a treatise which besides that addeth many thinges for profite and ornament; as a story, he is nothing but a narration of thinges done, with the beginnings, cawses, and appendences therof, in that kinde your method must be to have *seriem temporum* very exactlie. . . . In that kinde yow have principally to note the examples of vertue or vice, with their good or evell successes, the establishments or ruines of great Estates, with the cawses . . . and thus much as a very Historiographer.

Philip Sidney to Robert Sidney, 18 October 1580[42]

The story of the Queen's matrimonial maneuverings, at least from the perspective offered by nearly four hundred years distance, is capable of being reduced to "nothing but a narration of thinges done," even if some of the "beginnings, cawses, and appendences therof" are still reasonably obscure.[43] From the perspective of those living through them, however, the course of "true love" never did run less smoothly nor, from the perspective of the godly, was there ever more at stake in a marriage. To John Stubbs, for instance, were Elizabeth to marry a papist Monsieur, it would be no less than a second fall of man: "they have sent us hither, not Satan in body of a serpent, but the old serpent in shape of a man, whose sting is in his mouth, and who doth his endeavor to seduce our Eve, that she and we may lose this English paradise."[44] At the root of much of this despair lay the fear that Elizabeth's marriage to a French Catholic would mean a general overturning of religion and established order, a fear that those opposed to the marriage were quickly accused of creating. Elizabeth's proclamation of 27 September 1579 against Stubbs' book charged it with "seditiously and rebelliously stirring up all estates of her majesty's subjects to fear their own utter ruin and change of government, but specially to imprint a present fear in the zealous sort of the alteration of Christian religion by her majesty's marriage."[45] However inspired, the fear was fairly widespread, as Camden's account of Stubbs' punishment suggests: "I remember (being present thereat,) that when *Stubbs*, hauing his right hand cutt off, put off his hatt with his left, and sayd with a loud voyce, *God saue the Queene*; the multitude standing about, was altogether silent, either out of horror of this new and vnwonted punishment, or else out of pitty towards the man being of most honest and vnblameable report, or else out of hatred of the marriage, which most men presaged would be the ouerthrow of Religion."[46]

Although the story of Elizabeth's negotiations with François Hercule Valois, duke of Alençon, and, after the succession of his brother Henry to the French throne, duke of Anjou, or "Monsieur" as he is so often called in the pamphlet warfare generated by the attempts to make a match between Elizabeth and her "Frog," as she quickly dubbed him,[47] has been told with all the objectivity that some of our best twentieth-century historians can muster, I feel the need to retell it in an attempt to recapture some of the hysteria, doubt, anger, fear, and confusion rampant between 1578, when Anjou renewed his proposal of marriage, and early 1582, when he left England, never to return.[48] As Wallace MacCaffrey has reminded us, "Given our advantages of hindsight, we become impatient in focusing our attention on these intricate, inconclusive, and ultimately abortive negotiations. . . . But it is important to recover a sense of the deep anxieties of contemporaries."[49]

To contemporaries, then, if the "narration of thinges done" defied comprehension, there were certainly "examples of virtue or vice, with their good or evell successes" a plenty. To Sidney, in his "Letter . . . to Queen Elizabeth, Touching Her Marriage to Monsieur," the cast of characters was clear. There was, first of all, Monsieur, "a Frenchman, and a Papist, in whom, howsoever fine wits may find further dangers or painted excuses, the very common people well know this: that he is the son of the Jezebel of our age, that his brother made oblation of his own sister's marriage, the easier to make massacres of all sexes; that he himself, contrary to his promise, and against all gratefulness, having had his liberty and principal estates chiefly by the Hugenots' means, did sack La Charité and utterly spoil Issoire with fire and sword. This, I say, even at the first sight, gives occasion to all the true religious to abhor such a master" (*MP*, 48). Nor did Monsieur improve much on further reflection:

His will, to be as full of light ambition as is possible, besides the French disposition and his own education; his inconstant attempts against his brother; his thrusting himself into the Low Country matters; his sometimes seeking the King of Spain's daughter, sometimes your Majesty; are evident testimonies he is carried away with every wind of hope, taught to love greatness any way gotten, and having for the motioners and ministers of his mind only such young men as have shown they think evil contentment a sufficient ground of any rebellion; whose age gives them to have seen none other commonwealth, but in faction; and divers of which have defiled their hands in odious murders. With such fancies and favourites, is it to be hoped for that he will be contained within the limits of your conditions? [*MP*, 49]

The best that Sidney can say for him is that "as long as he is but Monsieur in might and a Papist in profession, he neither can nor will greatly stead you" (*MP*, 56); if his ability to help is limited, however, his potential for harm should the marriage occur, is not:

[I] t were strange, he that cannot be contented to be second person in France and heir apparent, would come to be the second person, where he shall pretend no way sovereignty. His power, I imagine, is not to be despised, since he is to come into a country where the way of evil doing will be presented unto him; where there needs nothing but a head to draw together evil affected humours; himself a prince of great revenues, of the most populous nation of the world, full of soldiery, and such as are used to serve without pay, so they may have show of spoil; and without question shall have his brother in such a case ready to help him, as well for old revenges, as for to divert him from troubling France, and to deliver his own country the sooner from evil humours. [*MP*, 49-50]

Next in the cast came Elizabeth, and little need (or could) be said of her. If she continues as she has, Sidney says, she will continue to be as she is, "the example of princes, the ornament of this age, the comfort of the afflicted, the delight of . . . [her] people, the most excellent fruit of all . . . [her] progenitors, and the perfect mirror to . . .[her] posterity" (*MP*, 57).

The final party to the drama was the realm, which Sidney sees as a kingdom divided into "two mighty factions" (*MP*, 47), based upon religion. "The one is of them to whom your happy government hath granted the free exercise of the eternal truth. . . . These, therefore, as their souls live by your happy government, so are they your chief, if not your sole, strength" (*MP*, 47). These, of course, Elizabeth runs the risk of alienating should she marry Monsieur. The other party, "most rightly indeed to be called a faction, is of the Papists: men whose spirits are full of anguish; some being forced to oaths they account damnable; some having their ambition stopped, because they are not in the way of advancement; some in prison and disgrace; some whose best friends are banished practisers; many thinking you an usurper; many thinking the right you had, disanulled by the Pope's excommunication; all burdened with the weight of their consciences" (*MP*, 48). This second faction Elizabeth cannot hope to appease by marrying Monsieur, says Sidney; rather she will merely supply them with "a head, who shall in effect need but to receive their instructions, since they may do mischief enough only with his countenance" (*MP*, 49). The world, in short, divides into two parties, Elizabeth and those to whom her "happy government hath granted the free exercise of the eternal truth" on the one hand; on the other, Monsieur and the Papists, those "men whose spirits are full of anguish." The choice should have been so simple.

The "inability" of Elizabeth (not to mention Burghley and the Earl of Sussex) to see and understand this simple division was a cause of some anguish to the spirits of Sidney, Leicester, and Walsingham. Sidney, having been ordered to write (Languet tells us) by "those whom you were bound to obey," could not be blamed by any "fair-judging man" for "putting forward freely what you thought good for your country, nor even for exaggerating some circumstances in order to convince them of what you judged expedient."[50] Languet, however, did not have to face Elizabeth in the particularly foul temper into which she had worked herself; Sidney did, and no doubt found it prudent to visit his sister. Leicester, according to the more or less unreliable testimony of Bernardino de Mondoza, Philip II's ambassador in England, is described as thoroughly upset at the whole affair, even to the point of threatening open opposition to the marriage in Parliament.[51] Walsingham, implicated in the publication of the *Gaping Gulf* by rumors heard so far away as France,[52] likewise came in for his share of abuse, again according to Mendoza.[53]

The issue, of course, was far more complicated than the reduction into blacks and whites Sidney is trying to make, "exaggerating," as Languet observed, "in order to convince them of what you judged expedient." What was at stake was not merely the question of Elizabeth's marriage but the outcome of a political struggle between the policy of the Burghley-Sussex faction on the council (aided for religious reasons by the Earls of Oxford and Northumberland) for a continuation of the cautious, balance-of-power policy that tried to keep either France or Spain from becoming preeminent and the Leicester-Walsingham circle's attempt to instigate an aggressive, Protestant, war policy by which England, at the head of a Protestant league of Danes, Swedes, Germans, Huguenots, and "Netherlanders," would gain independence for the Netherlands, freedom for the Huguenots, and reduce the Guise party in France, the Spanish imperialists, and the Pope to a state of frustrated impotence.[54] It is in the light of this policy that Greville sees and praises Sidney's abortive attempt to turn his condolence call on the Emperor Rudolph II in 1577, occasioned by the death in 1576 of his father, the Emperor Maximilian II, into a means of stirring up a league "between us, and the *German* Princes" (*Life*, p. 44) that would frustrate the "fatall conjunction of *Rome's* undermining superstitions, with the commanding forces of *Spain*" (*Life*, p. 42).[55]

In the process of visiting with various continental Protestant leaders, Sidney received two invitations to contract marriage, the first with the sister of Duke John Casimir, second son of the late Elector Palatine, and, like his late father, a Reformed Protestant who was now on the outs with his brother Ludwig, the new Elector, a Lutheran.[56] The second, like the first an attempt to achieve a binding link between England and a continental Protestant state, came from William of Orange, who offered Sidney his eldest daughter. Mendoza's report of 12 April 1578 to Philip II is explicit about the political consequences of the proposed match (even if mistaken about the identity of the lady in question):

There is much talk here of a marriage between Philip Sidney, Leicester's nephew, the heir of Henry Sidney, of the earl of Warwick, and of Leicester's property, and a sister of Orange, who enters very willingly into the suggestion, and promises as a dowry to make him lord of Holland and Zealand, by this means and other gifts gaining over Leicester, who has now turned his back upon France, to which he was formerly so attached.[57]

Although the marriage negotiations fell through,[58] they suggested another possible direction in foreign policy which Leicester and Walsingham were quick to support. They succeeded momentarily in getting Elizabeth to support John Casimir and an army in the Netherlands at the same time that Monsieur was leading an army there.[59] Casimir soon proved more interested in intervening on the Reformed Protestant side of internal squabbles than in fighting the Spanish, and Elizabeth apparently decided that Anjou was the better bet.[60] When Casimir came to England in January 1579 to ask both for more money and for Philip Sidney to be his joint commander, he succeeded in neither request.[61]

Greville's description of Leicester withdrawing from the aspersions of the "French faction reigning" (*Life*, p. 60) thus has to be
seen within this struggle for control of policy between Burghley
and Sussex on the one hand and Walsingham, Leicester, and Sidney on the other. Walsingham's theory that "the prosperity or adversity of kingdoms dependeth of God's goodness who is so long
to extend his protection as we shall depend of his providence and
shall not seek our safety (carried away by human policy) contrary
to his word"[62] thus stood in opposition to Burghley's theory that
politics requires prudent consideration of all possibilities and the
maintenance of a political balance of power.

Walsingham, according to Read, "wished to build up for England
a foreign policy based simply on religious principles. He trusted
the religious bond of union as he trusted none other, partly because he felt that the religious instinct was one of the strongest of
human impulses, largely because he believed that God almighty
would fight for the faith. 'Let God arise,' was the burden of his
chant, 'and let his enemies be scattered.' "[63] Like Walsingham, Sidney was all for "imprudence" coupled with complete faith that
God would support their actions. Both in his letter to Elizabeth
and in one written nearly seven years later to Walsingham, Sidney
shows how clearly he shares his father-in-law's view that politics is
God's art not man's.

To Elizabeth he writes that she should ignore those who say her
safety lies in a French marriage, and "laying aside this dangerous
help, for your standing alone, you must take it as a singular honour God hath done unto you, to be indeed the only protector of
his church. And yet in worldly respects your Kingdom is very sufficient so to do, if you make that religion upon which you stand
to carry the only strength, and have abroad those who still maintain the same cause [i.e., the Netherlands and the German Protestant states] : who as long as they may be kept from utter falling,
your majesty is sure enough from your mightiest enemies" (*MP*,
56). To Walsingham, on 24 March 1586, he writes: "I had before
cast my count of dang[er] want and disgrace, and before God Sir
it is trew [that] in my hart the love of the caws [i.e., the war
against the Spanish in the Netherlands] doth so far over-ballance
them all that with Gods grace thei shall never make me weery of

my resolution. If her Majesty wear the fowntain I woold fear con-
sidring what I daily fynd that we shold wax dry, but she is but a
means whom God useth and I know not whether I am deceaved
but I am faithfully persuaded that if she shold withdraw her self
other springes woold ryse to help this action. For me thinkes I see
the great work indeed in hand, against the abusers of the world,
wherein it is no greater fault to have confidence in mans power,
then it is to hastily to despair of Gods work" (*Prose Works*, 3:166).

Unfortunately, however much God may have supported them,
it seemed clear Elizabeth did not. Against all reason, she seemed
determined to marry Monsieur. Even Mendoza, who had a nearly
unbelievable ability to see everything through Spanish-colored
glasses, looked on Elizabeth's doings and despaired: "It is difficult
to see whether all this is artifice or whether God intends to blind
her in order to bring her to submission."[64] It is, in a sense, irrelevant that from hindsight Elizabeth apparently never had any intention to marry Anjou;[65] what is crucial is that it was all too possible
for Sidney to believe that she did. From his perspective it was almost an inescapable conclusion, to paraphrase Mendoza, that God
had indeed decided to blind her because she thought she could
stand independent of His will.

It was, I suggest, in this frame of mind that Sidney, rejected by
Elizabeth, despairing of the prospects of either England or himself
having a role in "the great work . . . against the abusers of the
world," retired to his sister's estate at Wilton and, chafing under
his enforced inactivity, began writing the *Old Arcadia*. Fulke Greville, who apparently read the *Old Arcadia* in this frame of mind,
offers some suggestive clues to the political content a contemporary reader could find in the work. Of the action that generates
the *Old Arcadia*'s plot, Basilius' decision to withdraw from government for the space of a year in response to a threatening oracle,
Greville comments, "may not the most refined spirits, in the scope
of these dead images (even as they are now) finde, that when Sov-
ereign Princes, to play with their own visions, will put off publique
action, which is the splendor of Majestie, and unactively charge
the managing of their greatest affairs upon the second-hand faith,
and diligence of Deputies, may they not (I say) understand, that
even then they bury themselves, and their Estates in a cloud of

contempt, and under it both encourage, and shaddow the conspiracies of ambitious subalternes to their false endes, I mean the ruine of States and Princes?" (*Life*, pp. 11-12).[66] In this reading, he is echoing the comments of the narrator within the work:

He [Euarchus] saw the Asiatics of the one side, the Latins of the other, gaping for any occasion to devour Greece, which was no way to be prevented but by their united strength, and strength most to be maintained by maintaining their principal instruments. These rightly wise and temperate considerations moved Euarchus to take this laboursome journey, to see whether by his authority he might withdraw Basilius from this burying himself alive, and to return again to employ his old years in doing good, the only happy action of man's life.[67]

For both Sidney and Greville, the action that sets the plot in motion is a metaphor for the state of affairs that results when a ruler fails to balance the calls of "publique action" and private "visions."

I wish to be quite clear about the nature of the political content I have in mind. I do not wish to suggest that the *Old Arcadia* is a roman à clef or an "allegory" of any specific event arising out of the Alençon marriage. I share David Bevington's belief that this is not how Elizabethan literature was meant to have been read and would like to join myself to his comments about Tudor drama, whose applicability to the *Old Arcadia* seems to me to be clear: "politics is germane to a remarkable percentage of Tudor plays, but in terms of ideas and platforms rather than personalities. Even the allusions to kings or queens, although obviously referring in many cases to the reigning monarch, pertain to the office instead of the man."[68] Sidney, we should remember, has given his characters names of precisely this sort. Basilius (βασιλεύς, ruler), the Duke of Arcadia, Gynecia (γυναικεῖος, womanly), the Duchess, and Euarchus (εναρχος, good ruler, ruling well), the King of Macedonia, father of Pyrocles (πῦρ κλέος, fire and glory) and uncle of Musidorus (Μοῦσα δῶρον, gift of the Muses), form the trinity of rulers in the work, the first two functioning as foils to the third.

Greville also sees in the chain of events that transforms the "heroic" princes who come to Arcadia into an Amazon and a shepherd and lead them to be "accused and condemned of rape, paricide, adulteries, or treasons" the truth that "these dark webs of effeminate Princes be dangerous fore runners of innovation, even in a quiet, and equally tempered people" (*Life*, p. 13). From these political concerns, however, Greville passes to the other half of Sidney's "Architectonical art" (*Life*, p. 18), from the politic consideration to the ethical, "in the knowledge of a man's self" (*MP*, 82-83):

[I] n all these creatures of his making, his intent, and scope was, to turn the barren Philosophy precepts into pregnant Images of life; and in them, first on the Monarch's part, lively to represent the growth, state, and declination of Princes, change of Government, and lawes: vicissitudes of sedition, faction, succession . . . with all other errors, or alterations in publique affaires. Then again in the subjects case; the state of favor, disfavor, prosperitie, adversity, emulation, quarrell, undertaking, retiring, hospitality, travail, and all other moodes of private fortunes, or misfortunes. In which traverses (I know) his purpose was to limn out such exact pictures, of every posture in the minde, that any man being forced, in the straines of this life, to pass through any straights, or latitudes of good, or ill fortune, might (as in a glasse) see how to set a good countenance upon all the discountenances of adversitie, and a stay upon the exorbitant smilings of chance. [*Life*, pp. 15-16]

Greville's testimony, both as Sidney's closest friend (and his companion on his ambassadorial mission) and as a reader sympathetic both to his political stands and his ethical position, is too important to remain unremarked. From the occasion of the plot, Greville passes to the end of the work, and finds it to be that "as in a glasse" it enables the reader to see himself, and from this self-knowledge to find his course. Greville's final view of the *Arcadia* — and here both versions are equally well described — is that it enables us clearly to see that Sidney's end "was not vanishing pleasure alone, but morall Images, and Examples, (as directing threds) to guide every man through the confused *Labyrinth* of his own desires, and life" (*Life*, p. 223).[69]

From what may have been the political genesis of the *Old Arcadia* in Sidney's discontented reflections on his "corrupt age" (Pears, p. 143), we must be prepared to pass to a consideration of what in man's nature makes his age corrupt, to investigate why rational men, shown rational courses to follow, insist on acting with complete irrationality, to the clear detriment of both "public advantage" and "thorough self-examination; to which employment no labour that men can undertake, is any way to be compared" (Pears, p. 143). Of those in such a situation Sidney writes, and he writes to them as well. If, out of his consideration of his failure to persuade the Queen, he came to an understanding of his own limitations, he may have come to feel he could do the same for us.

III. Moving and Teaching: Sidney's *Defence of Poesie* as a Protestant Poetic

Whether we owe the *Defence of Poesie* to the accident of Stephen Gosson's logical but ill-received dedication to Sidney of his *Schoole of Abuse* (1579), to Sidney's conversations about poetry with Dyer, Greville, and possibly Spenser, to Sidney's own need to justify the investment of time he was making on the *Old Arcadia*, or to some combination of all of these, we are indeed fortunate that Sidney was for some reason moved enough by something to sit down, at approximately the same time that he was in the midst of composing and revising the *Old Arcadia*, and to write out a formal defence of the art of poetry embodying those principles he had perhaps reached as a consequence of his efforts.[70] Whatever his motives were, there was indeed "just cause to make a pitiful defence of poor poetry, which from almost the highest estimation of learning is fallen to be the laughing-stock of children" (*MP*, 73-74), and which had suffered nearly as much at the hands of her defenders as she had from the poet-haters. Rather than considering poetry's attackers (whether Gosson, whose target is really the popular drama and with whom Sidney, like Thomas Lodge in his *Defence*,[71] would probably have agreed insofar as he focuses upon particular "abuses" presented on the stage, or Plato, whose strictures, although flaunted by Gosson as often as possible, had had quite a while in which to have made an impact), I should like to turn to George Gascoigne's attempt at a defence of his own poems in the three introductory epistles added to the second edition of his poems, *The Posies* (1575), in response to objections raised after their first publication in *A Hundreth Sundrie Flowres* (1573).

In the first epistle, "To the reverende Divines," Gascoigne begins by acknowledging that to some readers some of his poems "have not onely bene offensive for sundrie wanton speeches and lascivious phrases, but further I heare that the same have been doubtfully construed, and (therefore) scandalous" (1:3).[72] Conceding "a generall reformation of maners more necessarie to bee taught, than anye Whetstone of Vanities is meete (in these dayes) to bee suffered" (1:4), Gascoigne goes on to claim that he is innocent of any willful or knowing provocation to vice and to offer a five-part defence of his considerations in publishing his poems. Gascoigne's first two points—that poetry is nothing to be ashamed of, even the poetry of one's youth, in a "reformed" man (and he later cites "the reverend father Theodore Beza" as an example [1:6]), and that it is possible and patriotic to write poetry in English—need only be noted for their lack of originality; his next three, however, are worth some consideration:

Thirdly, as I seeke advauncement by vertue, so was I desirous that there might remaine a publike recorde, some pledge or token of those giftes wherwith it hath pleased the Almightie to endue me: To the ende that thereby the vertuous might bee incouraged to employ my penne in some exercise which might tende both to my preferment, and to the profite of my Country. . . .

Fourthly, bicause I had written sundry things which coulde not chuse but content the learned and Godlye Reader, therefore I hoped the same should serve as undoubted proofe, that I had layed aside vanities, and delighted to exercise my penne in morall discourses, at least the one passing (cheeke by cheek) with the other, muste of necessitie persuade both the learned, and the light minded, that I could aswell sowe good graine, as graynes of draffe. . . .

Lastly, I persuaded my selfe that as in the better sort of the same [i.e., "morall discourses"] I shoulde purchase good lyking with the honourable aged: So even in the worst sorte [i.e., "vanities"], I might yet serve as a myrrour for unbrydled youth, to avoyde those perilles which I had passed. For little may he do which hath escaped the rock or the sandes, if he cannot waft with his hande to them that come after him. [1:4-5]

These three arguments, arising out of much the same intellectual context that we have already explored, suggest, by their very unsatisfactoriness, that Sidney would have seen his task as at least as much concerned with correcting the inadequate conceptions of the nature and function of poetry held by her practioners as by her attackers. In the first of these three arguments Gascoigne suggests that poetry, even in a "reformed" man, may be lawful as proceeding from one's God-given talents—that poetry is as fit a calling (in the Protestant sense) as any other and that it can play as useful a part as any other occupation in advancing virtue. Having thus prepared us to expect a defence of poetry on the grounds of its usefulness in encouraging that "generall reformation of maners" which is so much to be desired, it is a trifle disconcerting to find him apologizing in his last two points for not achieving it because, despite his own reformation, he, as a man, cannot avoid "draffe" in his poetry, even if that very flaw may enable "unbridled youth" to see their own flaws in the mirror of his. If we ask why the mirror should work, given that "wee are all *magis proni ad malum quam ad bonum*" (1:4), all we get from Gascoigne is a shrug of helplessness:

To the fourth and last considerations, I had alleged of late by a right reverende father, that although in deede out of everie floure the industrious Bee may gather honie, yet by proofe the Spider thereout also sucks mischeevous poyson. Whereunto I can none otherwise answere, but that he who will throw a stone at everie Dogge which barketh, had neede of a great satchell or pocket. And if the learned judgements and honest mindes doe both construe my doings aright, and take therein either councell or commodotie, then care I the lesse what the wicked conceyve of my conceytes. For I esteeme more the prayse of one learned Reader, than I regard the curious carping of ten thousande unlettered tattlers. [1:6-7]

For Gascoigne, the poet must provide either wholesome moral doctrine or a negative moral *exemplum*; if the reader chooses to ignore it, that, Gascoigne seems to suggest, is his problem.

This, of course, is an unsatisfactory position, and Gascoigne, realizing it, returns to the question in each of the next two epistles. In the epistle "To al yong Gentlemen, and generally to the youth of England," he makes an outright appeal to those most likely to relish his vanities because they share them and to ignore his moral discourses:

> To speake English it is your using (my lustie Gallants) or misusing of these Posies that may make me praysed or dispraysed for publishing of the same. For if you (where you may learne to avoyd the subtile sandes of wanton desire) will runne upon the rockes of unlawful lust, then great is your folly and greater will growe my rebuke. . . . I assure you, my yong blouds, I have not published the same to the intent that other men hereafter might be infected with my follies forepassed. [1:12-13]

Here Gascoigne clearly realizes that the responsibility for ensuring that his poetry has the moral effect that he desires is his; but, other than begging his readers not to misuse his poems, he seems to have no idea how to achieve his ends. Ultimately, in the final epistle, "To the Readers generally," he is reduced to reminding them that "All that is written is written for our instruction, as the holy Apostle witnesseth to the Romaines in his .xv. Chapter" and that "as I never yet saw any thing so clerkly handled, but that therein might be found some imperfections: So coulde I never yet reade fable so ridiculous but that therein some morallitie might be gathered" (1:15, 16).

Gascoigne's problem is a complex one. On the one hand, he must confront the fact that many of his readers are incapable of reading other than literally and cannot conceive that a poem need not mean merely what it literally says.[73] Like Lodge, exploding in exasperation at Gosson's refusal to acknowledge the conventional allegorizations of events in pagan poems, Gascoigne has come face to face with "*homo literatus*, a man of the letter, little sauoring of learning" (Smith, 1:65). On the other hand, he is faced with the more serious problem of the reader who understands what the poem means but refuses to act upon the knowledge which has been given him, who refuses to listen to the moral doctrine or to look in the mirror and to reject what he sees — in short, the reader who "chooses" the poison instead of the honey.[74] If the poet must concede that most of his readers will either misunderstand his poetry or will refuse to accept its moral doctrine, then he must concede also that poetry is, as Gascoigne despairingly puts it, "a two edged swoorde" in the "naked hands" of his readers (1:14), and he must ultimately acquiesce in Gosson's condemnation even of those plays (or poems) which are "without rebuke": "These Playes are good playes and sweete playes, and of al playes the best playes and most to be liked, woorthy to bee soung of the Muses, or set out with the cunning of *Roscius* himself, yet are they not fit for euery mans dyet: neither ought they commonly to bee shewen."[75] If poetry is to be judged within the context of its utility to society, then the damage done to the "ten thousande unlettered tattlers" must clearly outweigh the "prayse of one learned Reader."

The objections raised to Gascoigne's poems and which provoked his long defence are all the more serious since we are dealing not with a hack but with probably the best English poet between Wyatt and Sidney. Gascoigne gets into trouble not because he is immoral but because he is concerned about his society. But his sense of the need for a general reformation of manners leads him to reach out unsuccessfully to a wide audience rather than settling for the approbation of the "learned and Godlye Reader" who is familiar with the traditional conceptions of poetry and the allegorical interpretations of the poets contained in the mythographical handbooks and the humanist editions and commentaries on the classics.[76] As a result of the changed conception of man's nature and faculties that accompanied the Protestant Reformation, the medieval and humanist justifications of poetry could no longer be satisfactorily defended. But if the old defences had failed, could the old definitions stand for long?

For Boccaccio, as for Dante, Petrarch, Chaucer, or almost any other late medieval poet who has left us a comment on his art, "poetry . . . is a sort of fervid and exquisite invention, with fervid expression, in speech or in writing, of that which the mind has invented. . . . This fervor of poesy is sublime in its effects: it impels the soul to a longing for utterance; it brings forth strange and unheard-of creations of the mind; it arranges these meditations in a fixed order, adorns the whole composition with unusual interweavings of words and thoughts; and thus it veils truth in a fair and fitting garment of fiction."[77]

From this definition of poetry, that fair garment of fiction that veils truth, we must extract the important elements of the pre-Reformation aesthetic. First, the poet must not merely utter the truth, he must impel the reader towards it through his "fervid" invention and expression of what he has invented. But as Robertson has pointed out, this fervor is not an emotional stimulus but an intellectual desire for knowledge:

In one of his letters (55.11.21), St. Augustine asserts that those things which are said figuratively in the Scriptures move and inflame love more than those things which are said literally. When the mind is immersed in terrestrial things, it is slow to be ignited by the fire of divine love, but when it is directed towards similitudes based upon corporal things and thence referred to those spiritual things figured in the similitudes, it is excited by the transition from one to the other so that it is carried with more ardent love toward the peace it seeks.[78]

Second, poetry must be obscure, must have a "veiled" surface in order that the reader, having struggled to attain to the hidden wisdom, will value it the more. Boccaccio quotes Petrarch's *Invective contra medicum* to this effect, "Such majesty and dignity [of style in poetic narrative] are not intended to hinder those who wish to understand, but rather propose a delightful task, and are designed to enhance the reader's pleasure and support his memory. What we acquire with difficulty and keep with care is always dearer to us."[79]

Underlying this aesthetic and giving meaning to it are the related assumptions that man has the ability to act upon the basis of what he has learned, that man has a free will, and that "piously and ardently to love . . . [the Truth towards whom all of poetry's truths lead, God] is possible."[80] Yet, as we have seen, it is precisely these assumptions that the Protestants denied. The result is that the older defence of poetry—that poetry drives the reader to seek for knowledge upon which he can then act—will no longer hold, and we are left, as with Gascoigne, with poets who still write in the old ways even though they can no longer defend them because they have no other conception of poetry which will serve them any better. Under these circumstances, the only way to defend poetry was to redefine its function, reevaluate the importance of its teaching role, and create a new aesthetic. It was this, I suggest, that Sidney set out to do when he began the composition of *The Defence of Poesie*.

In setting out his *Defence*, Sidney's reading in classical and modern literature and literary criticism did not go for naught. His use of such critics as Scaliger, Minturno, Castelvetro, Robortelli, and Landino has long been known and noted; yet, as critics have been arguing for the past quarter-century, what he uses takes on new meaning, transformed by its new context and the new emphases given to what often start out as commonplaces.[81] Following de Mornay's strategy, Sidney seeks to echo as many traditional defences as he can manage in his attempt to lead his reader from what he knows to what Sidney would have him believe. In so doing, he created a work "built of commonplaces which concealed the novelty of his basic conception of the function of poetry, supported by authorities who drew attention from the audacity of his synthesis, and presented in an easy style which makes his elevation of aim seem homely and familiar."[82] By coming to the *Defence* as we have through our consideration of the intellectual, political, and social contexts that gave birth to it, Sidney's revolutionary program may be more clearly seen.

Following his introductory remarks and his discussion of the high esteem in which poetry was formerly held, Sidney turns, by way of etymology, to the first problem he must face—how poetry, the product of men, can be innocent of men's flaws. This, we recall, was one of the rocks upon which Gascoigne stumbled; Sidney, through a cleverly arranged sequence of arguments and allusions, does not. He begins with the Latin term *vates*, but his sights are set on bigger game: "Among the Romans a Poet was called *vates*, which is as much as a diviner, foreseer, or prophet . . . so heavenly a title did that excellent people bestow upon this heart-ravishing knowledge" (*MP*, 76). For Sidney, of course, the prophetic aspects of Roman poetry cannot be allowed much emphasis,[83] so he quickly switches to more orthodox examples:

And may I not presume a little further, to show the reasonableness of this word *vates*, and say that the holy David's Psalms are a divine poem? If I do, I shall not do it without the testimony of great learned men, both ancient and modern. . . . But truly now having named him, I fear me I seem to profane that holy name, applying it to poetry, which is among us thrown down to so ridiculous an estimation. But they that with quiet judgements will look a little deeper into it, shall find the end and working of it such as, being rightly applied, deserveth not to be scourged out of the Church of God. [*MP*, 77]

Since not even the most antipoetical critic could object to David's Psalms—composed as they were by the "holy Ghost, who did endite the Psalmes, and set them foorth by his secretaries, David and others"[84]—that which should not be "scourged out of the Church of God" can only be poetry.

Without giving the reader a chance to wonder what the "end and working" of poetry is which makes it, "rightly applied," useful within the Church of God, Sidney moves to capitalize upon the prophetic and inspirational aspects of poetry which he has already suggested by insisting upon the implications of the Greek and English names for poets, "makers":

There is no art delivered to mankind that hath not the works of nature for his principal object, without which they could not consist, and on which they so depend, as they become actors and players, as it were, of what nature will have set forth.... Only the poet, disdaining to be tied to any such subjection, lifted up with the vigour of his own invention, doth grow in effect another nature...so as he goeth hand and hand with nature, not enclosed within the narrow warrant of her gifts, but freely ranging only within the zodiac of his own wit. [*MP*, 78]

Although Sidney's purpose in asserting the poet's independence from Nature is usually seen as an attempt to undercut Plato's condemnation of poetry as the imitation of an imitation (Nature) of reality (the Ideas), within the context soon to be established of "that first accursed fall of Adam" (*MP*, 79), it is clear that he is rather declaring poetry's lack of complicity in that corruption of nature, following man's first disobedience, into her present "brazen" state.[85]

Because the corruption in nature proceeded from man's own corruption, however, Sidney is quick to assert that the honor for escaping nature's confines belongs not to man but to God:

Neither let it be deemed too saucy a comparison to balance the highest point of man's wit with the efficacy of nature; but rather give right honour to the heavenly Maker of that maker, who having made man to His own likeness, set him beyond and over all the works of that second nature: which in nothing he showeth so much as in poetry, when with the force of a divine breath he bringeth things forth surpassing her doings—with no small argument to the credulous of that first accursed fall of Adam, since our erected wit maketh us know what perfection is, and yet our infected will keepeth us from reaching unto it. [*MP*, 79]

Although it has recently been argued that "the divine breath" is merely "a *natural gift*, one given under natural law (not a super-natural gift beyond human potentiality and granted by a special grace),"[86] Sidney is clearly suggesting far more than this. Because of man's fall, his capacities have been so diminished that, in nature, his wit is almost as infected as his will. As Calvin pungently puts it:

For although there is still some residue of intelligence and judgment as well as will, we cannot call a mind sound and entire which is both weak and immersed in darkness. As to the will, its depravity is but too well known. Therefore, since reason, by which man discerns between good and evil, and by which he understands and judges, is a natural gift, it could not be entirely destroyed; but being partly weakened and partly corrupted, a shapeless ruin is all that remains. [*Institutes*, 2.2.12]

If the "heavenly image in man [which] was effaced" (*Institutes*, 2.1.5) is to be restored, it must be "by the grace of regeneration (2.2.12). That "the Poet hath that *idea*" is manifest proof that he sees "with the eyes of the mind, only cleared by faith" (*MP*, 77); that he can bring them forth "with the force of a divine breath" argues that he, like David, merely follows the promptings of the Holy Spirit.[87]

If this line of argument has permitted Sidney to solve one problem, it has raised another. What does it matter that the poet "hath that *idea*" or even that the reader can get it if, despite knowing what "perfection" is, "our infected will keepeth us from reaching unto it"? It is at this point that Sidney switches contexts, moving from this theological overview to a "more ordinary opening of him, that the truth may be the more palpable" (*MP*, 79).[88] By the time he has finished the third of the three statements about the end and working of "poesie" and the poet that follow immediately, we are right back where he left us, but with another direction in which to move open to us. He begins with a simple, noncontroversial statement: "Poesy therefore is an art of imitation, for so Aristotle termeth it in the word μίμησις that is to say, a representing, counterfeiting, or figuring forth to speak metaphorically. A speaking picture, with this end to teach and delight."[89] Of the "three general kinds" of poets, Sidney says little about the first two, the divine and the philosophical.[90] Of the third, "indeed right poets," in defence of whom he is writing, he says more: "For these third be they which most properly do imitate to teach and delight, and to imitate borrow nothing of what is, hath been, or shall be, but range, only reined with learned discretion, into the divine consideration of what may be and should be" (MP, 81). With this, Sidney has recapitulated the argument developed through etymology; in what follows he goes beyond it: "for these indeed do merely [i.e., only] make to imitate, and imitate both to delight and teach; and delight, to move men to take that goodness in hand, which without delight they would fly as from a stranger; and teach, to make them know that goodness whereunto they are moved" (MP, 81). It is no longer sufficient that poetry teach and delight; now it must move the reader, or the delight and teaching are pointless.

It is not enough to say that the end of poetry is to make the reader know, "and by knowledge to lift up the mind from the dungeon of the body to the enjoying of his own divine essence" (MP, 82). Unless the reader can be moved to "well-doing and not . . . well-knowing only" (MP, 83), he is left, as he was before he began to read, with an "infected will" blocking any action based upon that knowledge. Before the poet can teach he must move:

And that moving is of a higher degree then teaching, it may by this appear, that it is well nigh the cause and effect of teaching. For who will be taught, if he be not moved with desire to be taught? And what so much good doth that teaching bring forth (I speak still of moral doctrine) as that it moveth one to do that which it doth teach? For, as Aristotle sayth, it is not γνῶσις but πρᾶξις must be the fruit. And how πρᾶξις can be, without being moved to practise, it is no hard matter to consider. [MP, 91]

With this, Sidney has potentially overcome the problem which stymied Gascoigne and aroused not simply the Puritans but all Protestants against poetry, that men are *magis proni ad malum quam ad bonum*. If the poet can move readers to take goodness in hand, it does not matter any longer that given the freedom they would prefer to suck "mischevous poyson" from the poet's flowers instead of industriously gathering "honie"; the "right poet," according to Sidney, denies the reader that choice.

To be moved—but how? We are presented with what seems like a paradox by the *Defence*, for Sidney, although basing his defence of poetry on the poet's power to move the reader to action, seems never to explain how the poet is to go about his task. It is true that he tells us that the poet delights the reader to move him, but when he later tells us that "delight we scarcely do but in things that have a conveniency to ourselves or to the general nature" (*MP*, 115), we might begin to ask ourselves why the process of everyday living does not have the same power to move as the poet. That we do not may be attributed partially to Sidney's rhetorical skill and partly to the psychology which motivates it. Paul Alpers has suggested that "the heart of Sidney's defense of poetry lies in the passages in which he describes, sometimes in ravishing prose, the psychological effect of poetry—in particular, the way it makes us see and love virtue and virtuous acts,"[91] with such passages in mind as Sidney's account of why the poet is the monarch of all sciences:

For he doth not only show the way, but giveth so sweet a prospect into the way, as will entice any man to enter into it. Nay, he doth, as if your journey should lie through a fair vineyard, at the first give you a cluster of grapes, that, full of that taste, you may long to pass further. He beginneth not with obscure definitions, which must blur the margin with interpretations, and load the memory with doubtfulness; but he cometh to you with words set in delightful proportion, either accompanied with, or prepared for, the well enchanting skill of music; and with a tale forsooth he cometh unto you, with a tale which holdeth children from play, and old men from the chimney corner. And pretending no more, doth intend the winning of the mind from wickedness to virtue. [*MP*, 91-92]

While passages like this are certainly persuasive and do their part in carrying the reader along, there comes a point at which ravishing prose ceases to be able to sustain our assent, a point at which we wish to know what it is that we have agreed to take in hand. At that point we must turn to Elizabethan notions about human psychology.

The process by which sensory data became the basis for action was a fairly simple one. As Calvin, synthesizing various current formulations, put it, "According to the philosophers, there are five senses . . . by which all objects are brought into a common sensorium, as into a kind of receptacle: Next comes the imagination (*phantasia*) which distinguishes between the objects brought into the sensorium: Next, reason, to which the general power of judgment belongs; And, lastly, intellect, which contemplates with fixed and quiet look whatever reason discursively resolves" (*Institutes*, 1.15.6-7).[92] The will, looking to what the reason and the intellect have propounded, then acts. This chain, of course, was broken in three places by the fall: the senses, which now feed inaccurate information to the sensorium; the reason, which was darkened; and the will, which was "infected."[93] Although the imagination was similarly subject to distortion, it was also a potential force for good. As Puttenham says, "Euen so is the phantasticall part of man (if it be not disordered) a representer of the best, most comely and bewtifull images or appearances of thinges to the soule and according to their very truth. If otherwise, then doth it breed *Chimeres* & monsters in mans imaginations, & not onely in his imaginations, but also in all his ordinarie actions and life which ensues."[94] Here, then, we have a faculty for the poet to work upon.

What makes the imagination even more suitable for the poet's purposes is that it is not merely a passive "representer" but an active force in itself. As La Primaudaye says:

This imaginatiue power of the soule, hath moreover such vertue, that oftentimes the imagination printeth in the body, the images of those things which it doeth vehemently think of and apprehend. . . . Many times . . . wee see some that can hardly goe ouer a bridge without falling, by reason of the apprehension of the danger, which they haue conceiued in their fantasie and imagination. . . . Neither is it altogether without reason which we vse commonly to say: that fancie breeds the fact which it imagineth.[95]

Because the poet can appeal directly to the imagination, he avoids the corruption of the senses; because he controls what the imagination receives, he avoids the possibility of its disorder; finally, because the imagination can work directly upon the will, he can overcome the obstacle to virtuous action presented by our "infected will." As Sidney says, "Whom doth not the words of Turnus move, the tale of Turnus having planted his image in the imagination" (MP, 92). If the poet's "speaking picture" is vivid enough, he can not only present an image to the imagination, he can also control its reaction to that image.[96]

Although Sidney's insistence upon the primacy of the poet's function as a mover would seem to downgrade his more traditional role as a teacher, Sidney is far from dismissing it entirely. Thus he is faced with still another problem: How is the poet to teach *homo literatus* what that goodness is whereunto he has been moved? For the medieval or humanist writer, this would have been no problem, for everyone knew that poetry was to be read allegorically. Why then could not the Elizabethan writer make the same assumption? For the answer, we must look to the effect of the Reformation upon the reading habits of those who accepted the "new learning."

The real difference between "Catholic" and "Protestant" attitudes toward allegory may be seen by contrasting the views of Erasmus and William Whitaker on the way to read the scriptures.[97] For Erasmus, the value of the literal sense is enriched by the hidden meaning it contains:

You should observe in all your reading those things consisting of both a surface meaning and a hidden one—comparable to body and spirit—so that, indifferent to the merely literal sense, you may examine most keenly the hidden. Of this sort are the works of the poets and of the Platonists in philosophy. But especially do the Holy Scriptures, like the Silenus of Alcibiades, conceal their real divinity beneath a surface that is crude and almost laughable.[98]

Though the Protestants did not deny that scripture could have a spiritual sense, they did insist that it did not have an existence separate from the literal sense:

There is but one true and genuine sense of scripture, namely the literal or grammatical, whether it arise from the words taken strictly, or from the words figuratively understood or from both together; and that allegorical expositions are not various meanings, but only various applications and accomodations of scripture. Such allegories, indeed, we may sometimes use with profit and advantage to give pleasure, not to coerce assent; especially when scripture explains a thing allegorically, for otherwise we should be frugal of inventing allegories.[99]

Whitaker's distinction between a figurative reading (which is nonetheless the literal sense, since the meaning of the words as figuratively understood is the "literal" meaning of the passage)[100] and allegorical expositions of the literal meaning by way of giving pleasure is significant for us because it suggests the key to the distinction implied by Sidney in a parallel passage in the *Defence*:

What child is there, that, coming to a play, and seeing *Thebes* written in great letters upon an old door, doth believe that it is Thebes? If then a man can arrive to that child's age to know that the poets' persons and doings are but pictures what should be, and not stories what have been, they will never give the lie to things not affirmatively but allegorically and figuratively written. And therefore, as in history, looking for truth, they may go away full fraught with falsehood, so in poesy, looking but for fiction, they shall use the narration but as an imaginative ground-plot of a profitable invention. [*MP*, 103]

Although the Protestants admitted the existence of a spiritual sense, they were extremely chary about searching out allegories in the text. William Tyndale's outburst in *The Obedience of a Christian Man* is not untypical:

The greatest cause of which captivity [under "antichrist the pope"] and the decay of the faith, and this blindness wherein we now are, sprang first of allegories. For Origen and the doctors of his time drew all the scriptures unto allegories: whose ensample they that came after followed so long, till they at last forgot the order and process of the text, supposing that the scripture served but to feign allegories upon. . . . Then came our sophisters with their anagogical and chopological sense, and with an antitheme of half an inch, out of which some of them drew a thread nine days long. . . . Yea, they are come unto such blindness, that they not only say the literal sense profiteth not, but also that it is hurtful, noisome, and killeth the soul.[101]

Tyndale did not deny that allegories could be useful "to express a text or an open conclusion of the scripture, and as it were to paint it before thine eyes, that thou mayest feel the meaning and the power of scripture in thine heart,"[102] but he insisted that they could not be employed to prove anything.[103]

If allegories were held to be best used sparingly and chiefly for the purpose of arousing delight or moving the reader, there is, nonetheless, a real appreciation of the spiritual sense in Protestant commentaries. This spiritual sense, however, is not so much allegorical as figurative, as Whitaker indicates: "In dealing with words we should consider which are proper, and which figurative and modified. For, when words are taken figuratively, they should not be expounded strictly. 'It is,' says Augustine, in his books of Christian Doctrine, 'a wretched bondage of the soul . . . when what is spoken figuratively is expounded as if spoken strictly.' "[104] The Protestant habit of reading figuratively grew out of their controversy with the Catholics on the sacraments, especially the sacrament of communion. In answer to Catholic assertions that the wafer and the wine are literally transformed into the body and blood of Christ, the Protestants pointed to the Augustinian doctrine of signs in the *De Doctrina Christiana* and insisted that the wafer and the wine are not literally transformed into the body and blood of Christ by the priest, but that they are a sign to the communicant by which he may remember Christ's sacrifice.[105] As such, their operation depends solely upon the faith of the individual. As Henry Bullinger wrote:

The truest and most proper cause, why sacraments be instituted under visible signs, seemeth partly to be God's goodness, and partly also man's weakness. For very hardly do we reach unto the knowledge of heavenly things, if, without visible form, as they be in their own nature pure and excellent, they be laid before our eyes: but they are better and more easily understood, if they be represented unto us under the figure of earthly things, that is to say, under signs familiarly known unto us. As therefore our bountiful and gracious Lord did covertly and darkly, nay rather, evidently and notably, set before us to view the Kingdom of God in parables or dark speeches; even so by signs it pleased him to lay before our eyes, after a sort, the very same thing, and to point out the same unto us, as it were painted in a table, to renew it afresh, and by lively representation to maintain the remembrance of the same among us.[106]

Signs, read figuratively, thus operate in much the same way that the rhetoricians conceived allegory to function, as a means of transforming the sense of the literal meaning to deepen and change the meaning of the narrative from the specific to the general and universal.

Within this context of contemporary polemics, the stress Sidney places upon poetry's ability to "figure" things takes on an increased importance. As we have seen, Sidney defines poetry, "metaphorically," as a "figuring forth,"[107] and the term recurs in passages essential to Sidney's argument. For example, in the refutation, he concedes that man's "wit" may make poetry "which should be ἐικαστική (which some learned have defined: figuring forth good things), to be φανταστική (which doth, contrariwise, infect the fancy with unworthy objects)" (MP, 104). It is because Sidney has defined poetry as a "figuring forth" that he can claim that the poet is superior to the philosopher because he gives "a perfect picture" of "whatsoever the philosopher saith should be done. . . . A perfect picture I say, for he yieldeth to the powers of the mind an image of that whereof the philosopher bestoweth but a wordish description, which doth neither strike, pierce, nor possess the sight of the soul so much as that other doth" (MP, 85). Without this perfect picture, Sidney goes on to say, no one can "satisfy his inward conceit with being witness to itself of a true lively knowledge" (MP, 85), for while the philosopher's counsels can replenish "the memory with many infallible grounds of wisdom," those grounds "lie dark before the imaginative and judging power, if they be not illuminated or figured forth by the speaking picture of poetry" (MP, 86). That is to say, without the "illumination" provided by the images the poet figures forth, poetry would lose its status as "monarch" of the sciences (see MP, 91-92).

Despite the importance of this concept in Sidney's Defence, only one serious attempt has been made to define precisely what Sidney means by "figuring forth," and that attempt leaves a great deal to be desired. Forrest G. Robinson, citing Thomas Cooper's definition of "Idea" as "a figure conceived in Imagination, as it were a substance perpetuall, being as paterne of all other sorte or kinde,"[108] narrowly defines "figuring forth" as the evoking of "vivid images" which present "the precepts of moral philosophy in such a way that . . . [the poet's] audience can see them."[109] He then proceeds to limit this conception still further by specifying the kind of "figure conceived in Imagination":

Clearly, then, the poet's Idea or fore-conceit is not a word or a verbal definition, nor is it an image of a phenomenal object. Rather, it is a diagrammatic concept, a mental chart upon which the "reasons" of a poem are organized. Once this basic structure is clearly visualized, it must be filled out with the logical divisions of the poem's subject. When the "universal consideration" is fully divided and stretched in precise detail before his mind, the poet has only to submerge it in an individaul verbal fiction (a person or an incident). The resulting fusion of the particular with the general is the speaking picture of poetry."[110]

As his model for a "diagrammatic concept," Robinson offers the chart in John Dee's preface to John Billingsley's 1570 translation of Euclid's *Elements*. [111]

While Robinson finds support for this circumscribed notion of how the "vivid images" the poet figures forth illuminate his *"idea or fore-conceit"* in the tradition of visual epistemology he educes from Plato through the Middle Ages down to Renaissance Neoplatonism, hermeticism, and Ramism, he fails to consider either Sidney's Protestant conception of epistemology as revelation in the *Defence* or the examples of "figuring forth" provided there. Sidney's discussion of David's Psalms provides a necessary corrective to his arguments: "for what else is the awaking his musical instruments, the often and free changing of persons, his notable *prosopopoeias*, when he maketh you, as it were, see God coming in His majesty, his telling of the beasts' joyfulness and hills leaping, but a heavenly poesy, wherein almost he showeth himself a passionate lover of that unspeakable and everlasting beauty to be seen by the eyes of the mind, only cleared by faith?" (*MP*, 77). This description of David's "figuring forth" hardly suggests a "diagrammatic concept" or a "mental chart"; rather Sidney depicts

David's "heavenly poesy" as using language to evoke images that move us emotionally to a state in which we are able to see ("as it were") the *idea* which has made David feel the passions that show him ("almost") to be "a passionate lover of that unspeakable and everlasting beauty."[112] By figuring forth God's "majesty" in this way, the poetical effect of the Psalms is to move us to desire the ability to see that "unspeakable and everlasting beauty" as David has. Sidney's description of the Psalms functions in the same way. Because in Sidney's Protestant epistemology we can only "see" properly when the "eyes of the mind" have been "cleared by faith," the diagrammatic charts of the Neoplatonists and Ramists will hardly do for the poet who must "imitate the unconceivable excellencies" (*MP*, 80) brought forth "with the force of a divine breath" (*MP*, 79) in the poetic consideration of "what may be and should be" (*MP*, 81).

For this reason, I cannot accept Robinson's argument that Sidney would have limited poetry perforce to "natural philosophy" on the grounds that what Robinson calls "divine philosophy"— *sapientia*—is a gift of grace and that there can be "no speaking picture, no delightful teaching, of wisdom received through grace but not learned, seen through the medium of faith but actually invisible to mortal eyes" (p. 101). As Calvin says, commenting upon 1 Cor. 2:9, while we may not be able to behold "the graces of God, which are dayly bestowed vppon the faythfull," in them we may always "behold" the cause ("the free goodnesse of God") and their effect upon those who receive them.[113] Although the "wisdom" of theology may not be transmitted through a "speaking picture," the poet may still "figure forth" its cause and effect, much as de Mornay, while utterly denying reason the power to define or "measure" faith, still feels that the way to "Waken such as are asleepe, to bring backe such as are gone astraie, to lift vp such as are sunke downe, and to chafe them a heat which are waxed cold" is to paint out "the true Religion liuely before their eyes, with the ioy, happines, and glorie which insue therevpon" (see de Mornay, *A Woorke*, sig. **6v, sigs. **4v-**5). There is, in short, no need to scourge Sidney's poetic of the divine nor to declare him a Neoplatonist philosophically even though he may be a Protestant theologically. While Sidney has no qualms about using

"Egyptian gold," he uses it in a way thoroughly in accord with his very Protestant notions about the natures of man and gold.

Although Sidney's faith in the efficacy of the images the poet figures forth may derive more from his knowledge of the *icones symbolicae* so ably discussed by E. H. Gombrich[114] than the visual epistemologies of which Robinson is so fond, we must note a key distinction even here. Gombrich posits that continental artists and philosophers may have found the "symbolic figures" attractive and illuminating because they offer a "free floating metaphor, a formula" upon which we may meditate and which "somehow . . . reveals an aspect of the structure of the world which would seem to elude the ordered progress of dialectic argument."[115] Sidney, however, would reject such "knowledge" as a false revelation; only when "cleared by faith" can the eyes of the mind see without distortion.[116]

This is not to say that because poetry is a figuring forth only the images themselves are significant or that because figurative writing employs images that function as signs all we need do is focus on those images and permit them to act upon us. Poetry is not a purely visual art nor is its function only to teach us. Because the whole of the poet's image cannot be completely apprehended simultaneously but must be constructed through the cumulative addition of verbal details, it may not be immediately recognizable. Contrariwise, the poet may choose to supply us with the general outline of his picture and then fill in the details as he goes along, making it recognizable without having fully defined it. In either case, however, rather than detracting from the image being figured forth, this lag—the silence while we wait for the picture to "speak" —may become an important part of the total effect. For the poet's "representing, counterfeiting, or figuring forth" must also move us emotionally and imaginatively. False starts, impatience for illumination, eagerness to see the slowly developing picture completed can all contribute to the poetic effect, for, as Sidney says, "who will be taught, if he be not moved with desire to be taught? And what so much good doth that teaching bring forth . . . as that it moveth one to do that which it doth teach?" (*MP*, 91).

In reading figuratively, then, we must attend not simply to the meanings the images figure forth but equally to the manner in which the images themselves are figured forth and to reactions elicited in ourselves along the way. When we read the products of this poetic, therefore, we must read with great care, for we will not fulfill our obligations as readers unless we give to the works the attention they demand. Through their reading of the scriptures and their attendance at sermons, the Elizabethans—even those who had not gone through the rigorous training of the schools—must have developed the habit of reading slowly and painstakingly and Sidney clearly expects his readers to bring the same reading habits to poetry. Bullinger's instructions for reading the scriptures might well form the basis of our study of the poetry Sidney is defending:

it is requisite, in expounding the scriptures, and searching out the true sense of God's word, that we mark upon what occasion every thing is spoken, what goeth before, what followeth after, at what season, in what order, and of what person any thing is spoken. By the occasion, and the sentences going before and coming after, are examples and parables for the most part expounded. . . . There is also, beside these, another manner of interpreting the word of God; that is, by conferring together the places which are like or unlike, and by expounding the darker by the more evident, and the fewer by the more in number.[117]

We must, in short, read attentively, perceiving not only the surface of the narrative but also the signs which may be embedded in it. We must also be very careful to observe the context of a given passage, for what a character says or does is often modified by the circumstances that frame and set off his speeches and deeds.

One final question remains. Since Sidney's defence of "poor poetry" has been largely based upon the theology of Reformed Protestantism, one might justifiably wonder why poetry "deserveth not to be scourged out of the Church of God" (MP, 77). The reprobate, who may well need the love of virtue and hatred of vice which the poet can instill, are ultimately immune from poetry's effects, since it hardly seems likely that Sidney could—or would—suggest that the poet can save those whom God has damned. Likewise, there would seem little reason to suggest that the elect ultimately need to be moved and taught by the poet since their salvation is assured in any case. Before we conclude that Sidney has defended poetry out of existence, however, we must recognize that Sidney has defended it not on eschatological grounds but within "ethic and politic consideration[s]" (*MP*, 83), as a "human" science, and "according to the human conceit" (*MP*, 91). We must not forget, as Charles Trinkaus has reminded us, that, like Bullinger and de Mornay, even Calvin "did not deprive man of an ability to control human affairs and to direct the course of nature through science. . . . Man could not save himself no matter how hard he tried; and moral virtue carried with it no merit toward justification and salvation, since the latter were predestined from eternity. It is significant, however, that in fact Calvin recognized the capacities of man in secular and social matters, though he denied them in spiritual things."[118] Poetry, if it can indeed "move men to take that goodness in hand, which without delight they would fly as from a stranger" (*MP*, 81), can indeed serve a "politic" function. If poets cannot make all things well, at least they can make some things better by making some men act better.

If we look at the manner in which Sidney formulates his definitions of the various genres, it is often precisely upon this "politic" consideration that he lays the most stress. Pastoral, for example, "can show the misery of people under hard lords or ravening soldiers, and . . . what blessedness is derived to them that lie lowest from the goodness of them that sit highest; sometimes under the pretty tales of wolves and sheep, can include the whole considerations of wrong-doing and patience" (*MP*, 94-95). The "bitter but wholesome Iambic" Sidney envisions as an instrument for the open and public rebuke of public misdeeds, rubbing "the galled mind, in making shame the trumpet of villainy, with bold and open crying out against naughtiness" (*MP*, 95). So too comedy is defined as an "imitation of the common errors of our life," represented "in the most ridiculous and scornful sort that may be, so as it is impossible that any beholder can be content to be such a one" (*MP*, 96). Comedy, moreover, can inspire its beholders not merely to desire not to "be such a one," but also to wish to see those who are punished, "although perchance the sack of his own faults lie so hidden behind his back that he seeth not himself dance the same measure, whereto yet nothing can more open his eyes than to find his own actions contemptibly set forth" (*MP*, 96). Similarly, Sidney's discussions of the other "public" genres, tragedy and lyric, focus upon the social "goodness" to which they move.[119] Tragedy "openeth the greatest wounds, and showeth forth the ulcers that are covered with tissue. . . . [It] maketh kings fear to be tyrants, and tyrants manifest their tyrannical humours" (*MP*, 96); lyric "giveth praise, the reward of virtue, to virtuous acts" and is "that kind most capable and most fit to awake the thoughts from the sleep of idleness to embrace honourable enterprises" (*MP*, 97). In all of these cases, the effect Sidney anticipates within the audience of a work falling within one of these genres is clearly contributory towards alleviating political miseries or promulgating societal improvements.

In a less obvious way, his discussions of the elegiac, satire, and heroic also contribute toward the improvement of human society by instilling within their readers the desire for personal improvement, largely by attacking the dominion of the passions. The elegiac helps by "rightly painting out how weak be the passions of woefulness," while satire "giveth us to feel how many headaches a passionate life bringeth us to" by making us "laugh at folly, and at length ashamed, to laugh at . . . [ourselves], which [we] cannot avoid without avoiding the folly" [*MP*, 95]. The heroical, finally, justifies its claim to being the "best and most accomplished kind" by being the genre that "most inflameth the mind with desire to be worthy, and inform[s] with counsel how to be worthy" by making "magnanimity and justice shine through all misty fearfulness and foggy desires," thus setting before us an attractively ravishing ideal, flying ever before us like Ariosto's Angelica and drawing us ever after her as Spenser's Arthur ever seeks his unmet image of perfection.

In this second group of genres, the "politic considerations" spring out of the "ethic" in a way suggestive of a further benefit. The "ending end" of all "earthly learning" is "virtuous action" (*MP*, 82), but there is an additional kind of learning, a kind of "knowledge of a man's self" whose end is to awaken us from that childishness that afflicts most of us until we are "cradled" in our graves (*MP*, 92). It is this kind of self-knowledge we are taught when we learn that "even Alexander and Darius, when they strave who should be cock of this world's dunghill" were merely occu-

pied in "contentions for trifles" (*MP*, 95); it is in this kind of reflection that we are engaged when, by "stirring the affects of admiration and commiseration" we are made to feel "the uncertainty of this world, and upon how weak foundations gilden roofs are
builded" (*MP*, 96). It is, finally, this revelation of our own limits
and of the limitations of the "too much loved earth" which is the
"brazen" stage upon which we act out our lives that justifies poetry's claim to remain useful to the "church of God."

If poetry cannot make man turn to God, faith being a gift of
God, not poets, it can instead give him the self-knowledge to feel
that he himself cannot free himself "from the dungeon of the
body to the enjoying of his own divine essence" (*MP*, 82). In this
view of poetry as a possible handmaid to the church, Sidney is
once again sharing in the position of de Mornay, who ascribes a
similar function to reason in the "Preface to the Reader" of *A
Woorke*:

And like as they [i.e., "some men in sundrie nations (who) haue mounted
aboue the common rate . . . and drawen some small sparks of truth and wisdom . . . as out of some little fire raked vp vnder a great heape of ashes; the
which they haue afterward taught vnto others"] haue caught some sparkes
from the fire, so will we kindle a fire of their sparkes: howbeit (in verie deed)
not to lead vs to saluation the hauen of our life; for in that behalfe we hathe
neede of God himselfe to be our Pilote: but to shew vs as it were from a
Tower; which way it standeth in the darke wherin we now be, to the end we
may call to God for helpe, and euer after make thitherward with all our
whole hart. [Sig. ***]

If the poet can teach us how much we need help, he will substan-
tially lighten our way along our journey to the "hauen of our
life."

CHAPTER *2*

"Notable images of vertues, vices, or what else": The Characters

Who Grace, for Zenith had, from which no shadowes grow,
Who hath seene Ioy of all his hopes, and end of all his woe,
Whose Loue belou'd hath beene the crowne of his desire,
Who hath seene sorrowes glories burnt, in sweet affections fire:
If from this heauenly state, which soules with soules vnites,
He be falne downe into the darke despaired warre of sprites;
Let him lament with me, for none doth glorie know,
That hath not beene aboue himselfe, and thence falne downe to woe.

Fulke Greville, *Caelica*, 83[1]

Sidney's *Old Arcadia* was largely written during the height of the political crisis precipitated by Queen Elizabeth's seeming determination to marry the Duke of Anjou. Against all of the objections advanced by the Leicester-Walsingham faction in the Privy Council, by Sidney in his letter to the Queen, and by Stubbs in his pamphlet, Elizabeth asserted her love for Monsieur, a love which appeared to outweigh all "rational" political and religious considerations.[2] The pessimism generated in the Sidney circle by Elizabeth's insistence upon continuing the marriage negotiations is reflected in the *Old Arcadia*, as we have seen, where Sidney is more concerned to show the "dark despaired warre of sprites" provoked in those who fall victim to the "unresistable force"[3] of love than the "heauenly state" in which the lovers seem to find themselves. Like Sidney's narrator, the reader finds himself a spectator at "a very stage-play of love" (p. 54), albeit a stage play framed not by "love" (p. 49) or "fortune" (p. 54), but (as Sidney's first draft to his sister has it) "by the almighty

51

wisdom," whose "fore-conceit" is "to show the world that by unlikeliest means greatest matters may come to conclusion; that human reason may be the more humbled, and more willingly give place to divine providence" (p. 265, textual variants).

To this end, Sidney assembles a cast of characters representative of some of the major classical formulations of the nature of man and of his purpose on earth and presents them in a pagan setting recreated by a narrator whose interjections mark him as distinctly Protestant in his conception of man's nature and capabilities and whose reading of "the ancient records of Arcadia" (p. 51) is done with an extremely jaundiced eye. The result, as I shall show in the next three chapters, is an *Old Arcadia*, conceived in terms of the poetic declared in the *Defence*, which presents a distinctly unflattering view of humanity based largely on sixteenth-century Protestant conceptions of human nature, here made even more dark by the absence, for the most part, of the workings of grace on Sidney's "pagan" stage. Augmenting this negative presentation, the still-unresolved political crisis lends its own air of despair to Sidney's "imitation of the common errors of our life," which he represents "in the most ridiculous and scornful sort that may be, so as it is impossible that any beholder can be content to be such a one" (*MP*, 95-96).

To read the *Old Arcadia* in this way is to define it as a comedy according to Sidney's discussion of the genres in the *Defence*. Yet with few exceptions,[4] critics of the *Old Arcadia* have seen it as a romance (either pastoral or heroic), largely on the basis of its setting or its matter. But both these readings and the usually accompanying claim that the characters represent the pinnacle of Renaissance heroism and are ideally virtuous besides have for too long passed unchallenged. In terms of Sidney's genre theory, this is tantamount to calling the *Old Arcadia* an "absolute heroical poem" (*MP*, 81), since Sidney's critical vocabulary does not seem to have included the term "romance," and works that we would normally call romances—such as *Amadis de Gaule* or Heliodorus' *Aethiopian Romance*—are included by Sidney in his discussions of heroical poetry.[5] One therefore cannot simply assert that the *Old Arcadia* is a romance without first demonstrating that it satisfies the criteria which Sidney establishes as identifying characteristics of the heroic genre in *The Defence of Poesie*:

There rests the Heroical—whose very name (I think) should daunt all back-biters: for by what conceit can a tongue be directed to speak evil of that which draweth with him no less champions than Achilles, Cyrus, Aeneas, Turnus, Tydeus, and Rinaldo?—who doth not only teach and move to a truth, but teacheth and moveth to the most high and excellent truth; who maketh magnanimity and justice shine through all misty fearfulness and foggy desires; who, if the saying of Plato and Tully be true, that who could see virtue would be wonderfully ravished with the love of her beauty—this man sets her out to make her more lovely in her holiday apparel, to the eye of any that will deign not to disdain until they understand. But if anything be already said in the defence of sweet poetry, all concurreth to the maintaining the heroical, which is not only a kind, but the best and most accomplished kind of poetry. For as the image of each action stirreth and instructeth the mind, so the lofty image of such worthies most inflameth the mind with desire to be worthy, and informs with counsel how to be worthy. [*MP*, 97-98]

Like every other kind of poetry, the power of the heroic to move an audience rests in its mimetic nature. However, since the mind would most like to be virtuous, it is most drawn to the beauty of virtue; hence the heroic is potentially the most moving (and thus the most effective) of the genres. It is, so to speak, the monarch of the genres—just as poetry is the monarch of the sciences (*MP*, 91) —because our admiration of the hero and our desire to imitate him makes it the most apt for the exhibition and inculcation of virtue. Thus Sidney urges us:

Only let Aeneas be worn in the tablet of your memory, how he governeth himself in the ruin of his country; in the preserving his old father, and carrying away his religious ceremonies; in obeying God's commandment to leave Dido, though not only all passionate kindness, but even the human consideration of virtuous gratefulness, would have craved other of him . . . lastly, how in his inward self, and how in his outward government—and I think, in a mind not prejudiced with a prejudicating humor, he will be found in excellency fruitful. [*MP*, 98]

If the characters are to be "in excellency fruitful" to the reader, their actions in the poem must show him how to be virtuous while they instill within him a desire to imitate them.

Thus one may not claim heroic status for the *Old Arcadia* without committing himself not only to proclaim the virtues of at least some of the major characters—Basilius, Pyrocles, Musidorus, Gynecia, Philoclea, and Pamela—but also to demonstrate how their virtues are manifested in their actions throughout the work. Unfortunately, this Sidney's critics have been either unwilling or unable to do. Some have chosen to point to a set of general kinds of behavior supposedly common to Sidney and the social class to which he belonged.[6] By this method, anything that seems to be morally questionable can simply be referred to the range of socially acceptable behavior of the time, and thus dismissed. This, of course, contradicts Sidney's belief that the poet should "borrow nothing of what is, hath been, or shall be; but range, only reined with learned discretion, into the divine consideration of what may be and should be" (*MP*, 81). Others have seen flaws in the characters—especially in the early parts of the book—only to interpret them out of existence by reference to the supposed conventions of a romance genre conceived more in terms of Shakespeare's romantic comedies than Sidney's comments in *The Defence of Poesie*.[7] Since Sidney has left us clear indications of the standards of behavior for characters in works of various genres and of how a reader of those works is to react to them, our first task is to examine the characters of the *Old Arcadia* and to determine how Sidney conceived of them and thus of his work. If we find ourselves responding positively to the positive virtues, we may assume that we are reading a heroic poem; if negatively to the "common errors" of mankind, a comedy.

I. Basilius

Sidney introduces us to both Arcadia and its ruling family at the very beginning of the work in a passage which stands as a prologue to the action, and, at the same time, provides us with a picture of the country and the people in stasis against which any movement during the course of the book can be measured. Arcadia, we are told, has always had a unique place among the Greek states, "partly for the sweetness of the air and other natural benefits, but principally for the moderate and well tempered minds of the people, who . . . were the only people which, as by their justice and providence gave neither cause nor hope to their neighbours to annoy them, so were they not stirred with false praise to trouble others' quiet" (p. 4). In contrast to this description of the setting, which is strikingly unhistorical in the stress it places upon the rationality of the people,[8] the narrator describes the Duke and his family in terms which, if they do not deny them rationality, certainly do not emphasize it:

In this place some time there dwelled a mighty Duke named Basilius, a prince of sufficient skill to govern so quiet a country where the good minds of the former princes had set down good laws, and the well bringing up of the people did serve as a most sure bond to keep them. He married Gynecia, the daughter of the king of Cyprus; a lady worthy enough to have had her name in continual remembrance if her latter time had not blotted her well governed youth. . . . Of her the duke had two fair daughters, the elder Pamela, the younger Philoclea, both so excellent in all those gifts which are allotted to reasonable creatures as they seemed to be born for a sufficient proof that nature is no stepmother to that sex. [*OA*, 4]

Unlike his predecessors, whose "good minds . . . had set down good laws," Basilius contributes to the preservation of order in Arcadia not by adding to the store of good laws but by administering them. But if he is merely "of sufficient skill to govern so quiet a country," the implication seems to be that any difficulties, internal or external, might be too much for him to handle. The doubt raised by this backhanded compliment to Basilius is augmented by the unspecified blight to come to Gynecia. In this context, the seeming praise of the two daughters is slightly tarnished. There is, moreover, some ambiguity about their gifts: keeping in mind the preeminence of reason over nature's gifts in the description of the Arcadian polity, we must wonder whether they are merely excellent in those things (such as beauty) which belong to the sphere of merely natural gifts. The total effect, in any case, is not that of whole-hearted praise.

Having presented the characters to us, the narrator begins his story with a view of Basilius in action which confirms the doubt raised by the prior description of him: "not so much stirred with the care for his country and children as with the vanity which possesseth many who, making a perpetual mansion of this poor baiting place of man's life, are desirous to know the certainty of things to come, wherein there is nothing so certain as our continual uncertainty" (p. 5), Basilius consults the Oracle at Delphi. His purpose is to discover if the rest of his life is to be as happy as it has been in the past, "whereupon he had placed greatest part of his own felicity" (p. 5). The passage makes it clear that Sidney's narrator is imposing a Christian sense of values upon a pagan world, and it thus comes as no surprise to see the Oracle of Apollo being referred to as "that impiety" (p. 5).[9] Our picture of Basilius has been considerably broadened. As one who has made "a perpetual mansion of this poor baiting place of man's life," it is clear that his behavior is at variance with the injunction of 1 John 2:15-16, "Love not the worlde, nether the things that are in the worlde."[10] This disregard must strike Sidney's reader as especially improper for rulers, who are to be God's vice-regents on earth, and whose power comes from God. As Sir Thomas Elyot advises, they should "first, and above all thing . . . consider that from God only proceedeth all honour, and that neither noble progeny, succession, nor election be of such force, that by them any estate or dignity may be so established that God being stirred to vengeance shall not shortly resume it, and perchance translate it where it shall like him."[11] But Basilius, far from remembering God, has begun to turn away from him. In consulting the Oracle, he is (as Philanax later tells him [OA, 7]) substituting vain curiosity for humility and patience; in then rejecting what he thinks is the future which the heavens have ordained for him, he is in the grip of a blind arrogance which thinks it can turn aside the will of God.[12] What we are watching, evidently, is a reenactment of man's original fall from God's grace. Like Adam, Basilius is tempted by "all that is in the world," and like Adam, he falls.[13]

Basilius' fall is of more than individual consequence, for he is the ruler of what we have called a prototype of the ideal political state. If each man has an obligation to control rationally his willful desires, the king has an even stronger obligation, for he must rule not only himself but also his people. In political terms, his actions —both in consulting the Oracle and in resolving to abandon active rule for one year in an attempt to escape the consequences foretold by the Oracle—represent a denial of reason and the substitution of curiosity, vanity, and arrogance as the foundation for political judgments. This is a clear violation of his kingly responsibilities, for the ruler "in all his actions . . . must vse reason as a heauenly guide, hauing chased away the perturbations of his soule, and es-teeme it a greater and more royall matter to commaund himselfe, than others. Hee must thinke that it is the true and proper office of king, not to submit himselfe to his pleasures, but to containe his own affections."[14] Through his actions, Basilius has undermined the stability of his kingdom, and its deterioration will become ap-parent as the narrative progresses.

Lest anyone mistake this characterization of Basilius, the nar-rator introduces Philanax, his friend and councillor, and has him condemn the Duke's actions, past and future. When the Duke con-fides that he plans to escape the dire predictions of the Oracle, Philanax counters by urging not flight from responsibility but trust in wisdom and virtue, and he rebukes Basilius for presumptu-ously prying into what should not concern him (*OA*, 7).[15] Basilius, however, refuses to listen to this wisdom, and insists upon fulfill-ling his intention to retreat from the world into a "solitary place" (p. 6) for one year. In doing so, as the narrator notes, he is "mak-ing his will wisdom" (p. 9). Following the dictates of the will in preference to those of "heavenly powers" is, of course, a clear and constant signal of impending disaster. Adam's fall occurred when he "followed his owne will, and left GODS commandement."[16] Basilius' decision to repair to his private lodge in the "desert" (*OA*, 16) is in every way, then, a choice of "will" over "wisdom," and no good may be expected to come of it.

Once in his retreat, the Duke completes the pattern which we have seen developing. He meets an "Excellent lady," (pp. 35-36) who identifies herself as an Amazon, and Basilius immediately an-nounces that he is hers to command. So that no one may doubt that he means us to remember the traditional identification of the Amazon as a figure of lust,[17] Sidney carefully controls our response to Basilius' inner struggle through his narrator's comments:

There hard by the lodge walked he, carrying this unquiet contention [be-
tween "honour" and "this new assault of Cleophila's beauty"] about him.
But passion ere long had gotten the absolute masterhood, bringing with it the
show of present pleasure, fortified with the authority of a prince whose power might easily satisfy his will against the far-fet (though true) reasons of the
spirit—which, in a man not trained in the way of virtue, have but slender
working. So that ere long he utterly gave himself over to the longing desire to
enjoy Cleophila, which finding an old broken vessel of him, had the more
power in him than, perchance, it would have had in a younger man. And so,
as all vice is foolish, it wrought in him the more absurd follies. [*OA*, 45] [18]

Soon Basilius is skipping through the woods, singing songs in praise
of the wisdom and constancy of old age as may be seen from him,
and acting, in short, like a fool.[19]

With his will firmly in control, Basilius is led ever more deeply
into the folly of vice. As his desire for Cleophila grows more in-
tense, she undergoes a series of transformations in his mind. From
a "Fair lady" (p. 35), she is soon changed to an "Excellent lady"
(pp. 35-36), and thence to a "heav'nly soul in human shape contained" (p. 95). Not satisfied with this, he soon hails her as a "heavenly woman or earthly goddess" (p. 114), and finally apotheosizes
her as a "goddess . . . towards whom I have the greatest feeling of
religion" (p. 177) and whom he will worship to the exclusion of
all other gods. As Cleophila, the object of this false devotion,
points out, this is blasphemy (p. 177). It is also idolatry, the worship of the creature, not the Creator.[20] The relationship between
Basilius' idolatry and his lust is quite natural and develops out of
the nature of both his sins: "And it was very agreeable (as St. Paul
teacheth [Rom. 1:18-32]) that they which fell to idolatry, which is
spirituall fornication, should also fall into carnall fornication, and
all uncleannesse, by the just judgementes of GOD, deliuering them
ouer to abominable concupiscences."[21] The common cause of
both is a defect of the will and a corruption of the reason.

While Basilius is occupying himself with thoughts only of his desires, he is faced with a rebellion. Some of his subjects, becoming
drunk while celebrating his birthday, resolve to remedy their country's want of a prince and, at the same time, end his domination

by a foreigner. To this end, they seize every implement which can possibly be used as a weapon, and rush off to Basilius' lodge. While this breakdown of order is not ultimately serious—the drunken rioters are put down by Cleophila, Dorus, and some of the shepherds—it should not have happened. Moreover, the responsibility for its occurrence beongs to Basilius, who should have been able to predict that it would happen.[22] Nonetheless, the scene provides us with a graphic picture of the political evils which follow from Basilius' removal of himself from governing and his doting love of Cleophila, whom we see soon after planning to participate in an invasion of Arcadia with her friend Musidorus, who is also attending upon the Duke, disguised as the shepherd Dorus.

Nevertheless, Basilius does not learn anything from the rebellion, and, after it has been thwarted, he returns to his doting. Finally Cleophila arranges a meeting with him, but the woman with whom he spends a night in a lightless cave is his wife, Gynecia. Upon awakening the next morning, he has nothing but scorn for his detested wife and praise for the sexual prowess of Cleophila. In his rapture, he resolves to rid himself of his wife, and to make the arrangement of the past night permanent:

"O Basilius," said he, "the rest of thy time hath been but a dream unto thee. It is now only thou beginnest to live; now only thou hast entered into the way of blissfulness. Should fancy of marriage keep me from this paradise? Or opinion of I know not what promise bind me from paying the right duties to nature and affection? O who would have thought there could have been such difference betwixt women?" [OA, 275]

Certainly not Gynecia, who, lying near him, is listening to him "prefer her to herself" (p. 276). With her, the reader can only muse at "how much fancy doth not only darken reason but beguile sense" and find "opinion mistress of the lover's judgement" (p. 276).

Basilius' inadequacies as a man, a husband, a father, and a ruler have been clear throughout the *Old Arcadia*, but Sidney, ever conscious of his responsibility to direct and to control the responses of his readers, chooses to have them restated once again. In another of the ironies that constantly inform his work, the means he utilizes for this task is Gynecia, who has come to the cave seeking precisely the same "paradise" as her husband. To Basilius' horror and amazement, the woman he has been praising so extravagantly arises and identifies herself as Gynecia, not, as he had fancied, Cleophila, and he can only stand there and listen to her "righteous" rebuke:

"Well, well, my lord," said she, "it shall well become you so to govern yourself as you may be fit rather to direct me than to be judged of me, and rather be a wise master of me than an unskilful pleader before me. Remember the wrong you do me is not only to me, but to your children, whom you had of me; to your country, when they shall find they are commanded by him that cannot command his own undecent appetites; lastly to yourself, since with these pains you do but build up a house of shame to dwell in. . . . Truly, truly, sir, very untimely are these fires in you. It is high season for us both to let reason enjoy his due sovereignty." [*OA*, 277]

Basilius, unfortunately, misses the point of her lecture. Although, grateful for being let off so lightly, he begs her forgiveness and vows to be faithful to her, he is not yet ready to "let reason enjoy his due sovereignty." Having become thirsty, he seizes a cup from Gynecia and drinks it, despite her warnings that she does not know what it contains. Once again, Basilius demonstrates that his physical demands take precedence over his reason. Upon drinking he falls down, crying out, somewhat cryptically, "O Gynecia, I die! Have care—" (p. 279). While his warning to his wife is certainly not unnecessary, it is again ironic that had he himself been capable of care, he could hardly have arrived at the position he was in when he uttered it.

II. Pyrocles and Musidorus

From this brief summary of the roles Basilius plays in the *Old Arcadia*, it is evident that he can by no means be considered either virtuous or heroic. From his first appearance to his exit from the action, Sidney is careful to shape our opinions of him in such a way that we can find little or nothing commendable about him. At first glance, however, the same cannot be said of the two young princes, Pyrocles and Musidorus, whose actions are the focus for our attention throughout most of the work. Unlike Basilius, whose capabilities, as Sidney insists, are minimal and whose virtues at best are passive (as a ruler, for instance, he is praiseworthy not because he is an able king, but merely because he is not a tyrant), the two princes have dedicated themselves from youth to the study and practice of virtue. "For they, accompanying the increase of their years with the increase of all good inward and outward qualities, and taking very timely into their minds that the divine part of man was not enclosed in this body for nothing, gave themselves wholly over to those knowledges which might in the course of their life be ministers to well doing" (p. 10). In the course of their travels—the result of being shipwrecked in Asia Minor while voyaging to join Pyrocles' father, Euarchus—they show themselves willing and able to put into practice the knowledge they have attained by defending innumerable ladies from wrong and restoring uncoutable disinherited persons to their rights. They have, in fact, come to Arcadia only because they desired "more and more to exercise their virtues and increase their experience" (p. 11).

Although their program may appear somewhat presumptuous to the modern reader, it is, in essence, in perfect accord with classical educational theory:

Thre thinges ther be that must concurre & agre in the accomplishing & perfecting of the warke, which I now purpose [i.e., educating children], that is to say Nature, Reason, and Custome. Reason I take for doctrine, custome for exercise. The begynninge and entre is to be taken of doctrine, Experience is won by meditacion & exercise. Of all those togyder is made a perfection: And where any of them do lacke or fayle, nedes must vertue halte.[23]

The princes welcome each new experience as an opportunity to test the doctrines they have learned, and in the morally uncomplicated adventures in which they have engaged themselves thus far they have been successful. In Arcadia, however, they are to be put to a more severe test. Pyrocles sees a picture of Philoclea, Basilius' younger daughter, falls in love with her, and soon can think of nothing but "how to come to the sight of his Philoclea" (p. 12). Thus when Musidorus prepares to leave Arcadia to continue their grand tour, "having informed himself fully of the strength and riches of the country; of the nature of the people, and of the manner of their laws" (p. 13), he is surprised and disconcerted to learn that his cousin for once does not share his desire to participate in the active pursuit of virtue. The stage has been set for another debate upon the conflicting demands of the reason and the will.[24]

Musidorus begins by rebuking Pyrocles for being unfaithful to the doctrines upon which they have based their previous adventures in the quest for moral excellence in much the same language Philanax had used to try to dissuade Basilius from retiring from active rule to his solitary place: "A mind well trained and long exercised in virtue, my sweet and worthy cousin, doth not easily change any course it once undertakes but upon well grounded and well weighed causes; for being witness to itself of his own inward good, it finds nothing without it of so high a price for which it should be altered" (p. 13). To this indictment, Musidorus adds the charge that Pyrocles is now indulging himself in solitude and idleness at the expense of virtue:

since our late coming into this country I have marked in you, I will not say an alteration, but a relenting, truly, and slacking of the main career you had so notably begun and almost performed . . . whereas you were wont, in all the places you came, to give yourself vehemently to knowledge of those things which might better your mind; to seek the familiarity of excellent men in learning and soldiery; and lastly, to put all these things in practice both by continual wise proceeding and worthy enterprises, as occasions fell for them; you now leave all these things undone; you let your mind fall asleep. [*OA*, 13]

Musidorus' doctrine is based on Aristotle's *Nicomachean Ethics*, and like him he argues for the excellence of the life governed by reason and devoted to the exercise of virtue. As Aristotle proclaimed, "A man fulfills his proper function only by way of practical wisdom and moral excellence or virtue: virtue makes us aim at the right target and practical wisdom makes us use the right means."[25] It is within this context that he adds the charge that Pyrocles' loitering about the forbidden lodges of Basilius and his family is foolhardy, "wherein, besides the disgrace that might fall of it (which, that it hath not already fallen upon you, is rather luck than providence, this duke having sharply forbidden it), you subject yourself to solitariness, the sly enemy that doth most separate a man from well doing" (p. 14). That Pyrocles' escape from disgrace is dependent upon fortune rather than providence follows from Aristotle's argument that virtue alone is excepted from fortune's sway,[26] and that to swerve from virtue is to lose the greatest aid man has in enduring fortune's blows.[27] Musidorus, in short, has accused Pyrocles of deserting the doctrines by which they had previously directed their lives in favor of a new course which can only end in solitude, idleness, and well-deserved disgrace.

In defense, Pyrocles shifts the base of the argument from his present behavior to philosophy, making the discussion turn on the permissibility of solitude for the purpose of contemplation:

I find not myself wholly to be condemned because I do not with a continual vehemency follow those knowledges which you call the bettering of my mind; for both the mind itself must, like other things, sometimes be unbent, or else it will be either weakened or broken, and these knowledges, as they are of good use, so are they not all the mind may stretch itself unto. Who knows whether I feed not my mind with higher thoughts? . . . And in such contemplations . . . I enjoy my solitariness; and my solitariness, perchance, is the nurse of these contemplations. [OA, 14-15]

There is, on the face of it, some support for this position in Aristotle's distinction between practical wisdom and theoretical wisdom or contemplation. Although the *Ethics* begins with the assertion that "the attainment of the good for one man alone is . . . a source of satisfaction; yet to secure it for a nation and for states is nobler and more divine,"[28] right before its conclusion, Aristotle turns to contemplation as holding pleasures "marvellous in purity and certainty."[29] Marvellous as they may be, however, those pleasures are not for man: "the activity of our intelligence constitutes the complete happiness of man, provided that it encompasses a complete span of life. . . . However, such a life would be more than human."[30] Accordingly, though praising contemplation, Aristotle returns to action as a prelude to the subject of politics and its relation to ethics: "insofar as he ["a man engaged in study"] is human and lives in the society of his fellow men, he chooses to act as virtue demands, and accordingly, he will need externals for living as a human being."[31] Musidorus feels that Pyrocles, given his political role as heir to the throne of Macedon, should be engaged in action to increase his virtues and prepare himself as a ruler, and has readied many arguments ("which the plentifulness of the matter yielded to the sharpness of his wit" [p. 16]), when a sudden change in Pyrocles' speech renders them unnecessary.

Dropping his pretense to philosophical justification for his retirement, "like a man unsatisfied in himself. . . . And so, looking with a countenance as though he desired he should know his mind without hearing him speak, and yet desirous to speak to breathe out some part of his inward evil" (p. 15), Pyrocles launches into an impassioned praise of the "pleasantness of this place" as grounds for a longer sojourn in it.

Do you not see how everything conspires together to make this place a heavenly dwelling? Do you not see the grass, how in colour they excel the emeralds, everyone striving to pass his fellow—and yet they are all kept in an equal height? And see you not the rest of all these beautiful flowers, each of which would require a man's wit to know, and his life to express? Do not these stately trees seem to maintain their flourishing old age with the only happiness of their seat, being clothed with a continual spring because no beauty here should ever fade? Doth not the air breathe health, which the birds, delightful both to the ear and eye, do daily solemnize with the sweet concent of their voices? Is not every echo here a perfect music? And these fresh and delightful brooks, how slowly they slide away, as loath to leave the company of so many things united in perfection! And with how sweet a murmur they lament their forced departure! [*OA*, 15]

How are we to react to this extravagant language? Although Pyrocles begins by considering the lilies of the field, the kingdom he is seeking is certainly not that of God (see Matt. 6:28-33). Neil Rudenstine has suggested that Pyrocles is here experiencing "a realm of feelings altogether inaccessible to Musidorus,"[32] and adds that "Pyrocles has suddenly discovered the beauties and delights of an ideal pastoral world, where there are no deeds to be done because there is no strife. He now finds even the commonest objects to be inexhaustibly rich. . . . The landscape is simply its own reward, and Pyrocles is content to be moved to contemplation and wonder by it."[33] From Pyrocles' description, however, one feels that what he has seen and what he has described can have only the most tenuous relationship. Rather than discovering the beauties of an ideal pastoral world, Pyrocles claims to have discovered the unattainable earthly Paradise which disappeared from men's view with Adam's expulsion from Eden. In the ideal pastoral world, the trees and flowers—however beautiful—are still trees and flowers, the products of nature. To these natural objects man's creations, if seen as perfected, can be compared and judged. In short, in the ideal pastoral world, man reaches his highest achievement when his achievements are in harmony with and comparable to nature's bounty.

Pyrocles' vision is not of this sort. Instead, the works of nature are secondary to man's artificial embellishments of them, and rather than nature being the standard by which man is measured, man (or, in this case, woman) becomes the filter through which nature is strained. The trees do not flourish because they are healthy, they flourish because of "the only happiness of their seat," because they have been privileged to grow in a place where, temporarily, Philoclea has been forced to dwell. The birds' song does not spring from the earth; it celebrates the "sweet concent" Pyrocles wishes to hear in Philoclea's voice. The landscape does not partake in the process of nature at all; instead it is exempted from the natural cycle of life and located in "a continual spring," and the beauty which here could never fade is, for Pyrocles, only a reflection of Philoclea's beauty.

Through Sidney's manipulation of the details which Pyrocles chooses to praise, we are prepared for his peroration even before utters it: "Certainly, certainly, cousin it must needs be that some goddess this desert belongs unto, who is the soul of this soil; for neither is any less than a goddess worthy to be shrined in such a heap of pleasures, nor any less than a goddess could have made it so perfect a model of the heavenly dwellings" (p. 15). In short, what makes this desert beautiful is that which makes it not a desert[34]—the presence of Philoclea. If Rudenstine's appraisal misses the point, however, so does Lanham's offhand condemnation of Pyrocles as one incapable of seeing anything but himself.[35] While Pyrocles has transformed the landscape into an unreal vision, he is not to be condemned for it but pitied. As yet unaware of his new state as lover, he is trying to rationalize his inner distress. Pyrocles, at this moment, is not completely selfish; he is, instead, momentarily selfless, having lost his grip on his rational being without realizing that he has come into the control of his willful being. His inner state is captured beautifully by the narrator's description of him at the conclusion of his speech: "And so he ended, with a deep sigh, ruefully casting his eye upon Musidorus, as more desirous of pity than pleading" (p. 15). Where Lanham sees Pyrocles' whole speech merely as consciously sophistical argument,[36] Sidney has his narrator point out that what we have seen and heard is a confused attempt at self-justification by one who knows that there can be no justification of his present actions according to the standards by which he has lived. Pyrocles is not a cool, rational debater scoring points against an opponent, but a self-condemned man desperately trying to understand why he is acting as he is.

Musidorus, listening to his friend and watching him while he speaks, is partially aware of Pyrocles' state, which is manifest in his expressions and gestures:

For, besides his eyes sometimes even great with tears, the oft changing of his colour, with a kind of shaking unstaidness over all his body, he might see in his countenance some great determination mixed with fear, and might perceive in him store of thoughts rather stirred than digested, his words interrupted continually with sighs which served as a burden to each sentence, and the tenor of his speech (though of his wonted phrase) not knit together to one constant end but rather dissolved in itself, as the vehemency of the inward passion prevailed. [OA, 16]

In an effort to discover the source of Pyrocles' discomfort, Musidorus abandons the arguments he had prepared against Pyrocles' defence of inactivity, and turns instead to "the excessive praises" Pyrocles gives to "this desert." Arcadia, to his rational mind, is "not unpleasant," but it is easily equalled by the countryside of Macedon or by the vale of Tempe in Thessaly, which must likewise be called heavens, "or find this no more than earthly" (p. 16). However, when Musidorus gently ridicules what he takes to be Pyrocles' hyperbolic description as akin to "words in the mouth of one of these fantastical mind-infected people that children and musicians call lovers" (p. 17), Pyrocles is stunned by the realization that he is, in fact, in love. His admission of that fact, coupled with his plan to disguise himself as an Amazon in order to gain admission to Philoclea's presence, unleashes a torrent of arguments from Musidorus attacking this surrender to love.

Musidorus' answer centers on the imperative that man must follow the dictates of his reason against the desires of his will:

Remember (for I know you know it) that, if we will be men, the reasonable part of our soul is to have absolute commandment, against which if any sensual weakness arise, we are to yield all our sound forces to the overthrowing of so unnatural a rebellion; wherein, how can we want courage, since we are to deal against so weak an adversary that in itself is nothing but weakness? Nay, we are to resolve that if reason direct it, we must do it; and if we must do it, we will do it; for to say I cannot is childish, and I will not womanish. [OA, 19]

Musidorus' Peripatetic argument that passion is a weakness which can easily be kept within bounds by reason stands in sharp contrast to the position Sidney adopts in *The Defence of Poesie* that man's will has become so corrupted since the fall that it cannot help but overcome the reason without the aid of grace. As Philanax's stoicism was preferable to Basilius' Epicureanism in the earlier debate, however, here Musidorus' Aristotelianism seems preferable to Pyrocles' confused and emotional appeals so long as we do not take Musidorus' arguments for Sidney's

Pyrocles, meanwhile, searching desperately for a rational justification for his behavior, abandons the Peripatetic position for the more hospitable Neoplatonic belief in the permissibility of loving a woman as the first step in the stairway leading to the love of God.[37] Pyrocles asserts that it is impossible to reach virtue through the pursuit of abstractions, but that it is necessary to find something concrete in which they are embodied, and to follow it until the pursuit of virtue becomes a habit:

For, if we love virtue, in whom shall we love it but in virtuous creatures? — Without your meaning be I should love this word of virtue when I see it written in a book. Those troublesome effects you say it breeds be not the fault of love, but of him that loves, as an unable vessel to bear such a power. . . . Even that heavenly love you speak of is accompanied in some hearts with hopes, griefs, longings, and despairs. And in that heavenly love, since there are two parts (the one, the love itself; the other, the excellency of the thing loved), I (not able at the first leap to frame both in myself) do now, like a diligent workman, make ready the chief instrument and first part of that great work, which is love itself. Which, when I have a while practised in this sort, then you shall see me turn it to greater matters. [OA, 22]

By opposing this Neoplatonic conception of love to Musidorus' more severe castigation of "this bastard love (for, indeed, the name of love is unworthily applied to so hateful a humour as it is, engendered betwixt lust and idleness)" (pp. 19-20), Pyrocles hopes to convince him that there is nothing unvirtuous in his love of Philoclea. However he cannot resist pointing out, in answer to Musidorus' charge of womanish behavior in giving way to his will, that despite his "woman's apparel . . . there is nothing I desire more than fully to prove myself a man in this enterprise" (pp. 22-23), and through this pun he unwittingly confirms Musidorus' assertions about the lustful basis for his "love" and undercuts his newly adopted Neoplatonism. As Ficino insists, love which desires physical consummation is not love at all: "Love regards as its end the enjoyment of beauty; beauty pertains only to the mind, sight, and hearing. Love, therefore, is limited to these three, but desire which rises from the other senses is called, not love, but lust or madness."[38]

Musidorus remains unmoved by Pyrocles' sophistries, and, in a reply to Pyrocles' defence of his love of virtue which is also a rejection of his Neoplatonism, points out that Pyrocles, not having met the lady, can know nothing of her virtue. " 'Well, well,' said he, 'you list to abuse yourself. It was a very white and red virtue which you could pick out by the sight of a picture. Confess the truth, and you shall find the uttermost was but beauty' " (p. 23). He further threatens, seeing Pyrocles "now upon the point of falling or rising" (p. 24) and unmoved by his arguments, to abandon his friend, rather than be forced to suffer "the continual pang of seeing your danger with mine eyes" (p. 24). However, what Pyrocles cannot accomplish by appealing to Musidorus' reason, he achieves by bursting into tears: Musidorus, too, abandons reason and agrees to help Pyrocles achieve his desires.

In describing Musidorus' reaction to his friend's breakdown, the narrator stresses that he is proceeding not from reason but, like Pyrocles, from his passions: "And this strook Musidorus's mind and senses so dumb, too, that for grief not being able to say anything, they rested with their eyes placed one upon another, in such sort as might well paint out the true passion of unkindness, which is never aright but betwixt them that most dearly love" (p. 25). Musidorus' submission, while almost unremarked by Sidney's critics, is crucial to our understanding of both Musidorus himself and Sidney's design.[39] His consent to Pyrocles' activities at once prepares us for his imminent descent to love on seeing Pamela and completes the parallelism between the fall of the two princes and that of Adam and Eve. In the commentaries on Adam's fall, Eve was often allegorized as the "carnal appetite" and Adam as reason. Seen thus, the fall did not occur until Adam, or reason, consented to the claims of the will, or Eve, and ate the apple himself.[40] In Sidney's evocation of this archetypal fall, Pyrocles is consistently accused by Musidorus of acting irrationally by following the demands of his will. When Musidorus, who has been playing the part of reason, capitulates out of love for Pyrocles, the analogy is complete. Just as Sidney figures Adam's fall in Basilius', he also establishes the similarity of the fall of the two princes to that of Adam and Eve. Although the scene is not an allegory of the fall, it is an echo of it, and the repetition figures the fallen state of the characters, constantly playing the narrator's Christian perspective against their various pagan ones. These conflicting sets of assumptions resonate throughout the *Old Arcadia* and force us always into the position of judge, not observer, always inviting us to become a partisan, not a neutral. If we accept this invitation, then we must see Pyrocles and Musidorus, like Basilius, as not simply unwise, but as seriously erring.

Throughout the debate, both Pyrocles and Musidorus are presented, if not with the narrator's approval, at least with his sympathy. Once they have committed themselves to the pursuit of Philoclea and Pamela, respectively, there is a decided shift in tone as he begins to mock them. After Pyrocles arrays himself as an Amazon in what Richard Lanham has described as a parody of an epic arming scene,[41] he, or rather "she" (for the narrator, ironically respecting Pyrocles' self-transformation into the Amazon, Cleophila, consistently speaks of him with the feminine pronoun)[42] sits down in a solitary place and, "with many sobs and tears" (p. 28), sings of her metamorphosis:

> *Transformed in show, but more transformed in mind,*
> *I cease to strive, with double conquest foiled;*
> *For (woe is me) my powers all I find*
> *With outward force and inward treason spoiled.*
>
> [OA 2, pp. 28-29]

In this sonnet, all of the self-deceptions Pyrocles clutched at in the debate with Musidorus are gone—including the temporary adoption of Neoplatonic attitudes. Pyrocles portrays himself as he sees "himself," as the womanish Cleophila who has permitted "herself" to abandon the guide of "his" reason for "her" will. His outward transformation thus mirrors Pyrocles' inner state. It is at once an admission of failure for not acting as he knows he should—and as he believes he can—as well as a statement of guilt for that failure. Pyrocles recognizes that, although the assault was external, the "treason" of submission came from within, as his reason surrendered control to his will. As in Musidorus' companion plaint, "Come shepherd's weeds, become your master's mind," the princes feel the fault lies not in their stars but in themselves: "Helpless his plaint who spoils himself of bliss" (OA 4.10, pp. 40-41).

The demeaning process is continued in Sidney's description of the birth of Musidorus' passion for Pamela. Unlike Pyrocles, whose struggles against love were at least capable of reminding us of his nobility and of the virtues he had mastered, Musidorus is quickly overcome almost in the act of protesting that his reason would never permit him to share Pyrocles' fate (see p. 40):

The beams of the princess Pamela's beauty had no sooner stricken into his eyes but that he was wounded with more sudden violence of love than ever Pyrocles was. Whether indeed it were that this strange power would be bravely revenged of him for the bitter words he had used, or that his very resisting made the wound the crueller . . . or rather that the continual healthfulness of his mind made this sudden ill the more incurable (as the soundest bodies, once infected, are most mortally endangered); but howsoever the cause was, such was the effect that, not being able to bear the vehement pain, he ran away through the grove, like a mad man. [*OA*, 41]

Despite all the ironies, however, Musidorus' sudden fall makes the point quite clear that his position in the debate earlier and his view of man do not adequately represent the reality of man's fallen state. Although the princes are not relieved of responsibility simply because their fallen nature is not strong enough to fight off the attacks of love, their descent into humanity serves fleetingly to make us recognize ourselves in them.

Where Pyrocles at least struggled against himself, Musidorus' opponent has no more nobility than an infection, and it reduces him to a madman. Pyrocles' reaction, too, is indicative of the change in their natures. Musidorus, we remember, was reduced to tears of compassion through his concern for his friend, and ultimately agreed, against his better judgment, to participate in Pyrocles' schemes out of love for him. In comparison, Pyrocles' first reaction (out of "perfect friendship") is to mock Musidorus because he "thought good a little to punish him" (p. 42), and the pity he finally accords Musidorus has its source largely in his own problems: "Cleophila's friendly heart felt a great impression of pity withal—as certainly all persons that find themselves afflicted easily fall to compassion of them who taste of like misery, partly led by the common course of humanity, but principally because, under the image of them, they lament their own mishaps; and so the complaints the others make seem to touch the right tune of their own woes" (p. 43). As we find ourselves alternating between condemnation and compassion, this speech may help to remind us—too late—that we have already cast the first stone.

Thus far, we have been discussing the love of Pyrocles and Musidorus primarily in terms of the effect which it has upon their outward behavior without paying too much attention to the nature of that love itself. Moreover, we have been considering their new state as lovers primarily from their varying points of view. The narrator's continual use of disease imagery provides another perspective on the meanings "love" is being made to figure forth.[43] The narrator's medical metaphors remind us of the tradition, going back to the Bible, of equating the state of sin with sickness. Thus Christ calls himself a physician (Mark 2:17), saying, "The whole haue no nede of the physicion, but the sicke: I came not to call the righteous, but the sinners to repentance." Thus also original sin was commonly considered to be an inbred disease.[44] By ceasing to struggle against his "infected will," Pyrocles' wit is rendered powerless, and, indeed, is made sick among the rest, for disordered love was regularly seen as a kind of madness.[45] When Pyrocles' reason ceases to struggle against his infected will, he is metaphorically decked with chains symbolizing his bondage and his lost liberty: "when he could fix his thoughts upon nothing but that, within a little varying, they should end with Philoclea; when each thing he saw seemed to figure out some part of his passions, and that he heard no word spoken but that he imagined it carried the sound of Philoclea's name; then did poor Pyrocles yield to the burden, finding himself prisoner before he had leisure to arm himself, and that he might well, like the spaniel, gnaw upon the chain that ties him, but he should sooner mar his teeth than procure liberty" (p. 12). It seems relevant to invoke Gal. 5:1: "Stand fast therefore in the libertie wherewith Christ hathe made vs free, and be not intangled againe with the yoke of bondage." Pyrocles, overwhelmed by the desire of his will, stands in need of the gift of Christ, "who rescued us from the tyranny of Sin, Satan, and death."[46] In place of the yoke of Christ (Matt. 11:29-30), Pyrocles wears the yoke of bondage (Eccles. 40:1).[47]

Having alerted the reader to just what kind of love Pyrocles has fallen prey, the narrator proceeds to exhibit the consequences of giving way to passion. In order to see Philoclea, Pyrocles decides to disguise himself as an Amazon. Besides remembering that the Amazon is a standard figure for lust, the narrator emphasizes that this change of sex is another inversion of natural order. Just as reason should control passion, so should man control woman. By submitting himself to a creature lower in the hierarchical scale than himself, Pyrocles is, in a sense, taking on the qualities of the woman. As Musidorus, not yet having himself given way to passion, reminds him, "as the love of heaven makes one heavenly, the love of virtue, virtuous, so doth the love of the world make one become worldly. And this effeminate love of a woman doth so womanize a man that, if you yield to it, it will not only make you a famous Amazon, but a launder, a distaff-spinner, or whatsoever other vile occupation their idle heads can imagine and their weak hands perform" (OA, 20).[48]

Despite his friend's warning, Pyrocles persists in his intention to seek out Philoclea. When he finally does succeed in meeting her, he is struck dumb: "The clouds of Cleophila's thoughts quite vanished, and so was her brain fixed withal that her sight seemed more forcible and clear than ever before or since she found it, with such strange delight unto her (for still, fair ladies, you remember that I use the she-title to Pyrocles, since so he would have it) that she stood like a well wrought image, with show of life, but without all exercise of life" (pp. 37-38). The narrator again points to Pyrocles' effeminacy and again insists that it is he who is responsible for his condition. He also suggests that Pyrocles' sickness has progressed even further since we last saw him. Then, he was still aware enough of his condition to complain, "with many sobs and tears" that he has been "false in my self" and that he has thus been egregiously transformed (p. 28). Now, in contrast, while he thinks that he has never seen so clearly before, he is actually completely unable to exercise any of his rational functions. His momentary stasis is the result of the complete victory of his will:

Some are so tossed and tormented, that they become senseles and out of their wits being ouertaken with looking vpon a beautiful face, which hath such pricks, that they pierce euen to the liueliest part of their heart and soule. Whereupon it commeth to passe, that the poore silly louers are so tormented and full of passions, that they stand altogether amazed, and are like to them that are rosted by a soft fire: yea their soule is so subiected to their concupiscence & desire, that she must obey them, as if she were some poore chambermaide and drudge.[49]

Transformed in will as in shape, the princes are no longer the exemplary images of classical ideals they began as, but something far more recognizable to a Protestant reader. They have become figures of fallen mankind.

The final episode of the first "book or act" of the narrative pro-

Figure 1. Lucas Cranach, "Hercules and Omphale." Copyright Statens Museum for Kunst, København. Reproduced with permission. (See n. 48.)

vides what seems like a definitive image of the princes' new psychic state.[50] Pyrocles and Musidorus, now accepted by all as a traveling Amazon and an apprentice shepherd, accompany the princesses to "the fair meadow appointed for their shepherdish pastimes," when into the scene rush "a monstrous lion, with a she-bear of little less fierceness" (p. 46). Although the princes spring to the defence of their princesses, the narrator makes it clear that Philoclea and Pamela should fear their defenders no less than they fear their assailants:

But Cleophila, seeing how greedily the lion went after the prey she herself so much desired, it seemed all her spirits were kindled with an unwonted fire; so

Figure 2. School of Lucas Cranach, "Hercules and Omphale." Copyright Southeby Parke Bernet, Inc., New York. Reproduced with permission (See n. 48.)

that, equalling the lion in swiftness, she overtook him as he was ready to have seized himself of his beautiful chase, and disdainfully saying, "are you become my competitor?"—strake him so great a blow upon the shoulder that she almost cleaved him assunder. [*OA*, 47]

While Pyrocles is busy with the lion, Musidorus, having killed the bear, uses the opportunity to fondle the unconscious Pamela, "(at that time in a swoon with extremity of fear) and softly taking her in his arms, he took the advantage to kiss and re-kiss her a hundred times" (p. 52). Clearly, the princes, having set loose the beast in themselves, are no less dangerous to the princesses than the wild animals they have slain.[51]

The fall of the princes is now complete. From the happiest of men, Aristotle's habitually virtuous wise men "most beloved by the gods,"[52] to confused men engaged in an all-out struggle between reason and will, thence to will-dominated effeminacy and mad witlessness, the princes finally reach their nadir when they are transformed into the equivalents of wild beasts. As the princes have changed, so too have our reactions to them. Our original admiration for their virtue is changed first to pity for the inner struggle they undergo, then to compassion (mixed with condemnation) for their losing effort, next to mockery for their new incarnations, and finally to distrust of their complete selfishness and animality. It is on this note that the narrator leaves us to dwell when he breaks off the action for the duration of the First Eclogues.[53]

Nothing occurs in the second act to make us change this conception of the two princes. Their part of the action is largely given over to their attempts to woo the princesses, and the narrator metaphorically describes this segment of the book as the incubation period for the disease that has been contracted by all the noble characters: "In these pastoral pastimes a great number of days were sent to follow their flying predecessors, while the cup of poison, which was deeply tasted of all this noble company, had left no sinew of theirs without mortally searching into it; yet never manifesting his venomous work" (p. 91). In this wooing, Musidorus has more success initially, and, having managed to convey his true identity to Pamela, is accepted by her as her lover. Pyrocles, plagued by the unwelcome attentions of Gynecia and Basilius, can find little opportunity to talk to Philoclea and is forced to unburden "her" love to the trees. Finally, Pyrocles is presented with an occasion to divulge his feelings and true identity to Philoclea, and she too admits her love for him.

Only at the very end of the second act is there any significant action. In the revolt of the Phagonians, Sidney forces us to consider Pyrocles and Musidorus in terms of the political effect they are having on Arcadian society. Stirred up by the knowledge that "a strange woman had now possessed their prince and government," the Phagonians—Arcadians living in a district near to Basilius' retreat—resolve to "deliver our prince from foreign hands, and ourselves from the want of a prince" (p. 127). Pyrocles, who is, of course, the "strange woman" in question, first repels the Phagoni-ans' assault, and then, sitting in the Duke's judgment seat, per-suades them that she does not intend them any harm. She pro-claims her innocence and takes refuge in the law of hospitality as "a stranger fled to your arms for succour" (p. 130). Her oratory is effective (if inaccurate) and the Phagonians, except for an unre-generate dozen, put down their arms.

It is traditional to see this episode as further proof of the ability of the princes (for Musidorus is also a minor participant in the epi-sode) and as a demonstration of their great courage. Similarly, the Phagonians are seen as the great Elizabethan bogeymen, revolu-tionaries, invoked only to be ridiculed and despised. These views, so far as they go, are not wholly incorrect. The princes are coura-geous and the mob is a drunken rabble. Nevertheless, the mob did have a legitimate grievance in its complaint that their ruler, now himself ruled by a "woman," was leaving them leaderless, and Py-rocles' speech in answer to them does not in any way refute their claims. Pyrocles (as Cleophila) has become the sole concern of Basilius, albeit unwillingly; and when, in the third book, Basilius decides to return to his court and active rule, Pyrocles dissuades him out of fear that his pursuit of Philoclea will be obstructed. The commonplace reaction to this kind of behavior in a prince is clear:

For how is it possible, that he which placeth his chiefe *Good* in the pleasure of the body, and in neuer feeling griefe, should make account of to imbrace vertue, which is an enemy to delights and pleasures, & commandeth vs rather to suffer a cruel & dolorous death, than to start aside against duty. It is cer-taine, that he which placeth his chiefe *Good* in pleasure hath no regard to do anything but for his priuate profite. Wherby he declareth sufficiently, that he careth not at al for vertue, especially iustice, which commandeth nothing so much, as to leaue our particular pleasure & profit, and to imbrace, though with our peril and losse, the publike welfare.[54]

The context provided by the opening of the third book also makes Pyrocles' arguments about the sanctity of established gov-ernments seem hypocritical. How can we possibly reconcile Pyro-cles' acceptance of Musidorus' plan to steal Pamela from Arcadia and to return leading an army to enforce Pyrocles' claim for Philoclea on Basilius (see p. 173) with his lecture to the Phagonians: "For such a hellish madness, I know, will never enter into your hearts as to attempt anything against his person; which no successor, though never so hateful to him, will, for his own sake, ever leave unpunished" (p. 130)?[55] Clearly, then, this episode serves two purposes. First, it reveals the disruptive effect which the abdication of rule and reason by princes can have on even the most rational of populaces (and we must remember that what makes Arcadia of singular reputation amongst the Greek states is the "moderate and well-tempered minds of the people" [p. 4]). Second, it shows the depths to which the princes have sunk, now that they are willing to subordinate the welfare of an entire country to the fulfillment of their desires. The infection of will first seen in Basilius, Pyrocles, and Musidorus is here shown to have reached the proportions of a plague.

In the third book, the action reaches a climax as the princes unleash the "inward evil" they have been nurturing. Since not even their strongest defenders have found much to praise in Musidorus' decision to elope with Pamela and return with an army or in Pyrocles' temporizing with Gynecia in order to buy time in which to continue his quest for Philoclea, I will reserve consideration of book 3 for my discussion of the *Old Arcadia*'s structure. The third book has ended with all of the noble lovers paired off, albeit some unwillingly, as Pyrocles and Philoclea sport in "bliss" (p. 243) while Basilius plays to Gynecia's discomfort (p. 227) and Musidorus turns from Pamela (whom he had been about to rape) to the "dozen clownish villains" who have proved "a most infortunate bar of his long-pursued and almost-achieved desires" (p. 202). When, after the Third Eclogues' exploration of marriage as occasioned by the nuptials of Lalus and Kala, we return to the various couples, we do so with the benefit of the narrator's newly offered perspective on their varied pursuits (albeit with particular reference to Pyrocles and Philoclea, whom Dametas has just discovered, naked, in bed together):

The everlasting justice (using ourselves to be the punishers of our faults, and making our own actions the beginning of our chastisement, that our shame may be the more manifest, and our repentance follow the sooner) took Dametas . . . (by whose folly the others' wisdom might receive the greater over-throw)[56] to be the instrument of revealing the secretest cunning—so evil a ground doth evil stand upon, and so manifest it is that nothing remains strongly but that which hath the good foundation of goodness. [*OA*, 265]

The lovers' bliss, seen in relation to the providential order of God, is now only "evil," and like all evils cannot endure. Rather than introducing the lovers, as they thought, to heaven, it seems more likely to lead them only to their own destruction.

Pyrocles, upon awakening, finds the door locked, his sword missing, and his activities with Philoclea common knowledge. To protect Philoclea, he resolves to kill himself, so that "it might justly appear that either Philoclea in defending her honour, or else he himself in despair of achieving, had left his carcass proof of his fact but witness of her clearness" (p. 291). He is, however, unable even to kill himself, and falls to the ground, merely stunned. Philoclea awakes, and a debate on the lawfulness of suicide ensues. Great thematic significance has been attributed to this debate, during which Pyrocles agrees to give up the idea of self-destruction. Walter Davis sees it as an essential step in the process of Pyrocles' working "out of the limited and cloudy perspective of the cave into the enlarged perspective of man in the universe, superior to the beasts and subject to God."[57] Davis continues:

She ["the humble and innocent Philoclea"] awakens to find him on the floor like Gynecia in the cave, beside him the iron bar with which he has just attempted suicide. She raises him up, like Boethius's Lady Philosophy, in order to educate him. The imperative she sets before him is this: a man must use his every effort to establish justice in his soul by the triple subjection of body to soul, of the lower parts of the soul to Reason, and of the whole soul to God. She gives him the strength to approach such an image by convincing him of the presence of God's providential order in the universe. The scene occurs as dawn breaks its way through the bedroom windows.[58]

Such an interpretation seems to me to romanticize the text. As Sidney wrote it, the scene serves only to reinforce our sense of the distance between Pyrocles' perspective and that of the narrator, which we have made our own.

Philoclea, to be sure, does raise him up from the ground, but her initial reaction is not that his act would lead to his damnation, but to hers. " 'My comfort, my joy, my life,' said she, 'what haste have you to kill your Philoclea with the most cruel torment that ever lady suffered? Do you not yet persuade yourself that any hurt of yours is a death unto me, and that your death should be my hell?' " (p. 293). She then urges Pyrocles against suicide on the grounds that such a course is not an act of virtue but of fear: "The killing oneself is but a false colour of true courage, proceeding rather of fear of a future evil, either of torment or shame" (p. 294). Pyrocles prefaces his answer with the declaration that the cause is not fear but love, then defends the act itself with the standard classical arguments.[59] In reply, Philoclea argues that suicide is a denial of God's goodness. When this fails, however, she threatens to confess to her father that she had given her consent to her seduction, then to put out her eyes, and finally to "give herself so terrible a death as she might think the pain of it would countervail the never dying pain of her mind" (p. 299). It is only after this threat that Pyrocles agrees not to kill himself.

Taking the scene as a whole, then, it is clear that Philoclea does not raise Pyrocles up to educate him; she raises him up because she loves him. She does not convince Pyrocles of "the presence of God's providential order in the universe"; she merely convinces him that "his end should but deprive them both of a present contentment, and not avoid a coming evil" (p. 299). Both end the scene as they began it, concerned more with their desire for the other than anything else and subject not to God but their passions.

With Pyrocles and Philoclea captives of Philanax, whose arrival coincides with the discovery of Basilius' "death," the narrative moves back to Musidorus, whom we had left in the middle of an attempted rape, foiled only by the appearance of the remnants of the Phagonian rebels, whose arrival the narrator attributes to the guidance of "the everlasting justice" (p. 307). The narrator begins by confirming our suspicions of Musidorus' motives: "the every way enraged Musidorus rase from her—enraged betwixt a repentant shame of his promise-breaking attempt and the tyrannical fire of lust (which, having already caught hold of so sweet and fit a fuel, was passed the calling back of reason's counsel)" (p. 306). The narrator takes pains to direct our response. The combat is not that of worthy enemies, but a skirmish between beasts. The rebels "who . . . as they were in the constitution of their minds little better than beasts" (p. 307), scatter when Musidorus runs at them "like so many swine when a hardy mastiff sets upon them" (p. 308). Clearly any difference between the prince and the rebels is quantitative, not qualitative. Musidorus' ultimate indignity comes when he is forced to surrender to them after, in his unthinking rage, he lets them capture Pamela. Finally, the two princes are united in Philanax's custody (the rebels having met and been slaughtered by Philanax's men).[60]

Between the princes' reunion in captivity, now physical as well as spiritual, and their next appearance in the fifth "book or act," a new ironic twist has been added to the situation. Pyrocles' father, King Euarchus, has come to Arcadia to see if he might persuade Basilius to return to his duties and to attempt to arrange for the marriage of Basilius' daughters to his son and nephew. All that the princes have lied and schemed for, everything for which they have degraded and deformed themselves would have been theirs with complete propriety and conformity to the laws of man and God had they not taken matters into their own hands. As all of Sidney's metaphors become literal, Euarchus, finding himself too late to persuade Basilius to return to his proper duties and stop him from "this burying himself alive," agrees to serve as a judge over his encoffined body. Among the defendants are Pyrocles and Musidorus, engaged now not in a metaphysical trial of their virtue between doctrine and experience, but in a real trial whose outcome will mean life or death for them.

Before the trial, however, the two princes engage in a discussion of their spiritual health. If we accept their own valuations of themselves, they have little to fear. When Pyrocles calls the heavens unjust in punishing Musidorus along with himself, Musidorus casts the excuse of destiny over all of their actions: " 'O blame not the heavens, sweet Pyrocles,' said Musidorus, 'as their course never alters, so is there nothing done by the unreachable ruler of them, but hath an everlasting reason for it. And to say the truth of those things, we should deal ungratefully with nature if we should be forgetful receivers of her good gifts, and so diligent auditors of the chances we like not' " (p. 371). Musidorus then goes on to tally all their good deeds: "We have lived, and have lived to be good to ourselves and others. Our souls (which are put into the stirring earth of our bodies) have achieved the causes of their hither coming. They have known, and honoured with knowledge, the cause of their creation. And to many men (for in this time, place, and fortune, it is lawful for us to speak gloriously) it hath been behoveful that we should live" (p. 371). In speaking thus, the princes are trying to prepare themselves for death according to Peripatetic dictates. They are, following Aristotle, thinking of the real good of life: "The attainment of the good for one man alone is, to be sure, a source of satisfaction; yet to secure it for a nation and for states is nobler and more divine."[61] Although they may not have achieved all they sought for themselves, they have done much for others in their pre-Arcadian exploits. Apparently this is enough to tilt the balance decisively for them. According to their interpretation, the ills they have experienced (and their part in these ills) are merely the gifts of chance, and may thus be ignored, leaving them free to contemplate only their "honourable purposes," whether or not they have fulfilled them, and to remember with a good conscience the good they have done in the world. They also give rein to their speculations on what it will be like after the death of the body, agreeing that they will live as pure intelligence, void of all human cares, "And shall, as I hope, know our friendship, though exempt from the earthly cares of friendship, having both united it and ourselves in that high and heavenly love of the unquenchable light" (p. 373).

For some critics, such as D. P. Walker, it is "fairly evident" that Pyrocles and Musidorus "are saved, judging by their discussion on the after life."[62] Yet in that case, we might wish to say the same of such as Plato, Socrates, Cicero, or Seneca, in whose works we can find similar discussions: "Picture to yourself how great is the glow when all the stars mingle their fires; no shadows will disturb the clear sky. The whole expanse of heaven will shine evenly; for day and night are interchanged only in the lowest atmosphere. Then you will see that you have lived in darkness, after you have seen, in your perfect state, the perfect light—that light which you now behold darkly with vision that is cramped to the last degree. And yet, far off as it is, you already look upon it with great wonder; what do you think the heavenly light will be when you have seen it in its proper sphere?"[63] Yet however touched we may be by the odd passage, we must remember that, although there were some Renaissance Christians, like Erasmus, who were willing to give the pagans the benefit of the doubt, most, like Calvin and de Mornay, attribute any sentiment resembling Christian truth to the inspiration of God while yet finding it insufficient to lead anyone to salvation. Just so de Mornay, after approvingly quoting Cicero's description of the Law as everlasting and unchangeable, goes on to define that Law as the one Jesus gave, "which yet not withstanding doth more surmount our abilitie to performe, and more bewray our corruption, and more condemne whatsoever is in vs of our owne, than doth the Lawe it selfe vniversally in all mankind" and to contrast this Law with the writings of the pagans: "On the contrarie part, what find we in all the writings of the Heathen, but a Hireling vertue, and a teaching to cloke vice, that is to say Hypocrisie?" (sig. Oo⁴). For de Mornay, who recognized only one God and only one religion, the pagans, however close they came, did not and could not ever get close enough to the revelation delivered by Christ, without which there can be no salvation for anyone.

Before we accept the princes' estimate of themselves and their destiny as Sidney's, we must consider, as we have done so often, the distance between the response Sidney expects us to have to his characters' speeches and the response they have.[64] In a passage already cited, the narrator insists that the whole process of divinely instituted justice in which the princes are now taking part has as its end the "making our own actions the beginning of our chastisement, that our shame may be the more manifest, and our repentance follow the sooner." Although their shame may be manifest, repentance is the furthest thing from their minds:

"Add this to your noble speech, my dear cousin," said Pyrocles, "that if we complain of this our fortune, or seem to ourselves faulty in having one hurt the other, we show a repentance of the love we bear to those matchless creatures, or at least a doubt it should be over dearly bought, which for my part (and so dare I answer for you) I call all the gods to witness, I am so far from that no shame, no torment, no death, would make me forgo the least part of the inward honour, essential pleasure, and living life I have enjoyed in the presence of the faultless Philoclea." [P. 372]

However healthy their state may seem to them, we know that those who set "their mindes upon vaine pleasures of this World, doe liue in sinne without repentance, not vttering the fruites that doe belong to such an high profession; vpon such presumptuous persons and wilful sinners, must needs remayne the great vengeance of GOD, and eternall punishment in hell, prepared for the vniust and wicked liuers."[65]

The scene thus becomes an ironic inversion of reality since Musidorus' hymn, which "he had made before love turned his muse to another subject" (p. 373), must be seen not as a statement of fact but as an unrealized prayer.[66] Since "the whole sum of their thoughts rest[s] upon the safety of their ladies and their care one for the other" (p. 370), it is clear that Musidorus' request in the hymn has gone unanswered:

> *Our owly eyes, which dimmed with passions be,*
> *And scarce discern the dawn of coming day,*
> *Let them be cleared, and now begin to see*
> *Our life is but a step in dusty way.*
>
> [*OA* 77.9-12, pp. 373-74]

If the princes have not achieved a reconciliation with God, however, they have been able to come to better terms with themselves. With the spur of desire temporarily removed from their sides, they have been able to regain the control over their emotions that they had originally possessed. Even though they cannot forget the princesses, the seeming impossibility of rejoining them has permitted their reason to regain a position of influence. Through their recollection of the virtues to which they had previously adhered, they are able to accept the thought of death and separation from their loves, "like men indeed (fortifying courage with the true rampire of patience)" (p. 370). Having ceased to aspire solely to worldly joys, they once again "did rather appear governors of necessity than servants to fortune" (p. 370). This is a significant change, of course, and calls for a modification in our response to them.

In the third book, the princes—Pyrocles in the cave and Musidorus with his attempted rape of Pamela—had become exemplars of the beast running rampant within fallen humanity. With the return of reason, however hesitantly, in prison, the princes have begun to re-ascend. Although their attitde toward the princesses is fundamentally unchanged, the danger into which the princes have put them and the absence of opportunities for physical contact combine to effect a change in their feelings for the ladies, as selfish lust is transmuted into loving concern for their welfare. Combined with their efforts to reason—and to reason about things uncovered with this world—the total effect is to permit the virtues they had once possessed to begin to reestablish themselves. To guard against overemphasizing this change, however, Sidney is careful to delineate its limits. The princes have not ceased their idolatrous love for the princesses; they have, however, added to it the thought of things to come. They have not accepted divine providence; they have merely ceased to accede passively to the whims of fortune. Finally, and most significantly, as the narrative moves to the trial which will be the culmination of their adventures, they have not been moved to repentance. Instead, still loving, they have determined to place themselves outside the bounds of justice by resolving that "the first care they would have should be, by taking the fault upon themselves, to clear the two ladies" (p. 374). Although their apparent proximity to death has made them reorder their priorities, those priorities are still ordered according to earthly values.

During the course of their trials, all their claims for special consideration are denied, forcing them to an admission of their human fallibility. After appealing for the exoneration of their ladies to the assembled citizenry, the time comes when they are forced to speak in their own defence, and they first attempt to exempt themselves from the procedures of justice: "they demanded to know by what authority they could judge of them, since they were not only foreigners, and so not born under their laws, but absolute princes, and therefore not to be touched by laws" (p. 385). The reply to the claim comes immediately: "whatsoever they were, Arcadia was to acknowledge them but as private men" (p. 385). They are, before the law (and before God), indistinguishable from other men. With the rejection of this defence, the princes pose another. If they are not exempt from justice because they are princes, they will be exempt because they are men, and it is unavoidable for man to escape error (see pp. 392 and 402). The answer to this argument, again, is inescapable. As Euarchus says,

> There resteth, then, the second point: how to judge well. And that must undoubtedly be done, not by a free discourse of reason and skill of philosophy, but must be tied to the laws of Greece and municipal statutes of this dukedom. For although out of them these came . . . yet because philosophical discourses stand in the general consideration of things, they leave to every man a scope of his own interpretation; where the laws, applying themselves to the necessary use, fold us within assured bounds, which once broken, man's nature infinitely rangeth. [*OA*, 404]

The human community can survive only if its members keep "free discourse of reason and skill of philosophy" subservient to the law, for without laws, which "fold us within assured bounds," no man would be safe from the consequences of human desires since "man's nature infinitely rangeth."[67]

The judgment that follows is not unfair, even though the judge is ignorant of some of the particulars of the preceding events. The princes are convicted of being "accidental, if not principal, causes of the duke's death" (p. 405), and of raping the princesses, literally in the case of Pyrocles and figuratively ("although he ravished her not from herself, yet he ravished her from him that owed her, which was her father" [p. 406]) for Musidorus. For these crimes they are sentenced to death. Suddenly, however, the princes are identified to Euarchus as his son and his nephew, and the general expectation is that they will be pardoned. As they are being urged to "joy in the good hap the gods had sent them" (p. 410), Euarchus dashes their hopes by reaffirming the principles of justice: "No, no, Pyrocles and Musidorus, I prefer you much before my life, but I prefer justice as far before you. While you did like yourselves, my body should willingly have been your shield; but I cannot keep you from the effects of your own doing" (p. 411). The princes are guilty, and, however unhappy their judge is at condemning them, they must suffer the consequences of their actions.

This is our final judgment of the princes, and to it we must adhere despite their ultimate escape from punishment when Basilius, suddenly returned to consciousness, pardons them. Through five books, we have watched them turn aside from the "exercise" of virtue and the pursuit of goodness to love, and fall from love to desire, from desire to lust, and from lust to the pursuit of evil and the exercise of crimes. Following the guidance of the narrator, our response to them has changed from admiration, first to pity, then to distrust and mockery, and finally to a knowledge of the complete folly of their actions. Though there is much that is virtuous in the princes, the evils they have done are not mitigated by their good deeds. Instead, with Euarchus, we must acknowledge that "no man, because he hath done well before, should have his present evils spared, but rather so much the more punished, as having showed he knew how to be good, would against his knowledge be naught" (p. 405). Within the terms of the book, we cannot pardon Pyrocles and Musidorus, and any inclination we may have to do so is discouraged by the conclusion. The sympathy provoked by their movement in the direction of self-control earlier in book 5 is there dissipated by the sight of them taking turns execrating the grief-stricken Euarchus (see pp. 412-14). Having refused to repent, they remain criminals in the eyes of both human and divine law.

III. Gynecia

If most critics have been too kind to Pyrocles and Musidorus, they have moved in the opposite direction with Gynecia. It is not fair to call Gynecia a "harried whore," as Walter Davis does, without recognizing that her sin is no different from that of all the other major characters.[68] Gynecia, though no less guilty than the other major characters, is certainly not the principal cause of the evils which occur during the course of the action. Why, then, is she condemned so harshly for the same kind of behavior for which the others are either praised or dismissed with a light slap on their wrists? The answer is probably to be found in the elements of her characterization that the narrator singles out for special attention. If one were to generalize, one might say that Basilius is notable for his ignorance and folly, the princes for their mistaken confidence in wisdom's ability to keep them virtuous and their willful disregard for anything standing between them and their desires. In a like manner, one would have to say that the narrator's delineation of Gynecia focuses on the conflict between her awareness of evil and her inability to turn away from it.

Despite her "well governed youth" (p. 4), Gynecia falls in love with Pyrocles with a "new wonderful passionate love" (p. 48) at the moment when her suspicions that he is a man masquerading as an Amazon are confirmed. Unlike the other characters, however, who struggle only fitfully, if at all, and then accept their new condition with little complaint, Gynecia cannot ever escape from the knowledge that she should not be acting as she is. Unable to rest and aware of the cause of her unrest, she leaves her lodge to wander in "the solitary places those deserts were full of" (p. 91), while she tries to solve her emotional and moral problems. Unlike the others, who value the satisfaction of their desires as the supreme good, Gynecia cannot forget the lessons of reason:

There appeared unto the eyes of her judgment the evils she was like to run into, with ugly infamy waiting upon them; she saw the terrors of her own conscience; she was witness of her long-exercised virtue, which made this vice the fuller of deformity. The uttermost of the good she could aspire unto was but a fountain of danger; and the least of her dangers was a mortal wound to her vexed spirits; and lastly, no small part of her evils was that she was wise to see her evils. [OA, 91]

Although she knows that virtue demands that she use her reason to control her will, she finds herself unable to do so, and despairs at this very inability:

O sun . . . whose unspotted light directs the steps of mortal mankind, art thou not ashamed to impart the clearness of thy presence to such an overthrown worm as I am? O you heavens, which continually keep the course allotted unto you, can none of your influences prevail so much upon the miserable Gynecia as to make her preserve a course so long embraced by her? O deserts, deserts, how fit a guest am I for you, since my heart is fuller of wild ravenous beasts than ever you were! . . . O imperfect proportion of reason, which can too much forsee, and so little prevent! [OA, 91-92]

It is her very hopelessness which makes her so desperate that she will try anything if only it will let her satisfy her obsession. Where the other lovers have a goal toward which they are working, Gynecia knows that the consummation she so devoutly desires cannot resolve the torment which afflicts her, since it is wholly self-inflicted and totally contradictory. She burns, at once, with the twin fires of lust and shame. This paradox becomes explicit as Gynecia, "pricked with the flames of love and torments of her own conscience," cries to Pyrocles, "O Cleophila, Cleophila . . . dost thou offer me physic which art my only poison" (p. 94). Unable to control her will through the use of her reason, Gynecia can satisfy her lust only by enflaming her guilt and ease her shame only by obeying her desires, which would then burn all the more strongly.[69]

To this combustible mixture is applied the spark of jealousy, as Gynecia becomes convinced not only that Cleophila is a man, but that he is in love with her daughter. The narrator aptly describes her as being full of "envenomed heat" (p. 122), as her combined afflictions constantly trouble her. This is Gynecia's state of mind when Pyrocles stumbles upon her in the cave. Unable to withstand her pains, she blasphemes the heavens and curses her life:

> Hark, plaintful ghosts! Infernal furies, hark
> Unto my woes the hateful heav'ns do send —
> The heav'ns conspired to make my vital spark
> A wretched wrack, a glass of ruin's end!
> Seeing, alas, so mighty powers bend
> Their ireful shot against so weak a mark,
> Come cave, become my grave; come death, and lend
> Receipt to me within thy bosom dark!
> For what is life to daily dying mind
> Where, drawing breath, I suck the air of woe;
> Where too much sight makes all the body blind,
> And highest thoughts downward most headlong throw?
>   Thus then my form, and thus my state I find:
>   Death wrapped in flesh, to living grave assigned.
>   [OA 40, pp. 180-81]

Unlike the other noble lovers, Gynecia realizes that by pursuing an illicit lust, she is making dark all that had previously enlightened her life. Unfortunately for her, she is, like the others, unable to refrain from seeking to satisfy the demands of her will. What makes her state so pitiful is that she knows that any joys she may experience will be brief and hollow compared to the joys of the virtue she has lost. As she says, comparing herself to the cave in which she is hiding, "This cave is dark, but it had never light . . . I darkened am, who once had clearest sight" (*OA 43*.1, 4, p. 182). Gynecia is too weak to be good and too conscience-stricken to enjoy being evil.

Even at her moment of apparent success, when Pyrocles arranges to meet her in the cave and to satisfy her desire for him, she cannot forget the lessons of virtue. She agrees to come by "closing her eyes, and letting her head fall, as if she would give her [Cleophila] to know she was not ignorant of her fault, although she were transported with the violence of her evil" (p. 222). In a sense, it is supremely decorous that she be the one who restates Sidney's judgment on Basilius' folly, for none of the main characters knows so well as she the disgrace and shame that comes from loving unwisely. Yet at the same time that she sees "how much fancy doth not only darken reason but beguile sense" (p. 276), she cannot refrain from scheming about how best to fulfill her thwarted plans for Pyrocles.

Her passions are uncontrollable, in fact, until the moment her husband cries out at her feet, "O Gynecia, I die! Have care—" (p. 279). This finally proves too much for her long-neglected reason:

Her painful memory had straight filled her with the true shapes of all the forepassed mischiefs. Her reason began to cry out against the filthy rebellion of sinful sense, and to tear itself with anguish for having made so weak a resistance; her conscience (a terrible witness of the inward wickedness) still nourishing this debateful fire; her complaint now not having an end directed to it, something to disburden sorrow; but as a necessary downfall of inward wretchedness. [*OA*, 279]

In her unhappiness and her awareness of her sins, Gynecia falls into an even greater sin. Thinking only of the magnitude of her evils, she forgets God's goodness and mercy, and denies the possibility of forgiveness for herself:

O bottomless pit of sorrow in which I cannot contain myself, having the fire-brands of all furies within me, still falling and yet by the infiniteness of it never fallen! . . . For wither should I recommend the protection of my dishonoured fall? To the earth? . . . To men . . . ? To the heavens? O unspeakable torment of conscience whch dare not look unto them; no sin can enter there! O, there is no receipt for polluted minds! Wither, then, wilt thou lead this captive of thine, O snaky despair? [*OA*, 279-80]

Gynecia's agony is terrifying in its intensity, yet all it does is feed her despair and thus further increase her suffering. Her reason, newly recovered, is still helpless in the face of the universe of absolute justice it has posited.

Sidney here forces us to reconsider not only Gynecia's attitude toward sin, but also her original feelings about her virtue. Her earlier complaint about falling in love is relevant here. Surely, one who can call herself the "professed servant" of virtue and imply that she has seen its "lovely presence" (p. 92) should have had a firm foundation of good with which to withstand the temptations of evil. This, however, is not the case. The reader has fallen along with Gynecia into complacency. Through Gynecia's agonies, we are reminded that "All men, Jewes and Gentiles, are vnder sinne, there is none righteous, no not one: there is none that vnderstandeth, there is none that seeketh after GOD."[70] Gynecia's confidence in her virtue before it has been put to test is a manifestation of pride, and when her virtue fails her, her complacency turns to despair. Even in her new awareness of her weakness she cannot avoid pride, thinking that she alone cannot be forgiven for her sins. Although Gynecia professes to believe in the gods, her faith is not strong enough to sustain her in this time of need, and she cannot bring herself to believe that the mercy she so desires could be granted.[71]

The immediate consequence of her despair is that she takes "a certain resolution to embrace death as soon as it should be offered unto her, and no way to seek the prolonging of her annoyed life" (p. 280). And yet, despite all her sins, the narrator refuses to permit his reader the luxury of an easy condemnation. When the shepherds come upon the scene, she runs away and is overtaken by them. Their reaction to her is unexpected: instead of vilifying her, they are apologetic, for "besides the obedient duty they owed to her state, they had always carried a singular love for her courteous liberalities and other wise and virtuous parts which had filled all that people with affection and admiration" (p. 281). Nor should we really be surprised by this, for the narrator takes great pains with all his characters to avoid arousing a single response, trying constantly to balance motives and actions, past deeds and present, awareness of evil and memory of good. While the reason for this strategy may not yet be apparent, the reader's awareness of it is guaranteed by his constantly changing reactions to the characters.

With the arrival of Philanax, Gynecia too is made a prisoner. Locked up in a cell, with "nothing left by her but a little lamp, whose small light to a perplexed mind might rather yield fearful shadows than any assured sight" (p. 367), Gynecia again gives way to unreason, and begins to "crucify her own soul," thinking that "the justice of God" demands her destruction (p. 366). Having only natural law to guide her, she begins "to fear the heavenly powers she was wont to reverence, not like a child but like an enemy" (p. 367).[72] Gripped by the "ugly claws" of "despair," she falls into "blasphemous repining against her creation" and attempts to lay the blame for her actions upon God: "O gods . . . if you love goodness, why did you not give me a good mind? Or if I cannot have it without your gift, why do you plague me? Is it in me to resist the mightiness of your power?" (p. 367). The consequences of this turning away from God are immediate: "Then would she imagine she saw strange sights, and that she heard the cries of hellish ghosts" (p. 367).[73] Having rejected God, damnation seems the only alternative. Again, however, the narrator ensures a reaction more complicated than simple condemnation. When at the trial, Gynecia condemns herself and begs for a speedy death, her "words and behavior stirred . . . [her audience's] hearts to a doleful compassion. Neither, in truth, could most of them in their judgements tell whether they should be more sorry for her fault or her misery, for the loss of her estate or loss of her virtue. But most were moved most with that which was under their eyes, the sense most subject to pity" (p. 382). Though she is finally condemned by Euarchus, the narrator maintains a balance between understanding and condemnation in his final appraisal of her:

Thus the excellent lady Gynecia, having passed five and thirty years of her age even to admiration of her beautiful mind and body, and having not in her own knowledge ever spotted her soul with any wilful vice but her inordinate love of Cleophila, was brought, first by the violence of that ill-answered passion, and then by the despairing conceit she took of the judgement of God in her husband's death and her own fortune, purposely to overthrow herself. [*OA*, 384]

To discover why Gynecia has been treated so much more harshly than the other noble lovers by the critics, we need only consider the scene in the cave with Cleophila once again. This scene is Sidney's most vivid picture of the evils of disordered love, and in it Sidney succeeds in rendering the commonplace terrifying by showing in Gynecia the pains and disharmonies which are only implied in his pictures of the other noble lovers. At stake is not only the fate of one person, but the fate of each of us. Left to his own resources, man is reduced to the state Gynecia bemoans: "O strange mixture of human minds: Only so much good left as to make us languish in our own evils" (p. 183).[74] Gynecia's dramatic function is to make this state vivid, and thus moving.[75] Like Pyrocles, who can call the speaker of these words his "fellow" (p. 182) so long as she remains an abstraction cloaked in darkness but who recoils in horror and disgust when he recognizes the speaker as Gynecia, a reader can misinterpret any of the other characters, thinking them merely suffering the "customary" pangs of "happy" lovers, so long as their sufferings are merely conventional. Gynecia, by forcing us to consider all the implications of this kind of love, so darkens the tone that she compels us to see the other lovers as she sees herself, as the victims of their disordered wills and the slaves of their desires. If we are repelled by Gynecia more than by the other main characters, it is not because her actions are more evil than theirs, but because Sidney has succeeded in implicating us more deeply in them: since the Fall, all mankind has been "womanly" in the sense Musidorus invokes in his debate with Pyrocles. In Gynecia, Sidney's concept of the speaking picture is realized most triumphantly.

IV. Philoclea and Pamela

The reactions of Philoclea and Pamela to love stand in direct contrast both to Gynecia and to each other. But then, the two princesses are carefully distinguished from each other in almost every way possible during the course of the action. The narrator's initial descriptions of them establish the key distinctions which remain operative throughout the narrative. In speaking of Pamela, he stresses both her virtue and her nobility: "The fair Pamela, whose noble heart had long disdained to find the trust of her virtue reposed in the hands of a Shepherd, had yet, to show an obedience, taken on a shepherdish apparel" (p. 37). The emphasis in his description of Philoclea, on the other hand, falls on her beauty:

> But when the ornament of the earth, young Philoclea, appeared in her nymph-like apparel, so near nakedness as one might well discern part of her perfections, and yet so apparelled as did show she kept the best store of her beauties to herself; her excellent fair hair drawn up into a net made only of itself (a net indeed to have caught the wildest disposition); her body covered with a light taffeta garment, so cut as the wrought smock came through it in many places (enough to have made a very restrained imagination have thought what was under it. [*OA*, 37]

Each of these descriptions, however, contains some disturbing notes. Pamela, though she makes a show of obedience to her father's commands, mocks them in the *impresa* she designed and wears, "a perfect white lamb tied at a stake with a great number of chains, as it had been feared lest the silly creature should do some great harm" (p. 37). Given the great stress on the duty and reverence owed to parents by the Elizabethans, Pamela's disdain, even before it becomes outright rebellion, is another reminder of the unpleasant gap between what ought to be and what is.[76] Likewise, Philoclea's lack of awareness of the effects caused by her style of dress presages an "innocent" wantonness not likely to restrain the "wildest disposition" to which her flesh is heir. Like Pyrocles, to whom she is linked by a somewhat similar description, Philoclea acts as if she lived among fellow innocents in an unfallen world.[77]

On the heels of these reflections comes an event which suggests even further the precariousness of their hold on virtue, isolated from the social stays their rank should otherwise provide them. In their first test, the attack of the wild animals, both demonstrate a vulnerability to emotion—in this case fear—sufficiently great to endanger their reason's control. While their reaction is not unnatural, the narrator does point to its aftermath. Philoclea, "carried away with the violence of an inward evil" (p. 48), runs away with such fear that "much of those beauties she would at another time have willingly hidden were presented to the eye of the twice-wounded Cleophila" (p. 47). Pamela falls into a "swoon with extremity of fear," giving Musidorus the opportunity to "kiss and re-kiss her a hundred times" (p. 52). In the aftermath of their escape from this danger, Philoclea falls into an even greater one. In her "simplicity," she becomes full of "unquiet imaginations," for "desire she did, but she knew not what" (p. 54). Pamela, however, shows the strength of her virtue, for feeling "a certain working of a new-come inclination to Dorus," she "would needs make open war upon herself, and obtain the victory" (p. 55). Although the cause of her strength is not respect for her father's commands but "the consideration of his [Dorus'] meanness" (p. 55), the fact of her victory seems itself of great importance, for it suggests a possibility which all the other characters deny, if not in words then by their actions.[78]

But Pamela's triumph over her will does not last long; having been obliquely informed of Musidorus' true social status, "even love began to revive his flames, which the opinion she had of his meanness had before covered in her. . . . Full well she found the lively image of a vehement desire in herself, which ever is apt to receive belief, but hard to ground belief" (p. 106). Even her pride fails her as Musidorus finally wins her "secret consent" by appealing both to her love and to her resentment at seeing herself in an "unworthy bondage" (p. 107). By appealing to Pamela's self-image of her virtue, and by suggesting the baseness of those who doubt its strength, Musidorus succeeds in persuading her to flee from one unworthy bondage to another even more unworthy, as all Pamela's virtue and wisdom prove unable to control her wounded sense of self-esteem and her passions.

If wisdom cannot cope with passion, however, neither can simplicity. Philoclea, who "was in their degree of well doing to whom the not knowing of evil serveth for a ground of virtue," finds that even though that degree may be higher than that of "many who rather cunningly seek to know what goodness is than willingly take into themselves the following of it" (p. 108), it is still not sufficient to keep her from evil. In fact, the narrator suggests that her innocence is the cause of her coming failure in the trial of her virtue: "True it is that the sweet and simple breath of heavenly goodness is the easier to fall because it hath not passed through the worldly wickedness, nor feelingly found the evil that evil carrieth with it" (p. 108).[79] When approached by Pyrocles, she rejoices at his maleness and admits her love for him. She does, however, insist that he love her virtuously (pp. 121-22). In view of the weakness of virtue grounded not upon wisdom but simplicity, one may legitimately doubt how long she will require him to keep his promise. The narrator purposely emphasizes these doubts by his description of her feelings at the moment of Pyrocles' declaration of his sex:

The joy which wrought into Pygmalion's mind while he found his beloved image wax little and little both softer and warmer in his folded arms, till at length it accomplished his gladness with a perfect woman's shape, still beautiful with the former perfections, was even such as, by each degree of Cleophila's words, stealingly entered into Philoclea's soul, till her pleasure was fully made up with the manifesting of his being, which was such as in hope did overcome hope. Yet did a certain spark of honour arise in her well disposed mind, which bred a starting fear to be now in secret with him in whose presence, notwithstanding, consisted her comfort — such contradictions there must needs grow in those minds which neither absolutely embrace goodness nor freely yield to evil. But that spark soon gave place, or at least gave no more light in her mind than a candle doth in the sun's presence. [OA, 120-21][80]

While her mind may be "well disposed" to Pyrocles, it has not absolutely embraced goodness, and, as the examples of Pyrocles, Mu-

sidorus, Gynecia, and Pamela remind us, even a mind which actively seeks virtue cannot withstand the overpowering force of an "infected will." When she does indeed allow him to seduce her in the
third book, Pyrocles must only fight against "a weak resistance,
which did strive to be overcome" (p. 243).

Pamela's downfall also comes in the third book, but it is of a
different nature than Philoclea's. Philoclea's innocence leads to un-
chastity, but Pamela would never assent to *this* kind of weakness.
Paradoxically, the cause of her political irresponsibility in fleeing
the country is the strength of her pride in her virtue. Although she
agrees to escape from Arcadia partly because of her love for Musidorus, she is able to maintain a measure of control over her passions. Once in flight, she stops and takes stock of herself.

> But Pamela who all this while transported with desire, and troubled with fear,
> had never free scope of judgement to look with perfect consideration into her
> own enterprise, but even by the laws of love had bequeathed the care of her-
> self upon him to whom she had given herself, now that the pang of desire
> with evident hope was quieted, and most part of the fear passed, reason began
> to renew his shining in her heart, and make her see herself in herself. [*OA*,
> 196]

Pamela makes Musidorus promise to leave her chaste until they are
married and he agrees, although, as we have seen, his resolution
does not last.

In a sense, however, it is her overriding concern about her chastity which is at the root of her wrongdoing. Pamela feels that, provided she remains a virgin until Musidorus marries her in Thessaly,
her flight from her father and her responsibilities as heir to the
kingdom is justifiable: "What should I more say? If I have chosen
well, all doubt is past, since your action only must determine
whether I have done virtuously or shamefully in following you"
(p. 197). The narrator leaves no doubt that it is primarily her resentment at her father's doubt of her ability to keep herself chaste
which leads her to flee Arcadia with the prince in the first place
(pp. 172-73). However, the question with which we are continually confronted is whether her father's admittedly capricious behavior toward her is sufficient justification for her to flee the country.
The answer, finally, is that it is not. Euarchus' condemnation of

Musidorus' action in taking Pamela from Arcadia applies equally to her for voluntarily going with him:

> The other young man confesseth he persuaded the princess Pamela to fly her country, and accompanied her in it—without all question a ravishment no less than the other; for, although he ravished her not from herself, yet he ravished her from him that owed her which was her father. This kind is chastised by the loss of the head, as a most execrable theft; for if they must die who steal from us our goods, how much more they who steal from us that for which we gather our goods. And if our laws have it so in the private persons, much more forcible are they to be in princes' children, where one steals as it were the whole state and well being of that people, tied by the secret of a long use to be governed by none but the next of that blood. [OA, 406]

Like her father, Pamela has preferred her own private interests to that of the public welfare, which has thereby been injured. At the root of the whole issue is her disobedience to her father's command.[81] Her pride in her virtue has led her to fail the first test of a future ruler, who must learn how to obey commands before being able to give them. Pamela's "virtue," with its concomitant lack of humility, leads to her downfall; her inflated sense of self-esteem causes her public humiliation.[82]

Although the follies of Philoclea and Pamela are not so active as those of the other noble lovers, the princesses are far from blameless. Their sins are basically of the same kind as those of the others, and neither Philoclea's innocence nor Pamela's insistence upon the strength of her virtue can prevent them from becoming involved in the series of actions which leads to the complete disruption of order in themselves and their country. In discussing the willingness of both Philoclea and Pyrocles to commit suicide out of love for each other, Sidney's narrator remarks somewhat ironically on the "small diference . . . betwixt a simple voidness of evil and a judical habit of virtue" (p. 294). His comment may be applied to the two sisters as well. Where Philoclea falls into sin because she cannot recognize the evils she embraces, Pamela errs by assuming that the strength of her virtue is such that anything she does is justified by it. Ultimately, however, Sidney insists that we must recognize the evils for which they are responsible and react accordingly.

V

The cast of characters thus far presented has offered a number of differing perspectives on dealing with the problems encountered in the course of life, the chief of those being how to deal with the urgings of the will to undertake a course to which the reason cannot or should not consent. Basilius, whose Epicureanism (debased though it may be) urges him to make "his will wisdom" whenever it desires something that may seem conducive to happiness, has the least problems. His reason abdicates quickly and easily, leaving his will, effectively, in permanent control. Philoclea's simplicity leads her to almost the same position. Not knowing evil, she can consent to the urgings of her will with almost as little hesitation as her father, believing her innocence to be capable of sanctifying her every desire unless it is blatantly corrupt (as in her temporary inability to reconcile her desire for Cleophila with her repugnance at embracing an "uncouth" love – a problem which disappears when Cleophila identifies "herself" as Pyrocles).

Pyrocles, Musidorus, and Pamela have more difficulty in confronting the problem because their philosophical faith in their reasonable faculties makes of the onslaught of the will's desire a sharp, though brief, moral combat. In each case, however, their reason soon bows to their wills, as their belief in the sufficiency of the intellect as a guide to moral choices or of virtue's impregnability to the assaults of vice forces them into rationalizations of their will's desires, aided variously by pride, Neoplatonism, and trust in the worthiness of the object of their desire.

Gynecia, as we have seen, is least able to rationalize her moral dilemma out of existence. She alone is constantly tormented by guilt; she alone has an active conscience; she alone is unable to ignore her reason's complaints. Like all the others, though, her will's demands are stronger than any opposition. What makes her problem so difficult is her belief in the existence of good but just gods. Because she is unable to reconcile her belief in their goodness and justness with her inability to maintain the standards of justness and goodness her reason tells her they demand, she falls prey to despair and deems herself irretrievably lost to sin and irrevocably damned. Her position, to translate it into the language of sixteenth-century theology, is that of one who has an almost Pelagian sense of the need to win salvation through works but who has come to a very Protestant sense of the depravity of her own nature. Sidney's presentation of Gynecia should elicit the most pity from the reader because her sense of the insoluble nature of her dilemma is very strong and her attempts to reach a solution are desperate. For her, as for the others, however, there can be no solution within Sidney's pagan setting. The result is that the reader can only reject each character's philosophical starting point as he is forced to reject the conclusions to which each is led when he tries to put his beliefs into practice under the goad of love's assaults.

From our examination of the leading characters of the *Old Arcadia*, we can perceive that Sidney did not intend them to be exemplars of heroism or virtue. Neither Basilius, Pyrocles, Musidorus, Gynecia, Philoclea, nor Pamela can be considered heroic unless we are willing to ignore the preponderance of negative characteristics in Sidney's portraits of them. They illustrate, to paraphrase Sidney's comments in the *Defence*, not "magnanimity and justice," but rather "misty fearfulness and foggy desires" (*MP*, 98). The "images" of their actions do not enflame "the mind with desire to be worthy" (*MP*, 98), but rather make it impossible "that any beholder can be content to be such a one" (*MP*, 96) at the same time they convince us that "under the image of them" (*OA*, 43) we see ourselves.

While the "matter" of the *Old Arcadia* is that most commonly used in the shaping of heroic poems, the manner of presentation is that of a comedy. In reading Sidney's prose "poem" we come to an appreciation of goodness obliquely, and only if we are first able to recognize the evils resulting from the actions of the main characters. In the four sets of eclogues that follow each of the first four books, Sidney adopts a more direct mode of presentation, and it is in them—as well as in his presentation of Euarchus (to be discussed in Chapter 4)—that we are to see the "beauty of virtue" against the "great foil" of the "filthiness of evil" (*MP*, 96) shown in the five "books or acts" of the *Old Arcadia*.

CHAPTER 3

"Under hidden forms":
The Eclogues

I f love, as Sidney's narrator suggests at the end of the First Eclogues,[1] "is better than a pair of spectacles to make everything
seem greater which is seen through it" (p. 88), it can also provide the occasion for setting up a glass in which we may see a diminished picture of ourselves. In the *Old Arcadia*'s four sets of
eclogues we can see both impulses at work: in the eclogues of Pyrocles, Musidorus, Philisides, Agelastus, Strephon, and Klaius, love
produces a magnification of the beloved that demands (and usually attempts) a reordering of the universe around a new divinity. In
the songs of the Arcadian shepherds we find love viewed from a
different perspective, one that distinguishes the human from the
divine and exalts by diminishing the human to what it "may be
and should be." Although the subject matter of almost all of the
eclogues is love, they are more concerned ultimately not merely
with distinguishing love from lust but with discovering and teaching us a "grammar . . . of more congruities" (*OA 30.*142, p. 151)[2]
than the fruitless debates about the relative strength of passion,
will, and reason in which the main characters are prone to engage.

Despite the brilliance of their achievement, the eclogues have
found few sympathetic readers, and of those fewer still willing to
consider them as a functional part of the *Old Arcadia*. For most
readers they are, as they are for Hallett Smith, at best "a shepherd's entertainments for a court, since serious political and moral
ideas are dealt with sufficiently in the romance."[3] Nor, among
those readers who have sensed the seriousness of the eclogues, has
any critical consensus emerged, save that the eclogues belong to
the pastoral genre.

The problem, I think, is that we are too accustomed to think of pastoral in terms of what it came to be in the late 1580s and 1590s. In the romances of Greene and Lodge or in their dramatic transformations such as *The Winter's Tale* and *As You Like It*, we have pastoral used, in the words of one critic, "as a showcase that exhibited the ideal or holiday relationship of Nature to Art. . . . The ideal superiority of Nature to Art, glimpsed only imperfectly and intermittently in the world of post-lapsarian man, may be made to operate consistently and without qualification in the paradise of pastoral form."[4] These later Elizabethan pastorals seem reversions to what S. K. Heninger has called "pure pastoral":

> From its inception, pure pastoral has described some half-remembered place in archaic terms, a nostalgic reminiscence of an idealized child-scape, an Eden-like state of innocence and harmonious perfection. Any realistic elements in pastoral appear within this carefully constructed frame of psychological distance. . . . But all takes place at least one remove from the here-and-now.[5]

Love in these works is always central and is "generally idyllic, lending itself to lyrical treatment, fitting in with the idealized setting, timeless and remote."[6] If there are problems they are not love's fault: "Fortune and villains provide the difficulties; they do not lie in the nature of love itself."[7]

However useful these formulations may be for Lodge, Greene, et al., they do not strike me as particularly valid when it comes to the pastoral of the sixties and seventies. In opposition to what Heninger calls "pure pastoral" (or what Patrick Cullen terms "Arcadian" pastoral)[8] is a tradition which began in the fourteenth century with Petrarch and was developed throughout the fifteenth and early sixteenth centuries by such poets as Mantuan (Baptista Spagnuoli) and Aeneas Sylvius (later Pope Pius II). This tradition, which Cullen calls the "Mantuan" (and Heninger the Renaissance's "perversion" of pastoral,[9] began as more or less crude moral and political satire, before becoming, in the hands of Spenser and Sidney, an extraordinarily fine instrument for the portrayal of what is essential in man's nature. It is, finally, this tradition which is responsible for the understanding of pastoral that is reflected in Elizabethan critics like Puttenham and Webbe. Puttenham's definition of the eclogue, in fact, makes explicit reference to the "moderne" conceptions of the genre:

The Poet deuised the *Eglogue* long after the other *dramatick* poems, not of purpose to counterfait or represent the rusticall manner of loues and communication, but vnder the vaile of homely persons and in rude speeches to insinuate and glaunce at greater matters, and such as perchance had not beene safe to haue beene disclosed in any other sort. . . . These Eglogues came after to containe and enforme morall discipline, for the amendment of mans behauiour, as be those of *Mantuan* and other moderne Poets.[10]

It is with this assurance of finding informing "morall discipline" that Webbe reads *The Shepherdes Calender*: "The occasion of his worke is a warning to other young men, who, being intangled in loue and youthful vanities, may learne to looke to themselues in time, and to auoyde inconueniences which may breede if they be not in time preuented. Many good Morrall lessons are therein contained."[11] In this, of course, he is only following the lead E. K. offers in the prefatory epistle.[12] While this fashion may have continued unchallenged for only a little while longer, it was certainly at its height in the 1570s and the early 1580s, when the *Old Arcadia* was being written and circulated.[13]

Sidney, writing about pastoral poetry in his *Defence*, likewise stresses the eclogue's serious moral purposes and insists on the value of the perspective it offers:

Is it then the Pastoral poem which is misliked? (For perchance where the hedge is lowest they will soonest leap over.) Is the poor pipe disdained, which sometimes out of Meliboeus' mouth can show the misery of people under hard lords or ravening soldiers, and again, by Tityrus, what blessedness is derived to them that lie lowest from the goodness of them that sit highest; sometimes, under the pretty tales of wolves and sheep, can include the whole considerations of wrong-doing and patience; sometimes show that contentions for trifles can get but a trifling victory: where perchance a man may see that even Alexander and Darius, when they strave who should be cock of this world's dunghill, the benefit they got was that after-livers may say

Haec memini et victum frustra contendere Thyrsin:

Ex illo Corydon, Corydon est tempore nobis.

[*MP*, 94-95]

For Sidney the function of pastoral poetry is to reduce things to their unadorned natures so that we may more easily recognize them for what they are and see what they have to teach us about "ourselves or . . . the general nature" (*MP*, 115). Thus from the pettiness of pastoral singing contests, we may see the ultimate futility of all worldly struggles, as the pastoral perspective, according to Sidney, equates the wars of Alexander and Darius with the contest between Thyrsis and Corydon (see Virgil's Eclogue 7) for poetical mastery.[14] Rather than dwelling upon "pleasant rivers, fruitful trees, sweet-smelling flowers, nor whatsoever else may make the too much loved earth more lovely" (*MP*, 78), the poet must show that nature's world is indeed "brazen," that "the poets only deliver a golden" because paradise was lost with that "first accursed fall of Adam" (*MP*, 78-79) and is not to be found while "this world's dunghill" still exists.

In the *Old Arcadia*'s eclogues Sidney continues his exploration of the issues raised in the main prose narrative, but we are offered a different way of seeing them. As dukes and duchesses, princes and princesses watch the shepherds perform, we also watch and see how their "noble" enterprises are not only imitated by the shepherds but bettered; we see too that nobility comes not from birth or title but from quality of vision, as (in Musidorus's terms) the shepherds' "health" is pitted against the nobles' "infection" in a contest to discover a satisfying way of seeing life (see *OA* 7.21, p. 59).

In studying the eclogues, however, we must do more than merely observe how the issues raised in the narrative become the argument of the poems, for the four sets of eclogues do not consist solely of eclogues. They also contain—especially the first two groups—a great deal of narrative, and this narration not only provides a context for the poems, but also has a life of its own. In it, new characters are introduced and the scene is expanded from the Arcadian present to the past adventures of the princes in Asia Minor. Most important, the eclogues are insured a dramatic fluidity, and the stasis that might otherwise have settled upon what could have been taken merely as a collection of poems is avoided. Nonetheless, the presence of this narrative poses a problem: what is the principle of organization which relates the new story line to the eclogues? This is a question that we must try to answer as we read through the eclogues, but I should like to suggest that Sidney's use of the prose narrative in the eclogues is similar to his practice in the five "books or acts" where the narrative embodies the "speaking picture" that is the foundation of Sidney's imaginative edifice. That is, we may expect the narrative to set off the poems and to enlarge our understanding of Sidney's conceptions of the characters and the way in which we are supposed to react to them. We may also expect it to illustrate the more general statements of the eclogues by embodying them in a new set of particulars and to insist upon their universality by showing that they may be applied not only in Arcadia, the locus of the story, but elsewhere as well.

Another problem that we must confront is the relationship of the four sets of eclogues to each other and, ultimately, to the main narrative. While the latter might more properly be discussed when we come to consider the structure of the *Old Arcadia*, it will be useful in navigating the largely uncharted seas of the eclogues if we possess even the sketchiest of guides. The eclogues are not simply a break in the serious action during which the reader may pause and relax. They are complex, often dense, presentations of certain key themes which reverberate not only throughout the eclogues but also in the main narrative; their function is to present a viewpoint opposed to those of the nobles on the crucial questions of how men may love and live without falling into disorder and disharmony. Rather than merely echoing the action of the main narrative, they react to it in an attempt to persuade the reader that the kind of actions to be emulated are those imaged not by the princely characters but by certain of the shepherds.

This view, of course, is a rejection of Elizabeth Dipple's contention that the eclogues may be considered as a work in themselves without reference to the actions around which they occur. Rather than being an "interdependent unity," they depend instead on the work as a whole to structure them and to give them solidity. The First and Second Eclogues offer an ideal vision of life in opposition to that implicit in the action of the nobles in the first two books, contrasting the way of the shepherds with that of their "betters," first in a series of debates, and then through the narrator's comparison of their health and harmony with the infection and disharmony that Dorus and Cleophila reveal in the eclogues that conclude each of the groups. The Third Eclogues have a different pattern necessitated by different circumstances. In the third book, the main characters commit themselves in various ways to the active pursuit of the disordered desires of their wills, thus ending their "debate" with the shepherds. Consequently they do not even participate in the Third Eclogues, which first present an actualization of the previously enunciated ideal after which the shepherds are striving, then instance the threats to that ideal, and finally explain the difficulties of achieving it. The Fourth Eclogues, finally, have still another kind of organization, for their function is to condemn the kind of disordered living and loving which had led to the destruction (although it ultimately turns out to be temporary) of the peace and harmony of the shepherds' existence.

In short, the eclogues function, in Scaliger's terms, as a kind of chorus: "Sometimes the chorus ministers comfort, sometimes it bewails; it also blames, predicts, expresses wonder, passes judgment, admonishes, learns that it may teach, makes choices, hopes and doubts."[15] Although the eclogues have a narrative life of their own, they are dependent upon the main narrative. Their chief function is to present not merely the purely negative moral strictures that the main narrative offers but a vision of the golden world which only a poet can deliver by ranging, "only reined with learned discretion, into the divine consideration of what may be and should be" (*MP*, 81).

I. The First Eclogues

The narrator begins the first of the four sets of eclogues with a brief statement about their matter and manner. Echoing Sidney's comments in the *Defence*, he stresses the poetic possibilities of the pastoral, "wherein sometimes they would contend for a prize of well singing, sometimes lament the unhappy pursuit of their affections, sometimes, again, under hidden forms utter such matters as otherwise were not fit for their delivery" (*OA*, 56). The shepherds, if they are capable of uttering basic truths "under hid-

den forms," are obviously not bound, as Dametas and his family
are, by their low social rank, and, in fact, the narrator insists that
they are "not such base shepherds as we commonly make account
of, but the very owners of the sheep themselves, which in that
thrifty world the substantiallest men would employ their whole
care upon" (p. 56). They have, moreover, a great respect for their
songs, and delegate one of their number to write them down after
they have been sung and to "polish a little the rudeness of an un-
thought-on song" (p. 56). Like the pointing fingers in the margins of
sixteenth-century texts, the narrator is plainly trying to warn the
reader to pay careful attention to the shepherds' eclogues. This
message is immediately reinforced as the narrator stresses their
inner happiness in obvious contrast to the state of torment and
"inward evil" in which all of the noble characters find themselves
at the end of the first book: "But the peace wherein they did so
notably flourish, and especially the sweet enjoying of their peace
to so pleasant uses, drew divers strangers, as well of great as of
mean houses, especially such whom inward melancholies made
weary of the world's eyes, to come and live among them, applying
themselves to their trade" (p. 56). Clearly there is something for
those with "inward melancholies" to learn from the shepherds, and
others have been so attracted by their happiness that they have
abandoned their worldly positions to join the pastoral community.

After the main characters are seated, and we have been reminded yet again of their inward distress, the narrator announces that
we are now to "leave all those princely motions to their considerations that, untold, can guess what love means" (p. 57), and to
turn instead to the pastoral games. For those who cannot guess
what love means, however, he immediately provides an explanation through the dance and song of the shepherds. This first eclogue is extremely significant for an understanding of the system
of values which the narrator is beginning to erect as a counter to
those behind the illicit desires of the princely spectators, and a
careful study of it will be repaid by the light it sheds upon the
theme of the First Eclogues and the *Old Arcadia* itself.

After "leaps and gambols . . . (being accorded to the pipe which
they bare in their mouths even as they danced)" (p. 57), the shepherds cast away their pipes and begin a new song:

holding hand in hand, [they] dance as it were in a brawl by the only cadence of their voices, which they would use in singing some short couplets; whereto the one half beginning, the other half answered; as, the one half saying:

We love, and have our loves rewarded.

The others would answer:

We love, and are no whit regarded.

The first again:

We find most sweet affection's snare.

With like tune, it should be (as in a choir) sent back again:

That sweet, but sour despairful care.

A third time likewise thus:

Who can despair whom both doth bear?

The answer:

And who can hope who feels despair?

Then, all joining their voices, and dancing a faster measure, they would conclude with some such words:

As without breath no pipe doth move,
No music kindly without love.

[*OA 6*, pp. 57-58]

The most obvious observation to make is that, for the first time in the *Old Arcadia*, we are seeing people who are in love, yet are still happy and capable—even the shepherds whose love has gone unreciprocated—of participating in their normal activites, in contrast to the nobles who are watching them. The closing couplet seems to offer an explanation at the same time that it opens up some new possibilities.

Music, of course, is an obvious symbol of harmony, and harmony, as Elizabeth Dipple reminds us, "is the major term the Renaissance understood to represent the state of balance and divine perfection: this is the state in which man was created and which he has been reseeking since his first sin."[16] Music, moreover, is a means by which that lost harmony may be at least temporarily regained, as Sir Thomas Elyot points out in his relation of the story of Saul and David (1 Sam. 16:16-23): "Saul . . . declining from the laws and precepts of God, was possessed of an evil spirit which oftentimes tormented and vexed him, and other remedy found he none but that David . . . being at that time a proper child and playing sweetly on a harp, with his pleasant and perfect harmony reduced his mind into his pristine estate, and during the time that he played the spirit ceased to vex him."[17] The virtue of the music which David makes, of course, comes from "the Spirit of the Lord" which is upon him (1 Sam. 16:13), and that Spirit is Love.[18] To say, then, that no music can be "kindly" without love is to say that the music will not have the power to "reduce" our minds to their "pristine estate" unless it is motivated by the proper kind of love and that music will not be music unless the harmony it creates is in tune with the universal harmony created by God's love. As la Primaudaye says, "seeing God hath created and framed . . . [the world] by loue, no doubt but loue is dispersed and shed throughout the whole world."[19] The Arcadian shepherds, both those who have been successful in love and those who have not, are able nonetheless to create the harmony of their song because their love is not based upon desire, like the love of the nobles, but is instead in harmony ("as in a choir") with their love of God and His works.

There is significance also in the dance they perform while they sing. According to Elyot, dancing comprehends in it "wonderful figures, or, as the Greeks do call them, *ideae*, of virtues and noble qualities, and specially of the commodious virtue called prudence, whom Tully defineth to be the knowledge of things which ought to be desired and followed, and also of them which ought to be fled from or eschewed."[20] To instill this virtue more easily within children, Elyot "devised how in the form of dancing, now late used in this realm among gentlemen, the whole description of this virtue prudence may be found out and well perceived, as well by the dancers as by them which standing by will be diligent beholders and markers, having first mine instruction surely graven in the table of their remembrance."[21] In the brawl, Elyot notes two motions which he proceeds to imbue with significance. The first of these is the "honour," with which the brawl, like every other dance, begins: "The first moving in every dance is called honour, which is a reverent inclination of curtesy. . . . By that may be signified that at the beginning of all our acts, we should do due honour to God, which is the root of prudence; which honour is compact of these three things, fear, love, and reverence.''[22] Elyot's second motion—the brawl proper—is composed of two parts:

> By the second motion, which is two in number, may be be signified celerity and slowness: which two, albeit they seem to discord in thier effects and natural properties: and therefore they may be well resembled to the brawl in dancing . . . yet of them two springeth an excellent virtue whereunto we lack a name in English. . . . *Maturum* in Latin may be interpreted ripe or ready. . . . Therefore that word maturity is translated to the acts of man, that when they be done with such moderation that nothing in the doing may be seen superfluous or indigent . . . do neither too much nor too little, too soon nor too late, too swiftly nor slowly, but in due time and measure.[23]

Just as in the brawl the seeming discord of the dancers' disparate motions is resolved into the graceful flow of the dance, so in their lives the shepherds seek to resolve the discordances of their nature into harmony.[24] At the root of their harmony, as at the beginning of their dance, would seem to be the fear, love, and reverence which they have for God, and the expression of their harmony is their love, which, as the succeeding poems will show, is "neither too much nor too little, too soon nor too late, too swiftly nor too slowly, but in due time and measure."

Since there can be "no music kindly without love," Sidney devotes the First Eclogues to a depiction of the range of love, from the proper and harmonious love of the Creator and his creations down through the scale to cupidinous love and thence to idolatry. There is in this depiction, moreover, a curious bifurcation between the poems of the disguised princes and those of the shepherds. The princes, despite the veiled appeals to the princesses they are making, present curiously literal and unpoetic complaints which offer no insight into their general condition beyond providing a particular example of the sufferings of those who engage in the wrong kind of loving. The shepherds, however, constantly take us beyond the particular act to the general condition.[25] An explanation for this might be, as Dipple has suggested, that the princes are not participating in the eclogues, but rather are seizing an opportunity denied them thus far in the main narrative to approach the princesses.[26] It is for this reason, perhaps, that their eclogues are set off from those of the shepherds by the use of quantitative metrics.

Sidney begins his illustration of the ways of loving in a singing contest between the disguised Musidorus and Lalus, "a shepherd accounted one of the best singers among them" (p. 58). Lalus, "having marked in Dorus' dancing no less good grace and handsome behaviour than extreme tokens of a troubled mind" (p. 58), urges him to disburden himself of his sorrows by reducing them to song. When Musidorus refuses, on the grounds that to disclose his love would be to profane it (*OA* 7.12, p. 58), Lalus insists that so long as Dorus is one of them he must abide by their rules. In the poetic debate that follows Musidorus' submission, the differences between the way in which the shepherds love and the manner that the noble lovers suffer are contrasted. The issue is put directly by Musidorus, when, after having called upon his muse to "historify/Her [Pamela's] praise," he claims the victory in advance because Lalus' "health" is "too mean a match for my infection" (*OA* 7.21, p. 59). The remainder of the singing match illustrates his boast as in his sickness he flies to such heights of hyperbole that Lalus, in his healthy and natural prosaicness, feels overawed. This dualism is clear from the first efforts of each to describe his lady.

Unlike Dorus, who will claim to "reach . . . beyond humanity" (*OA* 7.64, p. 60) in his love, Lalus' beloved is a human being whose glories (and flaws) are proper to her place in the natural world of created things. His poetry is not an attempt to immortalize her, but a simple praise of her natural gifts. Thus he begins not by asking the aid of the muses but the assistance of the shepherds' god, Pan,[27] and his love for Kala takes the form of a magnification of the glories of the created world. Kala, observing moderation, is "A heap of sweets . . . where nothing spilled is" (*OA* 7.28, p. 59). The only miraculous thing about her is that "though she be no bee," she is nonetheless "full of honey" (*OA* 7.29, p. 59). She is comparable to a lamb in mildness and a rabbit in daintiness. She is, in short, an altogether natural and human girl, even to some minor flaws like her coyness and the affectedness of her studied speech. Lalus' love leads him not into the web of his desires, but to a greater appreciation of the beauty of God's creation.[28]

The woman whom Musidorus loves, however, is of another kind. Where Kala may be compared to the things of the world, Musidorus is forced to seek his comparisons beyond them. In part, Dorus' exaggerated language is forced from him by the situation, for if Kala, a shepherdess, is the embodiment of natural beauty, then his love, who is after all a princess, must be praised more extravagantly still. Nonetheless, we know enough about Musidorus' love to realize that even if the situation had not forced him into the posture he adopts, he would have chosen it because for him Pamela really "is" the compound of all virtues and the envy of the gods, who fear that her death would result in her apotheosis and their loss of godhead. She is perfection even in the eyes of the gods, and, quite obviously, is the most precious object to be found on the earth. Musidorus has gone beyond love to idolatry. He can no longer think of Pamela as a human being, a part of the natural order, and the creation of God. Instead, he has come to worship her, forgetting her Creator, and thus has transformed love, which seems, at least for the Arcadian shepherds, to be a natural and healthy response to another human being, into his unnatural sickness, a compound of lust and idolatry. Where Lalus can find pleasure in the "flow'ry field" and "pastimes make, as nature things hath made" (OA 7.125, 127, p. 62), Musidorus can neither find pleasure in nature nor even comprehend nature without changing it into a metaphor for his own tormented inner state:

> Despair my field; the flowers spirit's wars;
> My day new cares; my gins my daily sight,
> In which do light small birds of thoughts o'erthrown. . . .
>
> [OA 7.139-41, p. 62]

One final exchange between them before they conclude their singing match is also highly revealing of their own reactions to love. For Lalus, the desire he feels is painful and distracting, but it is not raging totally out of control:

> Thus doth my life within itself dissolve
> That I grow like the beast
> Which bears the bit a weaker force doth guide,
> Yet patient must abide;
> Such weight it hath which once is full possessed.
>
> [OA 7.157-61, p. 63]

Although the natural tendency of the desire that accompanies love is to challenge the will, the "beastly" faculty since it was corrupted by the fall, Lalus' will still wears the bit of control. Because his will is subordinate to his love, he is able to recognize that, despite the desire he feels, he "patient must abide."[29] For Musidorus, however, "love" is the cause of the total dissolution of all the bonds of obedience:

> Such weight it hath which once is full possessed
> That I become a vision,
> Which hath in other's head his only being
> And lives in fancy's seeing.
> O wretched state of man in self-division!
>
> [OA 7.162-66, p. 63]

The "wretched state of man in self-division" is man's state as a result of original sin, which has left him both divided within himself and against himself: "The subject thereof is the old man, with all his powers, mind, will, and heart. For in the mind there is darkness, and ignorance of God, and his will: and in the will, and heart of man there is concupiscence, and rebellious affections against the law of God."[30] Because Musidorus' "infected will" is firmly in control, he has rejected the easy way of Christ and fallen into what Ficino describes as the madness of the "earthly lover," that "anxious care" by which lovers are "vexed day and night" and which causes them "to rush into madness and raging passion. . . . But the worst effect from it is that by this madness, man descends to the nature of a beast."[31] The consequence of this descent to the level of the beast is the (metaphorical) death of the soul:

There are these two kinds of love: one simple, the other reciprocal. Simple love occurs when the loved one does not return his lover's affections. In this case the lover is completely dead, for he neither lives in himself . . . nor does he live in his loved one. . . . Where, then, does he live? In air, water, fire, earth, or in some animal carcass? In none of these, for the human soul does not live in any but a human body.[32]

Having rejected God's love and not yet having gained Pamela's, Musidorus is reduced to nothingness. His existence is confirmed only by the eyes of others; his own eyes, devoid of the light of reason, are sightless and comprehend nothing but the fancies of his disordered will.

After seeing the results of earthly love as manifested in Musidorus, we are well prepared for the blanket condemnation of it offered by an old shepherd, Dicus, who, "whether for certain mischances of his own, or out of a better judgment, which saw the bottom of things, did more detest and hate love than the most envious man doth in himself cherish and love hate" (p. 64).[33] Dicus bears upon his breast "a painted table, wherein he had given Cupid a quite new form, making him sit upon a pair of gallows, like a hangman . . . he himself painted all ragged and torn, so that his skin was bare in most places, where a man might perceive all his body full of eyes, his head horned with the horns of a bull, with long ears accordingly, his face old and wrinkled, and his feet cloven" (p. 64). From his eclogue, it becomes clear that Dicus, while retaining the various meanings associated with the mythographical "blind Cupid," is attempting to substitute a more fitting visual description for the symbol of cupidinous love.[34] Instead of "A naked god, blind, young, with arrows two" (OA 8.6, p. 65), Dicus claims that Cupid is really "an old false knave . . . / By Argus got on Io, then a cow" (OA 8.13-14, p. 65).[35] Dicus' new hangman Cupid—part human, part beast—signifies the power of the wrong kind of love to transform men into beasts and to cause their spiritual death. These are the qualities that Dicus stresses in his poem:

> Thus half a man, with man he easily haunts,
> Clothed in the shape which soonest may deceive:
> Thus half a beast, each beastly vice he plants
> In those weak hearts that his advice receive.
>> He prowls each place still in new colours decked,
>> Sucking one's ill, another to infect.
>
> [OA 8.31-36, p. 66]

In his conclusion, moreover, he makes explicit the dilemma of those wills "patient" do not "abide":

> Millions of years this old drivel Cupid lives;
> While still more wretch, more wicked he doth prove:

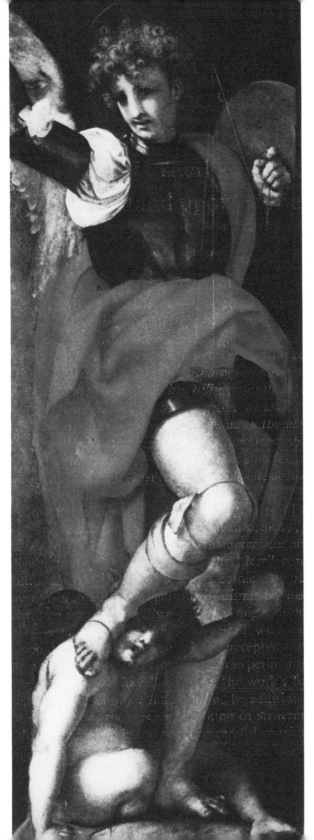

Figure 3. Jacopo Pontormo, "St. Michael." Copyright Museo della Collegiata di Empoli. Reproduced with permission. (See n. 34.)

Till now at length that Jove him office gives
(At Juno's suit who much did Argus love),
* In this our world a hangman for to be*
* Of all those fools that will have all they see.*

[OA 8.43-48, p. 66]

Cupidinous love has power over those whose will controls their soul, Dicus puns, because it is the will, itself infected since the fall of Adam, that is the source of the infection which breeds cupidinous love.

At the conclusion of Dicus' song, a young shepherd named Histor steps forth, and "with great vehemency desired all the hearers to take heed how they seemed to allow any part of his speech against so revengeful a god as Cupid was" (p. 66). As his name (history) suggests, he feels it unwise to dismiss so summarily such a potent force as cupidinous love. Histor then goes on to relate in prose the story of Erona, Princess of Lydia, who,

seeing the country of Lydia so much devoted to Cupid as that in each place his naked pictures and images were superstitiously adored, procured so much of her father (either moved thereunto by the hate of that god, or the shamefast consideration of such nakedness) utterly to deface and pull down all those pictures of him; which how terribly he punished quickly after appeared. For she had not lived a year longer when she was stricken with most obstinate love to a young man. [P. 67]

As a consequence of Erona's passion for Antiphilus, her father dies of grief, and the kingdom of Lydia is invaded by the King of Persia, an unsuccessful suitor of hers. Through the assistance of Pyrocles and Musidorus, the Persian king is killed and his army defeated. After the princes leave Lydia, Erona is betrayed to the sister of the dead Persian king, Queen Artaxia, by Antiphilus, her "mean" lover, who loves the idea of becoming the new king of Persia as much as he does Artaxia. His love is not reciprocated, however, and Artaxia has him slowly put to death. Erona is to be kept alive for two years as the bait in a trap for Pyrocles and Musidorus. Meanwhile, Plangus, a young Iberian nobleman in the court of Artaxia, falls in love with Erona and goes off in search of the two princes in the hope that they will be able to save her life. Just as Histor is about to repeat a complaint that Plangus had made to a wise Arcadian shepherd, he is interrupted by another shepherd, and the series of eclogues begins again.

There are several reasons for Sidney's introduction of Erona's tale into the First Eclogues. First, it gives him a chance to show us that Pyrocles and Musidorus were capable of heroic acts before they came to Arcadia and that they, above all, should have been more on their guard against the kind of love to which they have become enslaved, having seen how much disharmony it can create in both the individual and the state. Another function of the episode is to show us that cupidinous love is not restricted to Arcadia, but exists throughout the world. The most important reason for including this narrative, however, is to warn the reader. Following Dicus' contemptuous dismissal of Cupid as an "old drivel," the narrator wants to be sure that we do not underestimate the power of the force that he symbolizes. However ungodlike Cupid may be, cupidinous love can be the cause of great suffering and disorder. Moreover, as Erona's example shows, it is not enough just to hate all that Cupid stands for; one must find some way of preventing the passions from taking control. However willing the spirit may be, it cannot overcome the weakness of the flesh.

This struggle is very much at issue in the next eclogue, a debate between Geron, an old shepherd, and Philisides, a young non-Arcadian shepherd, who has thus far remained outside of the shepherds' harmony, neither singing nor dancing, "with so deep a melancholy that his senses carried to his mind no delight from any of their objects" (p. 71).[36] By now, we should not need anyone to tell us that we have before us another victim of the self-inflicted wounds of illicit love. Geron urges Philisides to let himself go in healing song, for "sweet tunes do passions ease" (*OA* 9.4, p. 72); his hope that by joining song to reason he can engage Philisides in a dialogue and so start the process of curing him is quickly dashed. Philisides, of course, refuses, having lost the desire to recreate his lost harmony in himself when he lost the desire to "ease" his passions and deified them instead. Geron then offers him some advice on how to curb his will and regain rational control of his mind:

> *Let not a glitt'ring name thy fancy dress*
> *In painted clothes, because they call it love.*
> *There is no hate that can thee more oppress.*
> *Begin (and half the work is done) to prove*
> *By raising up, upon thyself to stand;*
> *And think she is a she that doth thee move.*
>
> [*OA* 9.47-52, p. 73]

Geron's message to Philisides is a simple one. Recognizing that in the grip of his perverted love Philisides has allowed his will to turn away from God, in His place worshiping one of His creations, Geron bids Philisides to remember "thy mistress is a woman" (*OA* 9.61, p. 73). In doing so he is trying to make Philisides aware of his beloved's humanity and her proper place in the natural hierarchy as a first step toward reestablishing the proper relationship between his reason and his will in his soul. Just as the will should be subservient to the reason, so woman should be man's servant: "But consider thou againe, that the woman is a fraile vessel, and thou art therefore made the rule and head ouer her, to beare the weakenesse of her in this her subiection."[37] Philisides, however, has closed his eyes to the light and his ears to wisdom:

> *Hath any man heard what this old man said?*
> *Truly, not I who did my thoughts engage*
> *Where all my pains one look of hers hath paid.*
>
> [*OA* 9.135-37, p. 75]

With Histor, whose comment ends the eclogue, we can see

> *. . . how youth esteemeth age,*
> *And never hath thereof arightly deemed,*
> *Whie hot desires do reign in fancy's rage. . . .*
>
> [*OA* 9.138-40, p. 76]

Like Dorus, Philisides is obdurate and prefers his sickness to the possibility of health. His will is clearly not to be swayed by reason nor bound by courtesy.

Histor's observation suggests a critical question which Sidney has not yet answered. Thus far in the First Eclogues, we have been seeing the differences between health and infection, between the love which seems to take its beginning from the love we owe to God and all his creations and the love which begins in a turning away from God to the worship of a creature, between a love which is harmonious to reason and one which is a spur to an unbridled will. While Sidney has shown us how to recognize the symptoms of lust, he has not shown us how it may be cured. As Geron's unheeded advice indicates, the lover has closed his mind to the wisdom which might prove his cure. If wisdom alone cannot suffice to effect a return to peace and health, what else is needed? The answer does not come in the remaining poems of the First Eclogues —they simply indicate the depth of the problem by presenting to us the "infernal agonies" (*OA 11*.14, p. 80) which Pyrocles and Musidorus are enduring. However, Sidney returns to the problem at the beginning of the Second Eclogues.

II. The Second Eclogues

The Second Eclogues occur immediately after the Phagonian rebels have been dispersed, but they take their impetus as much from the conclusion of the First Eclogues as from the events of the second book. Just as the first two books of the prose narrative may be said to form one unit, so too the first two Eclogues function as one continuous group whose task is to provide an alternative to the ideals and values which guide the noble lovers in the main narrative. Sidney began this task in the First Eclogues by contrasting Lalus' love to the various ways in which the noble characters love. Having provided a touchstone, he was then free, through Dicus' eclogue, to pour scorn upon the passionate, idolatrous, cupidinous love that the nobles have "unwittingly" embraced. However, as the examples of Erona and Philisides informed us, once the passions and the will take control, the reason seems unable to function effectively. This is the problem to which the Second Eclogues are addressed.

Although the first poem of this group, "The skirmish betwixt Reason and Passion," occurs immediately after the abortive rebellion of the Phagonians, we must not assume that it is solely concerned with that revolt. As the narrator notes, the revolt does no more than give "occasion" (p. 135) to the dance of the shepherds, whose concerns arise equally from the issues left unresolved in the First Eclogues. The poem itself is the beneficiary of a considerable amount of tension created by the stichomythic responses of the two sides, to which is added the clarity gained from Sidney's customarily exact punning upon the key terms of his argument. Following the symbolic representation of the combat and reconciliation of reason and passion in the dance, the poem is in three parts. In the first, reason and passion advance their claims:

> Reason. *Thou rebel vile, come, to thy master yield.*
> Passion. *No tyrant, no; mine, mine shall be the field.*
> R.   *Can Reason then a tyrant counted be?*
> P.   *If Reason will that Passions be not free.*
> R.   *But Reason will that Reason govern most.*
> P.   *And Passion will that Passion rule the roast.*
> R.   *Your will is will; but Reason reason is.*
> P.   *Will hath his will when Reason's will doth miss.*

[OA 27.1-8, p. 135]

Taking its key from the context offered by the Phagonian revolt, Reason accuses Passion of rebellion and is in turn called a tyrant. Passion then cleverly proves its claim by forcing Reason to adapt itself to the language of passion: "But Reason *will* that Reason govern most" (my italics). In response to Reason's claim that Passion "by nature . . . to Reason faith . . . [has] sworn," Passion replies, "Not so, but fellowlike together born" (*OA* 27.11-12, p. 135). When reason tries to impose itself absolutely, it ceases to be reason, for reason can function not as an absolute prince but only as a guide:

Now although we said before, that reason held the soueraignty amongst the powers, vertues, and offices of the soule, yet wee must know, that reason reigneth not ouer will as Lady and Princesse, but onely as Mistresse to teach and shew it, what it ought to follow & what to flie from. For the will hath no light of it selfe, but is lightned by the minde, that is to say, by reason and iudgement, which are ioyned with it, not to gouerne and turne it from one side to another by commandement and authority, either by force or violence, as a Prince or Magistrate, but as a counseller or directer, to admonish and to conduct it.[38]

Passion's final argument, that Reason can see only "his own ill case" (*OA* 27.16, p. 135), is also a telling one, for we have seen the ultimately self-defeating effects of a reason which can admonish but not guide in Gynecia. On the other hand, Passion claims more power than it should have and is too unconcerned about the consequences of its rule:

> R.   *Whom Passion leads unto his death is bent.*
> P.   *And let him die, so that he die content.*
>
> [*OA* 27.9-10, p. 135]

We have seen too much of the effects of giving way to one's passions in the first two books of the main narrative to be able to delude ourselves, along with Passion, into believing that "content" is possible at the end of life ruled by passion.

Although Reason begins the second part of the poem on the offensive again, again the result is a standoff:

> Reason. *Dare Passions then abide in Reason's light?*
> Passion. *And is not Reason dimmed with Passion's might?*
> R.   *O foolish thing which glory dost destroy!*
> P.   *O glorious title of a foolish toy!*
> R.   *Weakness you are, dare you with our strength fight?*
> P.   *Because our weakness weak'neth all your might.*
> R.   *O sacred Reason, help our virtuous toils!*
> P.   *O Passion, pass on feeble Reason's spoils!*
> R.   *We with ourselves abide a daily strife.*
> P.   *We gladly use the sweetness of our life.*
> R.   *But yet our strife sure peace in end doth breed.*
> P.   *We now have peace, your peace we do not need.*
>
> [*OA* 27.17-28, p. 136]

Passions, as the abundant examples Sidney provides for us attest, most certainly do "abide" despite "Reason's light." In fact, as Passion suggests, they are capable of dimming reason's light. But then, the light that reason alone provides is but the "glorious title of a foolish toy":

And truelie, the reason of man, naturally ingraffed in his heart, which so far foorth as he is man, and according to his abilitie and manner of life he imitateth and followeth, is diuers from that which by special grace from aboue commeth to the elect, accompanieth them, and helpeth them in all their actions. This is full of faith, and of vndeceiueble assurance of eternall promises: the other, weake, troubled and wonderfully hindred, wherein a man can neuer haue any certaine resolution.[39]

Again, Sidney insists that reason is not a sufficient prop for a man to stand upon. Neither, however, is passion, which must not be allowed to "pass" despite the feebleness of the fortifications of reason. Those whom passions pillage can find only the peace of a ruined, burnt-out town, the peace of desolation and total destruction.

From the conclusion of the second section, it seems that war is inevitable, but the third section begins with an unexpected reconciliation in the dance as "the two square battles meet and, instead of fighting, embrace one another, singing thus":

> Reason. *We are too strong; but Reason seeks not blood.*
> Passion. *Who be too weak do feign they be too good.*
> R.   *Though we cannot o'ercome, our cause is just.*
> P.   *Let us o'ercome, and let us be unjust.*
> R.   *Yet Passion, yield at length to Reason's stroke.*
> P.   *What shall we win by taking Reason's yoke?*
> R.   *The joys you have shall be made permanent.*
> P.   *But so we shall with grief learn to repent.*
> R.   *Repent indeed, but that shall be your bliss.*
> P.   *How know we that, since present joys we miss?*
> R.   *You know it not; of Reason therefore know it.*
> P.   *No Reason yet had ever skill to show it.*
> R.P.   *Then let us both to heav'nly rules give place,*
>   *Which Passions kill, and Reason do deface.*[40]

[*OA* 27.29-42, p. 136]

After recognizing that it cannot overcome Passion by itself, Reason finally triumphs by going beyond itself. If the will can respond only in terms of what it desires for its "content," then reason must appeal to its latent desire for good by showing how a lasting pleasure may best be achieved. Thus instead of asserting its supremacy, Reason puts on the same "yoke" it desires Passion to wear, the yoke of obedience to "heavenly rules" or the yoke of Christ in Matt. 11:29-30. The surest guide to follow, as both Reason and Passion finally agree, is the guide of faith.

Sidney is here following the same strategy outlined in the "Preface to the Reader" to de Mornay's *A Woorke concerning the trewnesse of the Christian Religion*. Although de Mornay admits "that mans reason is so farre off from being the measurer of faith, which very far exceedeth nature, that it is not so much as the measurer of nature, & of the least creatures which lie farre vnderneath man; because of the ignorance and vntowardnes which is in vs and raigneth in vs," he insists that "mans reason is able to lead vs to that point; namely, that we ought to belieue euen beyond reason, I meane the things whereunto all the capacitie of man cannot attaine" (*Prose Works*, 3:194; *A Woorke*, sig. ** 6ᵛ). Similarly, in the "Skirmish" Sidney presents two positions each of which is inadequate in itself and each of which taken by itself is incorrect. From their mutual irreconcilability, he argues that a resolution can occur only by transcending the terms of the argument. If neither reason nor passion, taken by themselves, will suffice to guide man, then there must be something superior to them that will. By turning to "heavenly rules," the missing term is supplied; through faith, Sidney suggests, reason and passion can be brought to function harmoniously together.

The manner by which one may achieve a commitment to faith is suggested by the significance we have already seen Elyot assign to the dance. We must submit both our reason and our passion to a higher authority. This is in itself an act of reason, but it is reason fortified by grace and impelled by the awareness of one's limitations which comes from self-knowledge. Unless we have learned how unable reason is to control the passions that confront it and how unsafe it is to follow the desires of the will, we will not feel a need to attempt to surrender ourselves—reason, passion, and all —to the more comprehensive dictates of heavenly rules.

This poem and its companion, the first poem of the First Eclogues, together express the perspective of the first two Eclogues, which combine with the ironic overtones given to the actions of the noble characters is in the prose sections to establish a set of values in opposition to those held by the main characters and by which they may be judged. In them, in opposition to the painfulness of idolatrous love and the unrest caused by lust, are expressed the health and harmony which come from living and loving in accordance with "heavenly rules." Through them we may learn how to oppose to the desires of our "infected will" not the common sense of reason or even the intellectual subtleties of philosophy, but faith in God and his providential order gained through having "feelingly found the evil that evil carrieth with it" (p. 108) and through our recognition of the inability of fallen man to avoid evil by his own efforts.[41]

With one exception (*OA 30*), the remaining poems of the Second Eclogues add little to these statements; they merely provide a series of exemplifications of the consequences of not following them. Thus when Dorus and Dicus sing together, Dicus does not try to dissuade him from his folly (as earlier Geron had reproached Philisides) so much as to offer him sympathetic advice, pointing out that the fruits of his actions will be "late remorse" (*OA 28*.78, p. 139), and compassionately prays that he may have either "help or change of passion":

> *She oft her looks, the stars her favour, bend to thee:*
> *Fortune store, Nature health, Love grant persuasion.*
> *A quiet mind none but thyself can lend to thee,*
> *Thus I commend to thee all our former love.*
>
> [*OA 28*.99-102, p. 140]

Even here, however, the oppositions are clear: Dorus' hope can rest either on woman's fickleness and fortune's changeable gifts or, having a "change in passion," on the health of a love which is in harmony with man's nature.

The next poem, a singing contest between two young shepherds, parodies the high-flown phrases and low aspirations of Dorus and Cleophila.[42] Not only do the two reduce to farce the hopes of the princely lovers for favor, but their concluding riddles mock the fleshly consummation for which the nobles are scheming:

> Nico. *Tell me (and be my* Pan) *the monster's name*
> *That hath four legs, and with two only goes;*
> *That hath four eyes, and only two can frame.*
> Pas. *Tell this (and* Phoebus *be): what monster grows*
> *With so strong lives that body cannot rest*
> *In ease until that body life forgoes?*
>
> [OA 29.141-46, p. 146]

It takes a very restrained imagination indeed not to see that the monster of the first riddle is Rabelais' beast with two backs, while the second monster is the sexual desire that afflicts the noble lovers with whom the shepherds are sharing the stage.[43]

Following these two riddles, the narrator brings forth Histor to complete the tale of Plangus and Erona, in the process advancing our understanding of the manner in which reason is made to deface itself in favor of faith. Plangus, of course, is the exemplification of the cupidinous lover. His love for Erona, says Histor, began because Cupid was anxious to do "some greater mischief" (p. 70), and he has sacrificed everything so that he might devote himself to her service. Histor then relates the exchange between Plangus and Boulon which he has overheard.[44] From his complaint, it is clear that Plangus is in a state of despair. Having come to worship Erona, his unhappiness at not being able to help her leads him to blaspheme against God, whom he accuses of cruelly not permitting his quest for Pyrocles and Musidorus to succeed.[45]

Plangus begins as if he had understood all of the "skirmish betwixt Reason and Passion" save its concluding couplet:

> *Ah where was first that cruel cunning found*
> *To frame of earth a vessel of the mind,*
> *Where it should be to self-destruction bound?*
> *What needed so high sprites such mansions blind?*
> *Or wrapped in flesh what do they here obtain,*
> *But glorious name of wretched human-kind?*
>
> [OA 30.11-16, p. 147]

Like Gynecia, whose complaints in the fourth and fifth books echo these themes, Plangus is unable to move beyond the range of his reason. Being taught by the "common nature" of man that God is "good, and no author of evil" and having learned through his own experiences that man "is subject to passions, inclined to euill, weake vnto good and so forth" (*Prose Works*, 3:192; *A Woorke*, sig. **5ᵛ), he can only fall to questioning God's motives in creating man as He did. Behind this questioning lie two contrary syllogisms. The first might run something like this: "God is good, and no lover of evil. I am evil. God does not love me." The second, we may surmise, is along these lines: "God created me 'to self-destruction bound' for my evil. God is the author of evil. God is not good." Like Gynecia, Plangus has reasoned himself into a position where he must either abandon all trust in God or all hope of his own salvation. If God is good he must hate evil. If Plangus is evil, God hates him. If God hates him, can God be good? In this series of assumptions we can locate the immediate source of Plangus' despair. From this position, man's role in life seems as clear as it is unacceptable:

> Balls to the stars, and thralls to fortune's reign;
>> Turned from themselves, infected with their cage,
>> Where death is feared, and life is held with pain.
> Like players placed to fill a filthy stage,
>> Where change of thoughts one fool to other shows,
>> And all but jests, save only sorrow's rage.

[OA 30.17-22, p. 147]

Life for Plangus has become an obscenely meaningless play in which man is the tortured actor and God the amused spectator, jeering him on to ever greater degradations.

Boulon, disturbed by Plangus' insults to God, remembers some other of the "common principles" taught by the "common nature" of man, that God is "wise, and doth not anie thing in vaine. Also that man is borne to be immortall; that to be happie he ought to serve God and continew in his fauour" (*Prose Works*, 3:192; *A Woorke*, sig. **5ᵛ). He begins to expound on the "skirmish betwixt Reason and Passion," taking as his text, "But so we shall with grief learn to repent./Repent indeed, but that shall be your bliss":

> *O man, take heed how thou the gods do move*
> > *To causeful wrath which thou canst not resist.*
> > *Blasphemous words the speaker vain do prove.*
> *Alas, while we are wrapped in foggy mist*
> > *Of our self-love (so passions do deceive)*
> > *We think they hurt when most they do assist.*
> *To harm us worms should that high justice leave*
> > *His nature? nay, himself? for so it is.*
> > *What glory from our loss can he receive?*
> *But still our dazzled eyes their way do miss,*
> > *While that we do at his sweet scourge repine,*
> > *The kindly way to beat us on to bliss.*
> > > [OA 30.65-76, pp. 148-49]

Holding to his "reasonable" assumptions that God is good and does nothing without reason, Boulon resolves Plangus' logical dilemmas by faith in a justice "higher" than human reason can conceive, a justice which seeks not to punish man's proneness to evil but to correct it.[46] What reason cannot do, the "high justice" can, returning man's errant will to obedience through adversity and in the process recovering man's love for itself by making him dependent not on himself nor on the "grace" of others, but solely on God.[47]

Plangus, however, is still too caught up in his despair over Erona's fate and his own misery to be able to do anything but "repine" over God's "sweet scourge," which he sees beating him not to bliss but to destruction, since he acknowledges no god but Erona (see *OA 30.89-124*). Boulon tries again to bring him back to his senses by reminding him that his "mistress is a woman":

> *Yet reason saith, reason should have ability*
> > *To hold these worldly things in such proportion*
> > *As let them come or go with e'en facility.*
> *But our desire's tyrannical extortion*
> > *Doth force us there to set our chief delightfulness*
> > *Where but a baiting place is all our portion.*
> > > [OA 30.131-36, p. 150]

Boulon is concerned that having lost his sense of proportion, Plangus has also lost his sense of balance and chosen to dwell only in extremes:

> But still, although we fail of perfect rightfulness,
>   Seek we to tame these childish superfluities?
> Let us not wink though void of purest sightfulness;
> . . . .
>   Let us some grammar learn of more congruities.
>
> [OA 30.137-39, 142, pp. 150-51]

It is precisely this kind of "grammar" Sidney has been trying to teach us in the first two Eclogues: the fundamental rules of the science of harmonizing the parts of man's whole—passion, will, and reason—so that they cohere in obedience to heavenly rules.[48]

For Plangus, "who still doth seek against himself offences" (*OA* 30.167, p. 151), Boulon's lesson is not sufficient. Boulon cannot "lead" him "to salvation the haven of our life; for in that behalfe we have need of God himselfe to be our Pilote." All he can do is show him, "as it were from a Tower; which way it standeth in the darke wherein we now be, to the end we may call to God for helpe, and ever after make thitherward with all our whole hart" (*Prose Works*, 3:199; *A Woorke*, sig. ***). So long as Plangus insists on setting his "chief delightfulness / Where but a baiting place is all our portion," he will never be able to find his true "haven." Like those many who make "a perpetual mansion of the poor baiting place of man's life" (*OA*, 5), Plangus will not "avail" himself of the "pardon" the "high justice" has offered through adversity (see *OA* 30.167-68, p. 151). In so refusing, he is, in effect, rejecting the grace God has proffered.[49] While Plangus' sufferings are terrible, we must nonetheless distance ourselves from them, for Sidney warns us through Boulon against commiserating with Plangus too much:

> Betwixt the good and shade of good divided,
>   We pity deem that which but weakness is;
> So are we from our high creation slided.
>
> [OA 30.179-81, p. 152]

In this poem, Sidney makes the guilt that Plangus had tried to thrust upon God rebound back upon him. Plangus, like the rest of us, has, from his "high creation slided"; for him, however, a recovery does not seem likely. For those who can transcend their compassion for Plangus and see where he could not, blinded by the "foggy mist" of his "self-love," Sidney has suggested a way to walk where Plangus could only stumble and fall.

The reaction of Histor's audience to his recitation is interesting. Ignoring Boulon's warning, the nobles can think only of Plangus: "So well did Histor's voice express the passion of Plangus that all the princely beholders were stricken into a silent consideration of it; indeed everyone making that he heard of another the balance of his troubles" (p. 152). Since they are behaving much as Plangus did, their sympathy for him is not too surprising; as Boulon has noted, "Self-guilty folk" are "most prone to feel compassion" (*OA* 30.130, p. 150). Nonetheless, their sympathy is as clearly an insufficient response to the story they have heard as their lives are an inadequate effort to achieve the "bliss" to which their "high creation" seems to invite them.

At this point in the Second Eclogues, the narrator introduces a second long prose narrative, this time dealing with the adventures of Pyrocles and Musidorus after they had left Erona's court. In their first adventure, they destroy a giant who has been terrorizing the country of Paphlagonia, by taking in tribute each month two maids whom "he used at his beastly pleasure" and two young men whom he sacrificed to an idol (p. 153). Had Spenser written this episode, we might assume that Pyrocles and Musidorus had overcome beastly lust; in the context of the Eclogues, however, we may say only that we have been shown one more aspect of the beastliness of lust and of man's inability to learn from his experiences, for Pyrocles and Musidorus are prepared to sacrifice an entire kingdom to their idols, as book 3 will shortly reveal. In the following stories, the princes display, in addition to their wonted courage, justice and temperance as they reconcile the king of Syria to his brother, defend their chastity against the Lady of Palestina while protecting her kingdom against the prince of Arabia, and reconcile the king of Egypt to his son.[50] In each of these adventures, the difficulties the princes confront are caused by the abuse of love; their concern, however, is not with the causes but with the symptoms. "Why and how" these situations arose is of less concern to the princes than how to deal with them.

Following the princes' past adventures, the Second Eclogues return to the Arcadian present as Philisides, Sidney's alter ego, shows the capacity of the will to delude itself in an eclogue "betwixt himself and the echo" (p. 159). After being "told" by his echo that his "love" can only end in death, that the "heavenly woman" he worships is but a woman, and that the joys he seeks are toys which curse the only true bliss man can hope for, he engages in the following exchange:

> Mock'st thou those diamonds which only be matched
>   by the gods?   Odds.
> Odds? What an odds is there since them to the heav'ns
>   I prefer?   Err.
> Tell yet again me the names of these faire formed
>   to do ev'ls.   Dev'ls.
> Dev'ls? If in hell such dev'ls do abide, to the hells
>   I do go.   Go.
>   [OA 30.47-50, p. 162]

The persistence of sin and the strength of evil are also illustrated by Pyrocles, who, recognizing the inevitable end of his passion, nonetheless vows to be "faithful" to his "goddess":

> The life we lead is all love,
> The love we hold is all death,
> Nor aught I crave to feed life,
> Nor aught I seek to shun death,
> But only that my goddess
> My life, my death, do count hers.
>   [OA 32.52-57, p. 164]

Having closed their hearts to God and turned away from Him to both self-love and idolatry, Pyrocles and Musidorus (and Philisides and Plangus) are free to joy in the pleasures of their love.[51] The Second Eclogues end after two more eclogues by Cleophila and Dorus, in which they confirm again and again their wrongheaded love; then everyone wanders off "to counterfeit a sleep in their beds for a true one their agonies could not afford them" (p. 167).

Although the Second Eclogues conclude by expressing the discontent and disharmony of the noble lovers—and especially Pyrocles and Musidorus—the picture they present is, on the whole, a hopeful one. Beginning where the First Eclogues left off, the Second Eclogues suggest that even those over whom passion has gained control can, through repentance and faith, reestablish a harmonious relationship with God. Taken together, the first two Eclogues present an examination of the ways of living and loving. Against the backdrop of the willfulness of Erona and Plangus, Cleophila and Dorus, and Philisides, Sidney offers us the love of Lalus for Kala, the counsel of Dicus and Boulon, and the peace and harmony of the songs and dances of the shepherds. Even though the noble lovers seem destined to fates like those of the errant princes and princesses whom Pyrocles and Musidorus met in Asia Minor, we need not despair. With the announcement of the coming marriage of Lalus to the "fair Kala" (p. 159), there seems reason to think that the Eclogues' picture of life in a fallen world is far more hopeful than that of the main narrative.

III. The Third Eclogues

In several ways, the Third Eclogues differ markedly from their predecessors. With the exception of "the melancholy Philisides" (p. 245), who does not participate *in propria persona*, the cast is limited to the Arcadian shepherds. The nobles and the "Stranger Shepherds" are either unable or unwilling to be present. Consequently, the eclogues are all more directly concerned with the business at hand, the marriage of Lalus and Kala. Also changed is the time of day at which the shepherds meet. Unlike the other Eclogues, all of which take their impetus from the murky doings of the nobles, the Third Eclogues concern an event initiated by the shepherds. It is thus fitting that it takes place during the day instead of at night, for instead of being illuminated by the flickering torches of men it is bathed in the brilliance of the sun. So, too,

Sidney's ends are here being served not by the halting wisdom of men but by the presentation of a ceremony ordained by God.

Although Protestantism did not accord marriage the status of a sacrament, it held marriage in the highest respect both in itself and for what it signified.[52] As *The Book of Common Prayer* proclaims, "holy matrimony . . . is an honourable estate, instituted of GOD in paradise, in the time of man's innocency: signifying unto us the mystical union, that is betwixt Christ and his Church."[53] Marriage was considered to be the most holy of all human institutions:

First we haue to consider the beginning and antiquitie of mariage, the place where it was instituted, & who was the author therof, & that in the time of innocency. . . . Moreouer we must remember, that the heauenly word honored with his presence, & set forth a wedding feast with a miracle, euen with the first which he wrought in this world. Can any thing then be found more holy, than that which the holy of holyes, the Father & creator of all things hath established, honored & consecrated with his presence?[54]

Marriage was likewise thought to be the most honest and beautiful event that could take place on earth:

If we could (saith *Plato*) behold with bodily eies the beauty that honesty hath in her, we would be far in loue with her: but she is to be seene onely with the eies of the mind. And truely with the same eies wee may behold it in marriage, if wee consider narrowly the honesty of the coupled life, when it is in euery respect absolute, than the holy bond whereof, the earth hath nothing more beautifull or honest.[55]

Lalus' marriage is thus a major event in the *Old Arcadia*, with both a literal and figurative significance befitting the attention it receives. Through it, Lalus may best cement the loving relationship with Kala for which he has prepared himself and figure for us the loving relationship between man and his Creator which is figured in the marriage of Christ with his Church.[56]

Sidney sets the stage for the Third Eclogues by tracing the steps by which Lalus and Kala moved toward marriage:

Lalus, not with many painted words, nor false-hearted promises, had won the consent of his beloved Kala, but with a true and simple making her know he loved her; not forcing himself beyond his reach to buy her affection, but giving her such pretty presents as neither could weary him with the giving nor shame her for the taking. . . . Thus constantly continuing, though he were none of the fairest, at length he wan Kala's heart, the honestest wench in all those quarters. And so, with consent of both parents (without which neither Lalus would ask nor Kala grant), their marriage day was appointed. [P. 244]

Given the total contrast with the procedures adopted by the nobles, the narrator suggests that it would not be "impertinent to remember a little our shepherds while the other greater persons are either sleeping or otherwise preoccupied" (pp. 244-45).[57]

It would be not "impertinent" indeed for the "greater persons" to remember the ways of the shepherds, for, at the moment, two are committing what they think is adultery, two are sleeping after having unlawfully coupled, and of the last two, one has deserted her responsibilities as heir to the kingdom while the other, having been interrupted in mid-rape, is defending himself against the attack of the Phagonian rebels—"to the just punishment of his broken promise" (p. 202). Beyond the irony of this comparison of their pursuits, however, a deeper irony may be seen in the description of Lalus' courtship. Unlike Lalus, the princes have indeed used "many painted words" and "false-hearted promises" to win the love of Philoclea and Pamela. Moreover, neither the princes nor the princesses have observed the biblical commandment to honor their father and their mother, as the narrator's mention of the respect shown by Lalus and Kala in getting parental consent before becoming affianced reminds us. As we consider the conduct of Philoclea, Pamela, and Gynecia, the narrator's epithet for Kala —"the honestest wench in all those quarters"—becomes more than just an empty compliment.

Following the marriage feast, the shepherds begin to talk about various kinds of husbandry until finally the subject reaches its "highest point" as they turn to the "holiness of marriage" (p. 245). At this point, Dicus, whose hatred for the love over which Cupid presides we have already seen manifested in the First Eclogues, sings an epithalamion in praise not only of the lovers, but to the glory of "justest love." The harmony of man, nature, and God in the lawful love which Lalus and Kala have practiced here becomes the subject of his eclogue.

> *Let mother earth now deck herself in flowers,*
> *To see her offspring seek a good increase,*
> *Where justest love doth vanquish Cupid's powers*
> *And war of thoughts is swallowed up in peace*
>
> ·
>
> *O heav'n awake, show forth thy stately face;*
> *Let not these a slumb'ring clouds thy beauties hide,*
> *But with thy cheerful presence help to grace*
> *The honest bridegroom and the bashful bride,*
> *Whose loves may ever bide,*
> *Like to the elm and vine,*
> *With mutual embracements them to twine;*
> *In which delightful pain,*
> *O Hymen long their coupled joys maintain.*
>
> [*OA 63*.1-4, 10-18, pp. 245-46]

Dicus also calls upon the Muses to give their gifts to the two lovers "that they all vice may kill" (*OA 63*.23, p. 246), invokes the Nymphs to grant them "a long and joined life" (*OA 63*.92, p. 248), urges Pan to have care for them, and begs Virtue to be "the knot of this their open vow, / That still he be her head, she be his heart" (*OA 63*. 47-48, p. 247). Equally significant are those qualities that he banishes from the union: "churlish words," "self-seeking," "peacock pride," "vile jealousy," and Cupid, whose lustful love is again condemned (see *OA 63*.55-63, p. 247).

This song combines with the first poem in each of the first two sets of Eclogues to form an ideological core for the Eclogues comparable to the corresponding center of the main narrative, the third-act confrontation between Pyrocles and Gynecia in the cave. The opposites which are in conflict throughout the *Old Arcadia* are explicitly cataloged in these expositions as God/Cupid, love/lust, health/infection, faith/idolatry, selflessness/selfishness, harmony/discord, light/darkness, and obedience/disobedience. Despite the triumph this marriage figures, the balance between virtue and evil is not equal; as we have seen, it seems far easier to fall into sin than to stand upright. The remaining eclogues in this group explore some of the temptations to which those who walk in the way of virtue are subject, first in a fabliau about the fruits of jealousy (which, predictably, are horns) and then (after a prescription for keeping a wife honest) in a longer eclogue by Philisides.

His song is a "mean" between sorrow and mirth, and Sidney notes that "he had learned [it] before he had ever subjected his thoughts to acknowledge no master but a mistress" (p. 254). The poem itself, the oft-analyzed "on Ister Bank" (*OA 66*), is usually considered to be a political allegory about the establishment of tyrannies in the form of a beast fable, but it announces itself as of another kind.[58]

> *The song I sang old Languet had me taught,*
> *Languet, the shepherd best swift Ister knew,*
>
> . . . .
>
> *With his sweet skill my skill-less youth he drew*
> *To have a feeling taste of him that sits*
> *Beyond the heav'n, far more beyond our wits.*
> *He said the music best thilke powers pleased*
> *Was jump concord between our wit and will,*
> *Where highest notes to godliness are raised,*
> *And lowest sink not down to jot of ill.*
>
> [*OA 66*.22-23, 26-32, p. 255]

Since this is one of Languet's songs, our assumption must be that its intent is to teach us, too, to have "a feeling taste of him that sits / Beyond the heav'n" and to portray the alternative to the discord between our wit and our will which follows upon our new grammar of congruities.

The poem begins with a description of the world as it was before the creation of man:

> *For once the lion by the lamb did lie;*
> *The fearful hind the leopard did kiss;*
> *Hurtless was tiger's paw and serpent's hiss.*
>
> [*OA 66*.52-54, p. 256]

This description, of course, recalls as well Isaiah's prophecy of the future kingdom (11:6, 8): "The wolfe also shal dwell with the lambe, and the leoparde shal lye with the kid, and the calf, and the lyon, and the fat beast together, and a little childe shal lead them. ... And the sucking childe shal play vpon ye hole of the aspe, & the wained [i.e., weaned] childe shal put his hand vpon the cockatrice hole." The "spiritual meaning" of this passage has been described by Calvin in his commentary on Isaiah. The kingdom not only exists in the future but also in the past and present: "he again returns to describe the character and habits of those who have submitted to Christ.... But the Prophet's discourse looks beyond this; for it amounts to a promise that there will be a blessed restoration of the world."[59]

Before that restoration, however, those who have not "submitted" to Christ try to rule themselves without his aid. In asking for a King to rule over them (*OA* 66.64, p. 256), the animals are rejecting God, as in a similar situation the Israelites did (1 Sam. 8:7). Like Samuel (8:10-19), both the owl and Jove warn them of the consequences of their desire, but the animals persist. Man, accordingly, is created to be their King, and he gradually destroys their idyllic life. He begins by wounding the earth to seek iron (see Ovid, *Metamorphoses*, 1.125-31), and then proceeds to sow discord amongst the beasts.

Even without the traditional interpretation of the Ovidian material as an allegory of the fall of man, it is clear that the fall is the subject of this passage.[60] As Calvin says,

Whence comes the cruelty of brutes, which prompts the stronger to seize and rend and devour with dreadful violence the weaker animals? There would certainly have been no discord among the creatures of God, if they had remained in their first and original condition. When they exercise cruelty towards each other, and the weak need to be protected against the strong, it is an evidence of the disorder . . . which has sprung from the sinfulness of man.[61]

As the poem makes clear, however, the subject is not limited to Adam's original fall; the question at issue is rather the choice each man must make either to reenact Adam's fall into discord or to attempt obedience to Christ: "Yet we must attend to the spiritual meaning which I noticed, that all who become Christ's followers will obey Christ, though they may formerly have been savage wild beasts, and will obey him in such a manner, that as soon as he lifts his finger, they will follow his footsteps. . . . Let us, therefore, permit ourselves to be ruled and governed by him."[62] Philisides' summation, then, is not so much political as moral:

> But yet, O man, rage not beyond thy need;
> Deem it no gloire to swell in tyrany.
> Thou art of blood; joy not to make things bleed.
> Thou fearest death; think they are loath to die.
>
> [OA 66.148-51, p. 259]

Given its context, Philisides' warning is an exhortation to man not to permit his "infected will" to tyrannize over him, but to choose the way of humility instead, for "those who are not endued with this meekness do not deserve to be ranked among the sheep."[63]

Philisides' song repeats the theme of "the skirmish betwixt Reason and Passion" and the Plangus-Boulon debate that will and wit can be brought into concord only if both give way to "heavenly rules . . . / Which Passions kill, and Reason to deface." Curiously, the reaction of the shepherds, who, alone of all the characters, seem capable of understanding Languet's poem, is mixed, "some praising his voice; others the words, fit to frame a pastoral style; others the strangeness of the tale, and scanning what he should mean by it" (p. 259). Part of their problem is that Philisides' own conduct is at odds with the meaning of the song he has just sung. This Geron points out when he attacks Philisides' fable in revenge for the slight he had suffered at his hands in the First Eclogues: "he never saw thing worse proportioned than to bring in a tale of he knew not what beasts at such a banquet when rather some song of love, or matter for joyful melody, was to be brought forth. 'But,' said he, 'this is the right conceit of young men who think then they speak wiseliest when they cannot understand themselves" (pp. 259-60). In a way, Philisides does not understand his song, and in one sense, his song is out of "proportion" for *this* wedding. Ideally, at the celebration of virtuous love, it should not be necessary to dwell on the consequences of evil. That Sidney includes his song here is a reminder that the world itself is out of proportion, that harmony has been destroyed, and that health is the exception, not the rule; that the shepherds do not understand it is a reminder that they too live in a pagan world. Philisides' fable, like Nico's fabliau, thus becomes a sign that, in a fallen world, one cannot relax into complacency: virtue's triumphs are hard won and short lived.

The final eclogue in this group is a debate between Geron and Histor about the institution of marriage. Geron's arguments are in themselves indicative of a narrowing vision, for he conceives of marriage not as a commitment to the harmonious way of life but as an institution created to control man's sinful nature. For him "holy marriage" is but the "sweet and surest mean / Our foolish lusts in honest rules to stay" (OA 67.2-3, p. 260).[64] The joy of marriage is that it provides us with someone to share the burdens of life ("We made for pain, our pains they made to cherish," [OA 67.107, p. 263]), and to reproduce ourselves.[65] Histor objects that most women merely increase our suffering with constant strife, so that "A better life it is to lie alone" (OA 67.60) and to struggle for any good that he may get. Marriage is a dangerous proposition, most brides not being Kalas; as he notes, "The heav'ns do not good haps in handfuls bring" (OA 67.61, p. 261). Geron, no less than Philisides (or, for that matter, Languet), cannot escape from the knowledge of man's evil state, and his awareness shapes his praise of marriage, greatly reducing its symbolic value from the exemplification of heatlh to a precautionary measure against sickness. Histor, with his eyes on what "hath been" not "what may be and should be," likewise shows a retreat from faith to mere prudence.

The Third Eclogues, taken as a group, show a progressive diminishing of the visionary joy of Dicus' epithalamion. Moreover, they lessen, poem by poem, the possibility of an easy way to regain man's lost harmony with God and nature while enhancing the ominous probability that each man will fall, like Adam, into the disorder of sin. Taking place against a backdrop of treason, defection from duty, duplicity, rape, rebellion, and seduction, they seem to indicate that the balance between good and evil set up by the opposition of the first two Eclogues to the two acts which they conclude is not so even as we might have hoped and that even the "peace wherein . . . [the shepherds] did so notably flourish" (p. 56) may not be completely safe from the encroachments of evil.

IV. The Fourth Eclogues

The Fourth Eclogues are one long cry of pain and bereavement, the death of Basilius in the fourth book seemingly having ended all possibility of peace, harmony, and love for the shepherds. The backdrop against which they are placed is one in which the evils unleashed by the uncontrolled desires of the nobles have spread throughout Arcadia, regardless of the efforts of virtue to direct their course, and in which God has apparently limited His role to that of "the everlasting justice" who will punish those who commit evils without concern for righting the wrongs they have committed. The Fourth Eclogues begin where the fourth book ends, with "tumult upon tumult" arising from the "discords" of men (p. 326).

The first to sing in this group are the foreign shepherds, Strephon, Klaius, and Philisides, for whom the death of Basilius is an "occasion to record their own private sorrows" (pp. 327-28). The narrator begins with a brief account of Strephon and Klaius, who have been mentioned before only in connection with their absence from the Third Eclogues.[66] The two are gentlemen, "both in love with one maid of that country named Urania, thought a shepherd's daughter, but indeed of far greater birth" (p. 328). For her sake they have both become shepherds, but instead of being rivals they have remained friends through all of their trials: "they never so much as brake company one from the other, but continued their pursuit, like two true runners both employing their best speed, but one not hindering the other" (p. 328). Nevertheless, their pursuit has been fruitless: "But after many marvellous adventures, Urania never yielding better than hate for their love, upon a strange occasion had left the country, giving withal strait commandment to these two by writing that they should tarry in Arcadia until they heard from her. And now some months were passed that they had no news of her; but yet rather meaning to break their hearts rather than break her commandment, they bare it out as well as such evil might be." (p. 328).

There is something almost Job-like in their patient obedience to Urania's commandments and their resultant suffering that suggests the possibility that Urania may be hedged about with divinity. For

Strephon and Klaius at least, she is quite obviously a deity to be worshipped and obeyed, a deity who is the source of the harmony of the universe.

> Strephon. *For she, whose parts maintained a perfect music,*
> *Whose beauties shined more than the blushing morning,*
> *Who much did pass in state the stately mountains,*
> *In straightness passed the cedars of the forests,*
> *Hath cast me, wretch, into eternal evening,*
> *By taking her two suns from these dark valleys.*
>
> Klaius. *For she, with whom compared the Alps are valleys,*
> *She, whose least word brings from the spheres their music,*
> *At whose approach the sun rase in the evening,*
> *Who, where she went, bare in her forehead morning,*
> *Is gone, is gone from these our spoiled forests,*
> *Turning to deserts our best pastured mountains.*
>
> [OA 71.61-72, p. 330]

To Stephen and Klaius, Urania's attributes are a kind of combination of those of the celestial Venus and Christ.[67] Having been rejected by her, they are in the position of those who fear the wrath of the Lamb (Rev. 6:11), seeking sanctuary from judgment. By her hatred of them, she has thrown them into "eternal evening" and cut them off from God, man and nature:

> Strephon. *I that was once free burgess of the forests,*
> *Where shade from sun, and sport I sought in evening,*
> *I that was once esteemed for pleasant music,*
> *Am banished now among the monstrous mountains*
> *Of huge despair, and foul affliction's valleys,*
> *Am grown a screech-owl to myself each morning.*
>
> ·
>
> Klaius. *Long since the happy dwellers of these valleys*
> *Have prayed me leave my strange exclaiming music,*
> *Which troubles their day's work, and joys of evening.*
> *Long since I hate the night, more hate the morning.*
> *Long since my thoughts chase me like beasts in forests,*
> *And make me wish myself laid under mountains.*
>
> [OA 71.13-18, 31-36, p. 329]

Were Urania indeed divine, their lament would be an appropriate response to the hatred they have received from her.

Yet before we uncritically accept their own judgment of their condition—an acceptance which seems necessary if only to avoid the shocking breach of decorum that would otherwise result from their taking the occasion of Basilius' death as no more than an opportunity to express their "particular griefs" amidst "the general complaints of all men" (p. 328) in this moment of national mourning—we should consider whether their song presents anything new to the *Old Arcadia*. As the lament makes manifest, their mental state is one with which we have long been familiar through the complaints of Dorus, Cleophila, Gynecia, and Boulon. In each of these other cases, the cause for the lovers' despair was their entrapment in idolatrous passion, the love which is "all death." Any estrangement from God, nature, or other men that they had endured was of their own doing. Like them also, Strephon and Klaius share a hatred of the light and find comfort only in darkness. A careful consideration of the signs the narrator supplies in his introduction to their sestina suggests that the same situation is also at the root of Strephon's and Klaius' malaise.

In their continuing friendship, despite their relentless pursuit of Urania, the narrator says Strephon and Klaius are "like two true runners, both employing their best speed, but one not hindering the other" (p. 328). If we compare them to the true runners of 1 Cor. 9:24-25, the irony of the phrase becomes clear: "Knowe ye not, that they which runne in a race, runne all, yet one receiueth the price? So runne, that ye may obteine. And euerie man that proueth masteries abstaineth from all things: and they do it to obteine a corruptiel crowne; but we for an vncorruptible." Unlike the true runners, who strive for "a crowne of righteousness, which the Lord the righteous iudge shal giue me at that day: and not to me onely, but vnto all them also that loue his appearing," Strephon and Klaius are pursuing a corruptible crown, the love of Urania.[68] Moreover, the narrator's comment that the two would rather "break their hearts than break her commandment" to "tarry . . . until they heard from her" (p. 328) hints at the choice they have made, since to keep her commandment they must break not only their hearts but also God's commandment: "Heare me, ye stubborne hearted, that are farre from iustice. I bring nere my iustice: it shal not be farre of, and my saluacion shal not tary" (Isa. 46:12-13). What we are seeing is Sidney's most extended examination of the psychic state of the idolatrous lover. Strephon and Klaius, having transformed a woman into a deity who contains the attributes of Christ and the celestial Venus within herself, find the effects of her rejection of their love to be the same as those which they will experience when they come for judgment before Him whose love they themselves have rejected.[69]

The next eclogue in this group is another complaint by Strephon and Klaius which confirms our judgment of them, while it stresses that their actions had their root not in ignorance but in a willful disregard of the inevitable consequences of their disordered love. Strephon opens the poem with a series of paradoxes:

> *I joy in grief, and do detest all joys;*
> *Despise delight, am tired with thought of ease.*
> *I turn my mind to all forms of annoys,*
> *And with the change of them my fancy please.*
> *I study that which most may me displease,*
> *And in despite of that displeasure's might*
> *Embrace that most that most my soul destroys;*
> *Blinded with beams, fell darkness is my sight;*
> *Dwell in my ruins, feed with sucking smart,*
> *I think from me, not from my woes, to part.*
>
> [*OA* 72.1-10, p. 331]

Having rejected God, and having been rejected in turn by Urania, they are left spiritually adrift admist the storm of their passions and fears (see *OA* 72.41-50, p. 332). Their reason, too long neglected, cannot by itself help them because it simply defines their state for them, and, without faith to teach them that they may receive forgiveness if they can believe in the possibility of mercy after repentance, the only recourse left them is despair. In their despair, their only comfort is their consciousness of their constancy in adversity, but this is misusing adversity which, as the narrator informs us both in the Second Eclogues (*OA* 27 and 30) and at the beginning of the fourth book, is the means God uses to call us first to repentance and then to forgiveness. The conclusion of the poem reflects their awareness of the ultimate end of their folly, damnation:

> In earthly fetters feel a lasting hell
> Alas I do; from which to find release,
> I would the earth, I would the heavens sell.
> But vain it is to think those pains should cease,
> Where life is death, and death cannot breed peace.
>
> [OA 72.91-95, p. 333]

Strephon and Klaius may be caught in a trap of their own making —their desire for Urania is still so strong that they cannot see her for what she is, a woman, not a goddess—but they are also caught in one of Sidney's as well. As we cast about for some way to rescue them from the "lasting hell" in which they feel themselves to be, we are constantly brought up against the reality that for them there can be no rescue. They are pagans, and their naturally conceived notions of god, however plausible they may seem to them, do not permit them the recourse that our vision, based upon God's revelation of His providential design, affords us. Yet so closely have we come to identify with the shepherds during the first three Eclogues that this new realization of the gap between them and us is as difficult to confront as it is painful for us to do so. They have been our only alternative to the nobles for so long that we can hardly escape "Christianizing" them, as it were. Sidney makes it so easy for us to see them as figures for what should be and not pictures of what "hath been," that this sudden return to the literal facts of the story and its accompanying recognition of the fact of our misreading comes as a rude awakening from a kind of humanistic wish-fulfillment dream of human perfectability. Like the characters themselves, all we can do for the moment is engage in fruitless dialogues with them; yet ultimately the failure of our dialogues can serve to make us see the saving difference between their fate and our own more clearly.

With the remaining poems in the Fourth Eclogues, the distance between ourselves and the shepherds grows even greater. The next two poems (OA 73 and 74) emphasize the nature of the inner disharmonies which man must strive to resolve through the repetition of the already-established motifs of idolatry and despair. Thus

Philisides, having preferred Mira to the gods, suffers much as Dorus, Cleophila, Plangus, Strephon and Klaius have suffered in previous eclogues. The final two poems, Agelastus' two elegies on Basilius, illustrate the inability of men to understand or accept the ways of the "ever-lasting justice" which is responsible for the "death" of Basilius. Of the two laments, the first, based on Sannazaro's eleventh eclogue in his *Arcadia*, is the most interesting. As Ringler notes (*Poems*, p. 419), Sidney departs from Sannazaro toward the end of his poem because his pagan shepherd cannot find the consolation in Christian immortality that Sannazaro's can. That an Arcadian shepherd can question the justice of Basilius' death must make us pause, however, at the frailty of man's wisdom and the absolute faith in God's providence which seems to be required of all men who seek to reestablish in themselves man's lost harmony. The failure even of the Arcadian shepherds again forces us to seek elsewhere for a way of escaping from the fruits of the "common errors" of our lives. As the possibilities narrow to those held out by the revelation of the "eternal truth" (*MP*, 47) we alone have received, our options collapse into that Sidney offered Elizabeth, "make that religion upon which you stand to carry the only strength" (*MP*, 56).

The final song of the Fourth Eclogues offers us still another stark reminder of the consequences of failing to reach out to the consolation we have been offered. Agelastus' reaction to Basilius' death, in fact, is not unlike that of Strephon and Klaius to their rejection by Urania, a similarity emphasized by the images of the two poems:

> No, no, for ever gone is all our pleasure;
> For ever wand'ring from all good direction;
> For ever blinded of our clearest light;
> For ever lamed of our surest might;
> For ever banished from well placed affection;
> For ever robbed of our royal treasure.
>
> [OA 76.25-30, pp. 349-50]

Like all the idolatrous lovers, Agelastus' excessive love for Basilius, turning him away from God, has led him to the despair in which he wanders:[70]

Let tears for him therefore be all our treasure,
And in our wailful naming him our pleasure.
Let hating of ourselves be our affection,
And unto death bend still our thoughts' direction.
Let us against ourselves employ our might,
And putting out our eyes seek we our light.

[OA 76.31-36, p. 350]

Once again Sidney insists that those who reject God's providence and place all their hopes in earthly things are doomed to despair and self-hatred.

Upon this note the Fourth Eclogues end, leaving us to decide to what extent their depiction of the folly of men and the poor state of the world is meant to color our interpretation of the alternative to the disorderly careers of the main characters which the first three Eclogues seemed to provide. The conclusion that seems most valid is that the pervading despair of the Fourth Eclogues must be allowed its effect. Instead of what now seem the almost glib assertions of Dicus and Geron that man can and must live solely within the bounds of right, the Fourth Eclogues insist that living in harmony with God and the world is not so easy as we may have come to think. Although the possibility of regaining man's lost happiness which the other Eclogues offer us is not negated, it is qualified. The evil that is so prevalent in the world is not a force to be lightly dismissed; it can be dealt with only by those whose faith in the providential plan can support them and who take each occasion of despair to reinforce that faith. Sidney seems to be saying that man must constantly be aware of his weakness lest he try to face evil alone. As the Arcadian shepherds discover when they try to understand the meaning of Basilius' "death," such an effort is doomed to failure. Man cannot reason with God nor comprehend His ways. Instead, he can only accept events as they come, consoling himself not with his reason but through his faith. Ultimately, even the bitterest of griefs must give way to resignation. Seen in this way, the Fourth Eclogues are not wholly despairing, for in their closing moments, when the shepherds hope only for sleep so that they may forget and "ease their present dolors" (p. 350), they are met by a band of strangers. Although they do not yet know it, their griefs are about to be decisively eased, for the leader of the strangers is Euarchus, and it is through him that peace and harmony will come again to Arcadia.

Although the Eclogues should not be considered independently of the main narrative, they do offer—directly in the first three Eclogues and by a strategy of negation in the Fourth—a sustained view of life that is in opposition to the picture presented by the five books or acts of the prose narrative until their very end. From the actions of the noble lovers we might be justified in assuming that all our efforts are foredoomed to failure, and that even when the "everlasting justice" reaches out to help us our will is so corrupted that we must spurn God's assistance. Only the example of Euarchus mitigates this extreme pessimism in the prose narrative, but the Eclogues taken as a whole work against it. Although they portray man's folly and hard-heartedness—through the poems of Plangus, Cleophila, and Dorus in the first two Eclogues and the poems of Philisides, Strephon, Klaius, and Agelastus in the last two, as well as in the narrative of the princes' adventures in Asia Minor—the Eclogues suggest that there may be some hope for man if only his faith is great enough to sustain him. Through the Eclogues, we may attain to what Malcolm Mackenzie Ross has called "the sacramental vision of reality": "Though the flesh is frail, and though nature herself has suffered the wound of sin, the Incarnation redeems the flesh and the world, laying nature and and reasonable faculty open once more to the operation of the supernatural. . . . Existence becomes a drama which, no matter how painful it may be, is nevertheless meaningful."[71] Sidney shows us the meaning of existence in the peace and harmony of the shepherds through their dances and poems, and then suggests how we may reach out, however haltingly, beyond those states to the reality the shepherds can only figure for us. If only, Sidney suggests, we try to observe the rules of the game, we will not go unconsoled.

CHAPTER 4

"So evil a ground doth evil stand upon": The Structure

What is our life? a play of passion,
Our mirth the musicke of diuision,
Our mothers wombes the tyring houses be,
Where we are drest for this short Comedy,
Heauen the Iudicious sharpe spectator is,
That sits and markes still who doth act amisse,
Our graues that hide ve from the searching Sun,
Are like drawne curtaynes when the play is done,
Thus march we playing to our latest rest,
Onely we dye in earnest, that's no Iest.
Sir Walter Ralegh, "On the Life of Man"[1]

Like Ralegh's poem, Sidney's "stage play of love" (p. 54) takes a rather dim view of the human comedy, perhaps even more so since in this work the characters are not even allowed the dignity of dying "in earnest"—the "Iest" continues even there. Unfortunately, much of Sidney's comic view of man has been lost by critics intent upon ignoring or dismissing his "simplistic Terentian five-act structure" so that they might discuss the structure of his "romance."[2] If, as I have suggested, we are in fact dealing with a sophisticated attempt to use the accepted formal structure for a dramatic comedy as the basis for an experimental comedy in prose with four choric interludes, then the work's formal structure deserves some serious consideration. In addition to its formal pattern, however, there is another kind of structuring at work in the *Old Arcadia* and it too requires careful consideration. This other mode of structuring, as I have suggested elsewhere, is more dependent upon the reader's emotional reaction to the actions than upon the arrangement of actions per se.[3] These two structures— the formal and the rhetorical—must both be seen together, for both are essential to an understanding of "why and how" Sidney laid out the "ground-plot" (*MP*, 103) of his work.

Sidney's *Defence of Poesie* constantly insists that the function of poetry is to move the reader in order to teach him at the same time that it leads him to understand (by a kind of mental reenactment) what he is being taught (*MP*, 81). From his comment that "any understanding knoweth the skill of each artificer standeth in that *idea* or fore-conceit of the work, and not in the work itself" (*MP*, 79), it would almost seem that the critic is obligated to jump from the work itself to its "*idea*," and the resultant danger of reducing the work to a statement of its theme has not always been successfully avoided. This practice seems to me to distort Sidney's intent. While the poet's conception of his work's "truth" may be more important than his skill in setting it down (at least within the moral defence Sidney is making), the work shapes the form of that "truth" and so becomes an inseparable part of the poet's vision. To put it another way, if the initial response we have to the actions the poet imitates is the emotional response Sidney everywhere in the *Defence* assumes, then that response will define and color the intellectual formulation of the didactic teachings we are led to make by the work.

Sidney's example of Hercules in love is a case in point. The sight of Hercules, he says, "painted with his great beard and furious countenance, in a woman's attire, spinning at Omphale's commandment . . . breedeth both delight and laughter: for the representing of so strange a power in love procureth delight, and the scornfulness of the action stirreth laughter" (*MP*, 115-16). Given the careful manner in which Sidney insists upon a dual response, to interpret this action (or its equivalent in the *Old Arcadia*, Pyrocles' transformation into an Amazon) simply as showing the power of love to make an otherwise heroic figure act incongruously would be to distort Sidney's intent. Unless we are prepared to accord a validity equal to our understanding of the image's import to the emotional response Sidney anticipates to our imaginative "seeing" of this action—a feeling of scorn for the hero whose heroism is debased into voluptuousness in an unnatural perversion of "what should be"—we will never understand that the "strangeness" of love's power lies in its ability to demonstrate anew both how changed our nature is from what it was created to have been and how changeable it is in itself, for, as Sidney says, "delight we scarcely do but in things that have a conveniency to ourselves or to the general nature" (*MP*, 115). Consequently we will understand neither Sidney's attitude toward the cause of the transformation nor his reason for "making" the image to begin with.

Unless we "learne aright" both "why and how" Sidney has made his "Cyrusses," he will have succeeded in creating a mute picture rather than a speaking one (see *MP*, 79); if the work is to speak to us, if it is to be truly bestowed upon the world (*MP*, 79), then our imaginations, as Hippolyta suggests in *A Midsummer Night's Dream*, must play a part.[4] Both the poet's "speaking pictures" and our reactions to what he is "figuring forth," each using the other for a foil, each modifying the other's impact, must be amalgamated. What the poet "says" is not his fore-conceit; it is merely the verbal component. The manner in which we react to the poem provides us with an emotionally felt equivalent to the verbal component which inevitably qualifies our understanding of what we "hear" when we read the work.

It is at this point, then, that we may better understand the function of structure in Sidney's poetic. The formal Terentian structure gives Sidney a schema for arranging the plot of his comedy but it also organizes our emotional reactions to the narrative by sequencing them, and thus ordering them. This ordered sequence of emotional responses in turn becomes the work as the reader experiences it and, together with his reflections upon what he is experiencing, the means for understanding "why" the work says what it does at the same time that it defines "how" he says it.[5] As we now proceed to consider the structures of the *Old Arcadia*, we must observe not only the disposition of incidents within the plot and the relationship between the prose books and the eclogues but also the relationship between what Sidney is saying and how he makes us feel about it. Only then can we see how Sidney has structured the *Old Arcadia* to form a pattern that is at once archetypal and exemplary.

I

After a short prologue in which both the state of Arcadia and its royal family are described, the narrator introduces the argument of the *Old Arcadia* through the counsel of Philanax and Musidorus to, respectively, Basilius and Pyrocles. Although the two scenes are constructed to resemble each other, Philanax and Musidorus present two different conceptions of the function of virtue to justify their shared contention that constancy in an established course is the only safe procedure to follow. Since the positions of Basilius (that it is prudent to wish to know the future in order to avoid any coming unhappiness) and Pyrocles (that love is as heroic as the pursuit of virture) are clearly on the losing side within each of the two debates, the initial decision we are asked to make is whether either Philanax or Musidorus can be said to offer a sufficient argument in support of their position.

For Philanax, "the heavens have left us in ourselves sufficient guides" to see that "wisdom and virtue be the only destinies appointed to man to follow" (p. 7). Since these are "such guides as cannot fail," they function to show man "so direct a way of proceeding as prosperity must necessarily ensue" (p. 7). Although Philanax has couched his argument in terms calculated to appeal to the pleasure-loving Basilius, who has "placed the greatest part of his own felicity" in the continuation of his present "happiness" and "wellbeing" (p. 5), Philanax clearly has a different conception of what man's "wellbeing" is. Rather than worldly prosperity, he stresses the "inward comfort" (p. 7) man needs to sustain himself in adversity. Although man's outer state is subject to oppression by "the wickedness of the world . . . yet it could not be said that evil happened to him who should fall accompanied with virtue; so that, either standing or falling with virtue, a man is never in evil case" (p. 7). Man's knowledge of his own virture provides him with the "inward comfort" of his own "wisdom and goodness," than which nothing "can bring man's wit to a higher point" (p. 7).

Philanax sees the world, then, as a basically hostile place in which the best man can do is sustain himself against evil by his knowledge of his own inner "wisdom and goodness." He ends his counsel to the Duke by "beseeching" him to "stand wholly upon . . . [his]

own virtue" (p. 8). Musidorus, buoyed by the optimism of youth and a personal history of successful "well doing" (p. 10), has a vision of life which is slightly but significantly different from Philanax's. His youth as well as Pyrocles' has been given over "to those knowledges which might in the course of their life be ministers to well doing" since they believe that "the divine part of man was not enclosed in this body for nothing" (p. 10). Musidorus' argument begins by reminding Pyrocles of the harmony that follows a "yielding" to the "virtuous resolutions of the mind," a "right harmony" between "the very countenance and behavior" and "the inward good" which *is* a virtuous mind (p. 13). The point to which he wishes to move quickly, however, is a recapitulation of their youthful education: a praise of "honorable action" on the grounds that "in action a man did not only better himself but benefit others; that the gods would not have delivered a soul into the body which hath arms and legs (only instruments of doing) but that it were intended the mind should employ them; and that the mind should best know his own good or evil by practice; which knowledge was the only way to increase the one and correct the other" (p. 16).[6] Musidorus' stress on the necessity for virtue to be put to use suggests that for him virtue is not, as it is for Philanax, an end in itself but a part of a moral system in which the "inward comfort" supplied by a knowledge of one's goodness is less important than the benefits that may accrue to oneself and to others through the exercise of one's virtue.

This difference in emphasis, of course, is the difference between the Stoic and Aristotelian conceptions of virtue we have already observed in chapter 2. For Sidney, neither conception is viable. As de Mornay observes,

The Stoikes . . . giue vs another kind of happinesse or welfare; namely Morall vertue, which consisteth in the quiet reigning of reason in vs. But what is this els than a mere imagination: How will they answere to the Peripateticks, which say that man is not made for himselfe alone, but for common societie: That his vertue must ame at a further ende: That vertue neither in respect of that whereat it ameth, nor of that whereon it worketh can make men happie. . . . What then do the Peripateticks set vs downe: As the Stoiks left the Bodie to mount vp to the Soule, so these mount vp from the Soule to the Mynd. There are (sayth Aristotle) two sorts of Blessednesse. The one ciuill and pub-

like, called Policie; which consisteth in action; and the other private or household, called Wisedome, which consisteth in Contemplation. He thinks verely
that he hath sayd somewhat. But how can Policie be this blessednesse, considering that according to his own saying, Policie is but a cunning or skill to
leade things to a certeyne end, and is not the end it self: Or how can Wisedome
be it, seeing that (as he himself saith) our vnderstanding seeth as little in matters concerning God, as the eye of an Owle doth when she commeth nere the
Sunne: Our vnderstanding is dull, our iudgement vncerteyne, and our mem-
orie deceytfull. The deepest of our Knowledge (sayth Socrates) is ignorance
and all Philosophie (as Porphyrius vpholdeth) is but mere coniecture, easie to
bee overthrowne with every little push. [Sigs. Y_2 -Y_2^v]

The grounds for this scepticism about human nature and human
knowledge become clear as Sidney proceeds to undermine Musidorus' noble arguments about virture by making us doubt both his
motives and his self-knowledge.

Although we may see Philanax's position implicit in Musidorus'
arguments as a kind of fallback justification of virtue, what Musidorus is more concerned with when he speaks of action as a means
of bettering oneself is the opportunity for growth and improvement through experience. Despite his reference to the divine plan
for utilizing "well doing," it becomes clear as the debate between
Pyrocles and Musidorus continues that the growth and improvement Musidorus values is self-generated and self-centered. If, as
Musidorus comments, "the love of heaven makes one heavenly,
the love of virtue, virtuous . . . [and] the love of the world . . .
worldly" (p. 20), his love is directed not toward heaven but virtue,
which makes the pursuit of virture—conceived as Musidorus does—
ultimately a form of self-love.[7] Although we might say that, insofar
as Musidorus values virtue for the benefits it confers upon others,
he is defining virtue as charity and thus transforming it into a
Christian virtue, we may assume Sidney would agree with his friend
de Mornay that, unless virtue proceeds from the love of God, it is
neither virtue nor indeed charity.[8]

The failure of either Philanax or Musidorus to delineate an acceptable defence of virtue prepares the way for their charges' de-
cline into vice at the same time that it prophesies their own subsequent falls. It does not leave the *Old Arcadia* without a rationale
for "heroic" virtue, however, for sandwiched between the two de-

bates is a brief description of Euarchus, "who carried a heart prepared for all extremities (as a man that knew both what ill might
happen to a man never so prosperous, and withal what the uttermost of that ill was)" (p. 10). Although Euarchus is described only
briefly and his "philosophy" is not depicted at length until the fifth
book, the reader familiar with Sidney's letter to the Queen and
with his (and Golding's) translation of de Mornay need not proceed
darkly through the *Old Arcadia* until the final act—or even until
the Second Eclogues—without a sense of where its moral center
lies.

Sidney's letter to the Queen, like the counsel scenes portrayed in
the *Old Arcadia*, is an attempt to dissuade a ruler from embarking
upon a new and dangerous course (in Elizabeth's case, marriage to
the French King's brother). Sidney's real-life counsel, written at
about the same time as the fictional debates we have already witnessed, differs significantly. Her felicity, according to Sidney, being
known to lie not in "private pleasure nor self affection" (*MP*, 51),
but in the "precious reckoning of her people" (*MP*, 55), Elizabeth
must devote herself to the cause of those to whom her "happy government hath granted the free exercise of the eternal truth" (*MP*,
47). In so doing, she will deserve the "singular honour God hath
done . . . [her], to be indeed the only protector of his church"
(*MP*, 56). By making "that religion upon which . . . [she] stand[s]
to carry the only strength" (*MP*, 56), Elizabeth may be sure to
maintain in her kingdom the "virtue and justice" that are "the
only bands of the people's love" (*MP*, 54). The only "sufficient
stays" of her felicity, then, become "religion and equity" (*MP*, 54).
In Sidney's analysis, Elizabeth is, like Euarchus, a type of the "good
ruler," "a prince of such justice that he never thought himself privileged by being a prince, nor did measure greatness by anything
but by goodness" (*OA*, 10).

The humility Sidney portrays in Euarchus and claims to see in
Elizabeth is demanded of all men by de Mornay. Not simply rulers
but every man must make religion his only strength: "Religion (as
the men of olde time themselues haue taught vs) requireth of vs in
effect, that we should yield full obedience vnto God: ful obedience
say I, so as we should dedicate our selues to his glorie, both our
thoughts, words, and deedes, in such sort that our selues and all
that euer is in vs should be referred to his honour" (sig. Z). The

problem is that each man knows himself unable to do so: "But now ageine, seeing that Religion byndeth vs in so great a bond, euen by nature, that there is not any man which is not inforced to confesse the dette so witnessed by the whole worlde: surely there is no man that feeleth himselfe able to pay it, or which doth not willingly pleade giltie, yea and which is not inforced to say, that the most part of his thoughts, words and deedes, are not only farre of from God, but also tending directly to offend GOD" (sig. Z). Humility is born at the moment when man realizes his inability to satisfy this debt: "If a man bee too [i.e., "to"] humble himself, I would fayne have them to tell me, what other way there is than to know himselfe: what other way to knowe himselfe, than to behold himselfe: what other way to behold himselfe, then to looke into a faire deare glasse: And what clearer glasse is there, than the Lawe of God, and the perfect obedience which GOD requireth at mans hand?" (sig. Z₂). Clearly, the greatest obstacle to this kind of self-knowledge is belief in the self-sufficiency of one's own virtue and trust in one's own goodness.

The *Old Arcadia* begins, then, with the characters in need of a "faire deare glasse" in which they may see themselves and come to know themselves for what they are. To this goal the "knowledges which might in the course of their [i.e., Pyrocles and Musidorus] life be ministers to well doing" (p. 10) should have been directed, for, as Sidney says in the *Defence*, all learning is "directed to the highest end of the mistresss-knowledge, by the Greeks called ἀρχιτεκτοηὑκή, which stands (as I think) in the knowledge of a man's self, in the ethic and politic consideration" (*MP*, 82–83). As we have seen, however, this goal has not been realized. Instead, all of the major characters are soon hotly pursuing a quest of a rather different kind, the satisfaction of the desires aroused by love.

Paradoxically, however, it is the very fall from "virtue" prophesied by the Pyrocles-Musidorus debate that offers the most promise to this point in the work that the characters may eventually discover their true natures. Musidorus' comment that "the highest end . . . [love] aspires unto [is] a little pleasure with much pain before, and great repentance after" (p. 20) offers the possibility that at some point the characters will be compelled to precisely the kind of self-examination that Sidney requires in the

Defence. What the characters need most to learn is that they are not self-sufficient; the transformations promised by love (see pp. 18, 20) point to exactly that kind of awareness, as each of the lovers will become completely dependent for his happiness—indeed for his very existence—upon his beloved. While this is hardly the kind of dependency upon which de Mornay and Sidney insist, it may ultimately prove to be a step in the right direction.

Although Pyrocles cannot do as Musidorus asks when he urges him to "separate yourself a little, if it be possible, from yourself, and let your own mind look upon your own proceedings" (p. 19), love may prove to be more "persuasive" in this regard. By dissolving his single-minded preoccupation with his own virtues, love has made it impossible for Pyrocles to be contented with his own self-image. Although Pyrocles has not yet discovered what his "best proceedings" may be, his former proceeding has been rejected. Should love lead him—and the other characters—into a situation that shatters their belief in the sufficiency of love—or virtue, or wisdom, or happiness—as guides through life, they may be forced to look elsewhere for direction and assistance. In short, what reason and virtue cannot do, the consequences of giving way to passion may.

Whatever good may eventually result from the characters' falls into love, however, the immediate result is a turn toward what both the characters themselves and Sidney's narrator term "evil." Although love may ultimately lead the characters to good, it is itself an "inward evil" (pp. 15, 48), a "vice" (p. 45), a "thraldom" (p. 40), a "sensual weakness" (p. 19), a "pestilent fever" (p. 24), a "disease" (p. 12), and a "wound" (p. 12). Love begins an "unwonted war" (p. 54) in the spirit; yielding to love is "inward treason" (p. 28) and breeds "absurd follies" (p. 45). As the remainder of the first book demonstrates, it also breeds further evil as the "infection" (p. 49) of love spreads contagiously from Pyrocles to Basilius, Musidorus, Gynecia, Philoclea, and Pamela.

From the major incidents of the plot in the first book—the decisions of Basilius to make "his will wisdom" (p. 9) and later to attempt to satisfy his desire for Cleophila, of Pyrocles to disguise himself as an Amazon out of love for Philoclea, of Musidorus to aid Pyrocles in his pursuit and then to disguise himself as a shepherd to court Pamela, and of Gynecia to win Cleophila for herself—it is clear that reason and virtue are far less able supports than Musidorus and Philanax had supposed. Even Pamela's resolution to control her inclination toward the disguised Musidorus, which is based upon a lack of information about his true rank, is quickly overthrown as soon as her vanity is satisfied that he is a prince and not a shepherd whose low social status would be unworthy of her.

A more telling argument against Musidorus' assumptions is made in the incident that ends the first book, the encounter of the noble lovers with the wild beasts. Pyrocles in his new incarnation as Cleophila has just begun to make advances to Philoclea, "when suddenly there came out of the wood a monstrous lion, with a she-bear of little less fierceness, which, having been hunted in forests far off, had by chance come to this place where such beasts had never before been seen" (p. 46). Into the supposedly rational world comes a totally unforeseen disruption caused by "chance." Although we cannot be sure of the reasons why Sidney chose to make the beasts a lion and a female bear, the implications of the scene are clear enough. Having seen the wise and virtuous Pamela no less overcome with an "inward evil" (p. 48), fear, than the innocent Philoclea, we may doubt whether reason (or innocence, for that matter) can sustain us against the attacks of our emotions. Nor can we value courage as an absolute good when we have seen the wild beasts slain by the no less wild princes whose goals are surprisingly like those of the lion and bear. The Stoic belief in the harmony and goodness of nature is turned upside down as Sidney shows us Pyrocles and Musidorus following the Stoic injunction to imitate nature and transforming themselves into wild beasts. Instead of a world in which goodness is natural to man and reason guides men's actions to virtue, it is clear that we must view the actions with the awareness that they are occurring in a world in which the harmony between reason and passion and between man and nature has been broken. We have, moreover, seen the initial cause of this disharmony —the fall from obedience of Adam and Eve in the Garden of Eden —reenacted by Basilius, Pyrocles, and Musidorus. Once the harmony within man is destroyed, all other orderly relationships begin to dissolve. Through the intrusion of the wild animals, Sidney has pointed out the first consequences of sin—the disruption of nature.[9]

Throughout the first book, the narrator's tone remains fairly constant. His opinion of men in general and the leading characters in particular is fairly low. Most men, according to his generalizations, are full of "vanity" (p. 5), in love with what they have done (p. 31), given to "counterfeit" (p. 36; the term is described as a "womanish quality," but given Pyrocles as an example, it may be applied generally as a human characteristic), and lacking in true compassion (p. 43). Given the narrator's conception of love as a passion and an evil (pp. 45, 48, 49), it is no surprise to find him remarking on the folly of vice and the absurdity of vice's follies (p. 45). The prevailing tone of the entire first book, in fact, is sardonically mocking. As we have seen earlier, the narrator takes delight in laying bare the rationalizations of the characters by following their highly principled arguments with a depiction of the underlying passions—indeed the passionate selfishness and lack of self-knowledge—which have given rise to those arguments. If book 1 shows the "very stage-play of love fortune had framed" (p. 54), the narrator, telling his tale from the "ancient records of Arcadia" (p. 51), seems to feel an obligation to serve as a critic for the "fair" (p. 27) and "worthy" (p. 49) ladies who are his audience.[10]

The clarity with which the flaws in the characters are sketched and the tone adopted by the narrator define our response to the action of the first book. Yet the generally condemnatory reaction Sidney elicits from us is somewhat blunted toward the end of the book as the passions—fear, delight, love—are transformed from "inward" evils to powers external to the mind and heart of those afflicted. The narrator's description of Gynecia sounds a note of sympathy not heard since the very beginning of the first book: "And this doubt [about Cleophila's sex] framed in her a desire to know, and desire to know brought forth shortly such longing to enjoy that it reduced her whole mind to an extreme and unfortunate slavery—pitifully, truly, considering her beauty and estate; but for a perfect mark of the triumph of love who could in one moment overthrow the heart of a wise lady, so that neither honour long maintained, nor love of husband and children, could withstand it" (p. 48). While the process is similar to that by which Pyrocles likewise became love's captive, the narrator's pity invites us to reconsider our condemnations of Pyrocles', Musidorus', and

Basilius' falls, to transform their "longing to enjoy" into the "triumph of love," whose "unresistable force. . . . He must fly from himself that will shun his evil" (p. 49). Although the last sentence almost equates "love's evil" with the "evil" within those who are prisoners to love, it is still tempting to allow our newly evoked pity to limit the "evil" to love and to see its slaves as unwilling victims.

At this point in the narrative, however, Sidney introduces us to the shepherds in the First Eclogues, and simultaneously adds a new dimension to the testing process we have been following. Instead of violence and inner conflict, the shepherds live in harmony and peace. Moreover, Sidney insists that we compare the two different conditions that the shepherds and the noble lovers enjoy by explicitly contrasting their states at the very beginning of the First Eclogues. As opposed to the "peace wherein . . . [the shepherds] did so notably flourish" (p. 56), the noble audience is in a state of unrest:

[Basilius] sat himself down, having on the one side the duchess, but of his heart side the fair Cleophila. To whom speaking in looks (for as yet his tongue was not come to a thorough boldness), he sought to send the first ambassade of his passions—little marked of Cleophila whose eyes seemed to have changed sight with Philoclea's eyes (whom Gynecia had of purpose placed by herself), so attentive looks were mutually fixed between them, to the greatest corrosive to Gynecia that can be imagined, whose love-open sight did more and more pierce into the knowledge of Cleophila's counterfeiting, which likewise more and more fortified her unlawful desires; yet with so great and violent a combat with herself as the suppression of a long-used virtue comes to. But another place shall serve to manifest her agonies; this, being dedicated only to pastorals, shall bend itself that way, and leave all those princely motions to their considerations that, untold, can guess what love means. [OA, 57]

Rather than leaving these "princely motions"—a diverse set of desires maneuvering for position—Sidney immediately contrasts them again with the shepherds' motions in their opening dance, which, along with the Lalus-Dorus debate that follows, explains what love really "means" for those who cannot guess.

As we have seen, the shepherds' harmony and peace, which are expressed in their dances and songs, arise from their understanding of love, without which no music can be "kindly." Essentially, their love seems to be conceived as a natural process that occurs within a real world and has as its object the linking of two human beings, as opposed to the grand passion felt by the nobles which becomes simultaneously a form of worship of a divine creature and a means of gaining possession of a valuable object. Throughout the remainder of the First Eclogues, the peace that the shepherds have found is opposed to the disquietude that possesses the princely spectators as enunciated by Cleophila and Dorus, who participate in the Eclogues as a means of advancing their desires. At the same time, however, Sidney makes us reappraise our estimation of the seriousness of the consequences that may come from those desires by showing us what happened to Erona and the countries of Lydia and Persia when she was overcome by the same kind of love which the noble lovers have embraced. Histor's picture of "vindicative Cupid" (p. 69) manipulating the hearts of his victims makes it clear that, even though the initial assault may be external, the consequent desires aroused by love receive full support from the minds and wills of those afflicted. From the deceit and treachery that follow, it is clear that, to a lover, "virtue" and "wisdom" are mere words to describe the policy by which love's "wicked paradise" (p. 69) may be achieved. By the end of the First Eclogues, we have seen the peace and harmony that come from the shepherd's kind of loving and the uproars and unhappiness that come from the nobles' kind of loving; we are left with the unanswered question of how one can make himself love as he should and the uneasy feeling that there is worse to come.

II

Although our question is not answered in the second "book or act," our fears are realized in its depiction of the growing disorder in each of the characters. As the action begins again, the narrator informs us that "In these pastoral pastimes a great number of days were sent to follow their flying predecessors, while the cup of poison, which was deeply tasted of all this noble company, had left no sinew of theirs without mortally searching into it" (p. 91). The incidents of the second book illustrate the truth of this prologue, as we see the characters, both alone and with the object of their desires, show how far they have put aside the virtue, wisdom or innocence, and truthfulness by which they had previously ordered their lives.

The extent to which this infection has progressed is demonstrated by the final incident of the second book, which focuses upon the consequences of the disruption and disharmony in the noble lovers. Just as Gynecia, having chased away her daughter Philoclea (whom she now jealously despises), is about to "display to Cleophila the storehouse of her deadly desires," she and Cleophila are overrun by a "mutinous multitude" (p. 123). The Phagonians, some of Basilius' erstwhile loyal subjects who were, we must recall, the principal cause of Arcadia's "singular reputation" because of their "moderate and well tempered minds," have, while drunk, become enraged at the living arrangements which have deprived them of their rightful ruler. Resentful of Basilius' negligence, they resolve to "deliver our prince from foreign hands, and ourselves from the want of a prince" (p. 127).

Their behavior, which is emblematic of the actions of the noble characters they are about to threaten, is fully described by the narrator:

adding fury to fury and increasing rage with running, they went headlong towards the duke's lodge, no man in his own heart resolved what was the uttermost he would do when he came thither. But as mischief is of such nature that it cannot stand but with strengthening one evil by another, and so multiply in itself till it come to the highest, and then fall with his own weight, so to their minds once past the bounds of obedience more and more wickedness opened itself. [P. 128]

Evil, once unleashed by the mind, grows and spreads until all that it touches is contaminated. From the initial revolt against wisdom by the wills of Basilius and Pyrocles, the disease has spread to Musidorus, Gynecia, Philoclea, and Pamela. This evil is first manifested in the internal struggles of the characters, as their wills fight to overcome what they have believed in, and it is figured forth in the disharmonious harmony between fallen man and fallen nature which we saw at the end of the first book. Its next manifestation occurs in the second book as human relationships, first between individuals and then between previously orderly groups, disintegrate. What we are watching, evidently, is the progress of evil as it attacks and destroys the means by which an orderly existence may be maintained.

Yet neither the narrative nor the narrator have given us any reason to hope that there is a way to halt the progress of evil once it has begun to work or to avoid its initiation. Since evil in the *Old Arcadia* takes its origin from love and love has been shown to be a force capable of overpowering anyone and everyone who encounters it, how are we to avoid it? Musidorus' comment that his "love shall be proved no love, without I leave to love" (p. 102; see also *Astrophil and Stella 62*) comes in the second book to have a validity that seems incontestable.

Just as the narrator condemns the Phagonians' "barbarous opinion to think with vice to do honour, or with activity in beastliness to show abundance of love" (p. 126), we are led to see that where love is mixed with beastliness or honor with vice, there is neither love nor honor. The problem, however, as the narrator's comment on Philoclea suggests, is that in our nature there is precisely such a mixture: "such contradictions there must needs grow in those minds which neither absolutely embrace goodness nor freely yield to evil" (pp. 120-21). As the complaints of Gynecia (pp. 91-92), Pyrocles (p. 93), Musidorus (p. 105), Pamela (pp. 106-7), and Philoclea (pp. 108-9) show, none of the noble lovers (except Basilius, who is too besotted with himself to feel anything) can escape the "contradictions" love breeds. If the "sweet and simple breath of heavenly goodness is the easier to fall because it hath not passed through the worldly wickedness, nor feelingly found the evil that evil carrieth with it" (p. 108), neither the wisdom gained through confronting "worldly wickedness"—as Pyrocles and Musidorus have in Asia Minor—nor the feeling of the "evil that evil carrieth with it"—as Gynecia has as a result of her love for Pyrocles—have been able to do any better.

While the second book concludes with a hymn to Apollo asserting that "nothing wins the heav'n but what doth earth forsake" (*OA 26*, p. 134), that prayer must be set against the far more moving image of Gynecia's dream:

The dream was this: it seemed unto her to be in a place full of thorns which so molested her as she could neither abide standing still nor tread safely going forward. In this case she thought Cleophila, being upon a fair hill. delightful to the eye and easy in appearance, called her thither; but thither with much anguish being come, Cleophila was vanished, and she found nothing but a dead body which seeming at the first with a strange smell so to infect her as she was ready to die likewise, within a while the dead body (she thought) took her in his arms and said: "Gynecia, here is thy only rest." With that she awaked, crying very loud: "Cleophila! Cleophila!" [*OA*, 117]

Despite her terror, Gynecia is hardly ready to forsake the earth, even at the cost of losing heaven. She is, if anything, more wedded to what she fears, much as the disguised Pyrocles, who can recognize that "The life we lead is all love, / The love we hold is all death" and yet offer that death as a gift to "his goddess," embracing the death he knows is seeking to embrace him (*OA 32*, 52–57, p. 164). The second book contains nothing to suggest any of the other characters would react any differently.

It is against this backdrop that the Second Eclogues occur. Following hard on the heels of the Phagonian revolt, these poems not only show that the growth of evil is indeed inevitable if the characters cannot change their ways but also suggest that a way is open for them to break the hold of the passions that now grip them, but only if they reject not simply the principles by which they have lived but also their very image of themselves and their world. The first dance of the shepherds, the "skirmish betwixt Reason and Passion" (pp. 135–36), illustrates how the nobles may put aside the passions that possess them and reach out toward the peace and harmony that the shepherds enjoy. Instead of trusting to reason or giving way to passion, they must be brought to subordinate both their desires and their rationalizations; instead of following either their reason or their will, they must be made to look to "heavenly rules" for guidance.[11] In the eclogue that Plangus and Boulon sing, moreover, Sidney shows us how God sends adversity to call us from our self-conceived sufficiency to Him. If we do not heed that call, then our downfall must follow just as the erring princes whom Pyrocles and Musidorus encountered in their adventures in Asia Minor all came to ruin.

Yet Plangus rejects Boulon's counsel, his listeners are "stricken" only into a "silent consideration" of Plangus' "passion," which they identify with their own (p. 152), and the eclogues that follow ignore Boulon's warning and dwell only on the singers' passion and their devotion to the objects of their passions. At the same time that the princely lovers demonstrate their intentions to continue to "seek . . . offences" against themselves while they "employ" themselves to "hurt" themselves (see p. 151), we are warned that our compassion and pity are themselves signs of *our* "debility" since "self-guilty folk [are] most prone to feel compassion" (*OA 30*, p. 150). In consequence, we are made to feel that our attitude toward both them and ourselves must change. Unless we can separate ourselves from ourselves as well as from them, the way opened in the Eclogues by the "skirmish" and by Boulon will be closed to us.

III

The end of the Second Eclogues coincides with the conclusion of the first major structural movement of the *Old Arcadia*. Up to this point we have been concerned with the issues raised by Musidorus and Philanax in the opening pages of the work. We have been forced first to see the characters through their own eyes and then to balance that view against the general conceptions of right and wrong behavior that are established through Sidney's imagery in the narrative and through the system of values portrayed by the shepherds in the first two Eclogues. As the plot has progressed, we have seen the noble lovers transformed from active seekers after virtue to passive participants in evil, but the evil has been, for the most part, internal. The focus has been upon the growing distance between the characters as they are and as they think themselves to be. By the beginning of the third book, however, the incubation period of their disease has ended, and the evil with which the characters have been infected has triumphed. Henceforth, following the comic pattern, the princely characters will be shown in active pursuit of their desires as Sidney strips away the pretensions to virtue with which they have tried to mask their intentions both from others and from themselves. The first two books have functioned as the protasis, setting forth the argument and showing us the "sum of the business" that is to occur; the third book is modeled after the epitasis, "in which turbulences are either begun or made tense."[12]

So long as Sidney had not yet dramatically resolved the argument of the *Old Arcadia*, he was careful to maintain a balance in his narrator's presentation of the noble lovers, showing the foolishness of their present behavior but never letting us forget the state of virtue from which they fell. Thus the princes, although impelled toward whatever seems most expedient in their quest to satisfy their desires for the princesses, have still retained something of the aura of heroism for which they have become renowned throughout Greece in their slaying of the beasts and their thwarting of the Phagonian rebels. Now, however, Sidney begins to show us that their natures have been changed by their infection and that the part of them which was akin to the beasts and the rebels has become dominant. All of the incidents in the third "book or act" are designed either to lead up to or to illustrate the central truth illuminated in the blackness of the cave in which Pyrocles is confronted with the figure of what he has become.

As we trace Pyrocles' path to the cave, the princes are shown to have permitted not their conception of virtue but their desire for the princesses to determine the way they will act in a given situation. Musidorus plans to steal Pamela away from her father and to return with "such an army hither as shall make Basilius (willing or unwilling) to know his own hap in granting you [i.e., Pyrocles] Philoclea" (p. 173). Pyrocles' assent to this plan implicates him equally, and both of the princes are now reduced to the level of those against whom they had struggled in Asia Minor. Pyrocles, too, demonstrates his new nature when he meets Basilius after parting from Musidorus. Although he had previously scorned him, when Basilius announces that the revolt of the Phagonians has made him see "what dangers he might fall into" (p. 178) as a consequence of his retirement from court and that he is ready to return to his responsibilities as ruler, Pyrocles suddenly begins to fawn upon him, substituting "favours" for "disgraces" (p. 178) in an attempt to keep him from resuming his obligations. He is once again determining his responses according to expediency. The simple sequence of incidents makes clear the way that the infection of evil saps the strength of the will to resist and perverts the reason, preventing it from judging by making it rationalize the unworthy deeds committed on the way to the desired goal.

It is thus only after we have seen the way that evil works that Sidney introduces us to evil itself. After eluding Basilius, Pyrocles comes to a cave in which he tries to escape from the now painful light of the sun. In a sonnet, whose rhyme-words are "light" and "dark," Pyrocles plays upon the themes of reason and passion. His conclusion, however, is not so much a resolution as a surrender:

> *Since, as I say, both mind and senses dark*
> *Are hurt, not helped, with piercing of the light;*
> *While that the light may show the horrors dark,*
> *But cannot make resolved darkness light;*
> *I like this place where, at the least, the dark*
> *May keep my thoughts from thought of wonted light.*
>
> [OA 39.9–14, p. 180]

Pyrocles, having identified light solely with "beauty's light" (*OA 39.2*), which in turn has subverted the "windows" of his "inward light" (*OA 39.7*), comes to reject light completely in his frustrated state. Since Philoclea's beauty has aroused his dark passions and subjugated his reason to them, he has become unable—of his own will—to recognize any other light. Not only has he rejected Musidorus's arguments about the primacy of his "reason's light," but he has also become blind to divine illumination. As la Primaudaye notes, "if the minde be lightened and inflamed with diuine light, and the reason also that ruleth therein, then the heart will . . . burne with the loue of God and of his neighbour. Which if it fall out so, the heart will not be slacke in shewing forth those heauenly motions that are within it, and giuing matter to the soule to glorifie God.[13] Pyrocles' "inward powers" are "dark" (*OA 39.8*), and his heart burns only with desire. While he can thus see the "horrors dark," he cannot turn away from them. His taking refuge in the cave is an attempt to escape from both the pain caused by Philoclea's "light" and guilt which comes through God's light.

While Cleophila sits "musing upon her song" (p. 180), she hears a "lively . . . portraiture" of her "miseries," and immediately identifies herself with it: "It is surely the spirit appointed to have care of me. . . . But . . . whatsoever thou be, I will seek thee out; for they music well assures me we are at least hand fellow prentices to one ungracious master" (p. 181). Upon advancing further into the cave, she sees "a lady lying with her face so prostrate upon the ground as she could neither know nor be known" (p. 182). Curiously approaching, she hears the lady identify herself as Gynecia. "Cleophila no sooner heard the name of Gynecia but that, with a cold sweat all over her, as if she had been ready to tread upon a deadly stinging adder, she would have withdrawn herself, but her own passion made her yield more unquiet motions than she had done coming" (p. 183), and Gynecia, in a reversal of her dream, rises up and seizes him. What Gynecia's words cannot do, the sight of her can: Pyrocles is moved to a momentary recognition of what he has become. Having shut off his reason, Pyrocles can listen without distress and identify with a song describing his state as "Death wrapped in flesh, to living grave assigned" (OA 40.14, p. 181). When this same state is presented to his senses, the result is a mixture of fear, hatred, and disgust. As he was before the prisoner of love, so he is now the prisoner of evil, entrapped by his own passions. Pyrocles' perceptions of himself are here merged with ours, and through him Sidney makes us aware of the terrifying reality of evil. Pyrocles comes face to face with himself in the form of "the spirit appointed to have care of me"—his *daimon* Gynecia—and we see his instinctive repulsion. Yet the evil is not Gynecia; rather it is something dark within ourselves. Pyrocles, in trying to escape from Gynecia, is really trying to flee from himself and he cannot succeed. We cannot temporize with evil, Sidney suggests; we must either give in to it or call for aid in the struggle against it. Rather than acknowledge this new self-knowledge, however, Pyrocles rationalizes it as merely a means to an end.[14] As the scene concludes, Pyrocles, no longer afraid of this "deadly stinging adder," is about to embrace it.

From this point onward, the narrator switches back and forth from Musidorus to Pyrocles as Sidney shows through their adventures that the evil they have unleashed is growing ever stronger.

The chance or involuntary acts of disharmony which we have seen in the first two books are replaced by something more serious, as the values to which each of the characters has at least paid lip service dissolve under the pressure of the now uncontrollable demands of the will for the satisfaction of its desires. The characters' gestures toward the maintenance of order are replaced by conscious subversions of that order wherever it impedes their desires. Musidorus frees himself of Pamela's warders by playing upon their own vices and flees Arcadia with Pamela. Pyrocles likewise seemingly gives in to the desires of Basilius and Gynecia, but actually arranges for them to commit "adultery" with each other, thus leaving him free to sneak into Philoclea's bedroom. As the final scenes of the book—Musidorus' attempted rape of Pamela and Pyrocles' successful seduction of Philoclea—unfold, the scale of evil is broadened, and the revolt of the characters against God, implicit throughout and signaled by their reenactments of the archetypal fall, becomes the focus of our attention. Having successfully trampled upon all human institutions, Musidorus and Pyrocles unleash the divine justice by breaking oaths made before God.

Musidorus is the first to be caught up in the web of deceit he has spun. After he flees with Pamela, she has some second thoughts:

But Pamela who all this while transported with desire, and troubled with fear, had never free scope of judgement to look with perfect consideration into her own enterprise, but even by the laws of love had bequeathed the care of herself upon him to whom she had given herself, now that the pang of desire with evident hope was quieted, and most part of the fear passed, reason began to renew his shining in her heart, and make her see herself in herself, and weigh with what wings she flew out of her native country, and upon what ground she built so strange a determination. But love, fortified with her lover's presence, kept still his own in her heart. [OA, 196]

Although love's influence is powerful enough that she is still content to stay with Musidorus, she now adds the condition that he respect her virtue by letting her remain chaste. Musidorus swears that he will do so and makes the gods his pledge's guarantors. Pamela accepts his vows, and shortly thereafter, laying her head in his lap, falls asleep. Musidorus, however, is unable to control himself, and, "rising softly from her, overmastered with the fury of delight, having all his senses partial against himself and inclined to his well beloved adversary, he was bent to take the advantage of the weakness of the watch, and see whether at that season he could win the bulwark before timely help might come" (p. 202).[15] Just as he is about to rape her, timely help does indeed come in the person of "a dozen clownish villains" who "to the just punishment of his broken promise, and most infortunate bar of his long-pursued and almost-achieved desires" (p. 202) force him to defend both himself and her whom he had just been attacking. Given the context, I think we may see in "infortunate" not only the basic meaning of "luckless" (*OED*), but also the sense that the occurrence itself was not the result of chance but rather represents the workings of providence, for, as we later learn, the Phagonians were "guided by the everlasting justice to be the chastisers of Musidorus' broken vow" (p. 307).[16] This reading is confirmed by the narrator in his relation to Pyrocles' very similar adventures, to which he abruptly turns.

Since Sidney does not employ the technique of *entrelacement* in the first two books or in the fifth book, his use of it in the third book and at the beginning of the fourth book is noteworthy. Why are events narrated until a conclusion is reached in the other books, but here constantly interrupted before they have reached fruition? The answer, I think, lies in the structure of the work. In the first two books, Sidney is showing us the gradual growth of evil in the minds of the characters, and the best way to illustrate this is through the simple progression of incidents so that an impression of the increasing strength of the characters' inclination to sin is obtained by an additive effect. In the third and fourth books, however, we are shown the triumph of evil and the nature of the consequences of evil in the state and the characters. Since, as the narrator insists, "So evil a ground doth evil stand upon, and so manifest it is that nothing remains strongly but that which hath the good foundation of goodness" (p. 265), the best way to demonstrate the inconstancy of evil is to fragment the very imaging of it. By showing the inconclusiveness of evil, Sidney can at once implicitly contrast it with the patterned beauty of his providential order and show that once we opt against obedience to "heavenly rules," we are no longer able to control ourselves enough to prevent the accomplishment of evil.

Thus we return to the cave and see how Pyrocles, in attempting merely to escape from the immediate danger of Gynecia's desire for him, sets in motion a whole chain of events which ineluctably leads to his imprisonment, Philoclea's disgrace, Basilius' "death," and Gynecia's self-excoriation. After swearing his love to Gynecia and promising her that he will find a way to be alone with her without endangering her reputation, Pyrocles is allowed to leave the cave. He soon conceives a plan by which he may rid himself not only of Gynecia, but also of Basilius. By agreeing to spend a night alone in the cave with each of them—an appointment he has no intention of keeping—Pyrocles finds himself alone in the Duke's lodge with Philoclea, only to discover that she has been misled by his show of affection for Gynecia into believing that he no longer cares for her. Although he finally stumbles (almost literally) into bed with her, he has been forced to make the gods the pledges of his love for her: "There is none here to be either hinderers or knowers of the perfecting the mutual love which once my love wrought in you towards me, but only the almighty powers, whom I invoke to be the triers of my innocency" (p. 234).[17]

Throughout the third book, the narrator has allowed more and more contempt to show openly in his comments on the actions. And yet, paradoxically, it is in the third book that we are most drawn to the characters. The result is that we are repelled by the characters and yet forced to recognize the similarity of their natures to our own. We sympathize with them, despite our growing knowledge of their moral degradation, precisely because of that basic similarity. The narrator's reactions to his story are a case in point. One moment, commenting on Musidorus' unknitted words, sigh-broken eloquence, and dismayed color, he can interject "But, O feminine love, what power thou holdest in men's hearts!" (p. 174). The next, Dorus, torn between love of Pamela and his friendship with Pyrocles, is described as easily yielding to love, since, besides "all force of such arguments of which *affectionated* brains are never unprovided, the continual sting of insatiate desire, had (as you have heard) gotten the fort" (p. 185; my italics). At once victim and instigator, the lover is helpless before love's demands as he greedily anticipates the pleasures those demands will yield.

It is as hard, in fact, for the narrator to decide how he feels about the characters as it is for us. Gynecia demands our compassion as she yields to Pyrocles' plan to meet at the cave by wringing his hand, "closing her eyes, and letting her head fall, as if she would give her [Cleophila] to know she was not ignorant of her fault, although she were transported with the violence of her evil" (p. 222). And yet our sympathy is quickly dissipated when, later that night, Gynecia agrees to proceed to the cave before Pyrocles, "tickled thereunto by a certain wanton desire that her husband's deceit might be the more notable" (p. 223). So she leaves, drawing with her the narrator's parting comment, "for what dare not love undertake, armed with the night and provoked with lust?" (p. 224). But this contempt cannot be long sustained either. As Gynecia says, "O strange mixture of human minds: only so much good left as to make us languish in our own evils!" (p. 183). And yet how much good does this languishing do us? Our reluctance to sin, to wholeheartedly embrace and "freely yield to evil" (p. 121), can only make us miserable when we find ourselves "transported with the violence of . . . [our] evil" (p. 222).

Yet languish we do and so does the narrator. It is impossible to sympathize with the characters and impossible not to. Reason, clearly, will not help us in this situation. Besides its misuse in the third book, exemplified by Pyrocles' resolution "now with plainness to win trust—which trust she [i.e., Cleophila] might after deceive with a greater subtlety" (p. 203), the narrator undermines its use as a tool in his comment upon Gynecia's decision to trust Pyrocles' "plainness." Her decision, as it proceeds out of the "obscure manison" of her mind, is based on her need to believe what she wants to hear. The narrator's comment sums up our dilemma precisely: "O weakness of human conceit! . . . For such, alas, are we all! In such a mould are we cast that, with the too much love we bear ourselves being first our own flatterers, we are easily hooked with others' flattery, we are easily persuaded of others' love" (p. 206). The narrator's punning use of "conceit" equates thought with self-love and vanity, and thought, as it is presented throughout the third book, is nothing but the servant of self-love.

Turning the screw once again, however, Sidney manages to transform even our contemptuous rejection of the characters' vicious folly into self-love by forcing us to see ourselves in the "faire deare glasse" of the cave, the emblematic center of not only the third

book but the *Old Arcadia* itself. Gynecia, sounding less like the
Actaeon of myth and allegory than the David of the penitential
Psalms, makes the dilemma of the *Old Arcadia* explicit: "O accursed reason, how many eyes thou hast to see they evils, and how
dim, nay blind, thou art in preventing them! Forlorn creature that
I am, I would I might be freely wicked, since wickedness doth prevail; but the footsteps of my overtrodden virtue lie still as bitter
accusations unto me. I am divided in myself; how can I stand? I
am overthrown in myself; who shall raise me?" (p. 183).[18] In the
pagan world of the *Old Arcadia*, there can be no answer to her
question, yet her self-accusation stands mockingly before her—and
the reader—throughout the third book.

At this point in the development of the plot, Sidney places the
Third Eclogues, whose function is to contrast the orderliness of
God's ways with the disorderly disharmony of man's. In place of
the chaotic darkness of the cave in which we encounter evil, Sidney substitutes the almost visionary brightness of a sun-flooded
field in which the marriage of Lalus and Kala takes place. As we
have already noted, the Third Eclogues are the high point of the
Old Arcadia and conclude the movement that began in the First
Eclogues with the opening dance of the shepherds. In the marriage
which is the occasion of the Third Eclogues, Sidney shows us one
way of living in accordance with "heavenly rules" as Lalus and Kala
consecrate their love in the manner ordained by God. By not
shaking off the "bit a weaker force doth guide" (*OA* 7.159, p. 63),
Lalus and Kala have heard the "kindly" music of love of which
Languet had long ago sung:

> . . . *the music best thilke powers pleased*
> *Was jump concord between our wit and will,*
> *Where highest notes to godliness are raised,*
> *And lowest sink not down to jot of ill.*
>
> [*OA* 66.29–32, p. 255]

If we will please the heavenly powers, we must patiently "abide"
(*OA* 7.160, p. 63) like Lalus. Framed by the uncontrollable desires
and agonies of the princely characters in the third and fourth books,
the Third Eclogues' depiction of the goal toward which we must
reach takes on a beauty that transcends our normal conception of
marriage.

IV

According to sixteenth-century comic theory the fourth act should be "the full vigor and crisis of the play, in which the intrigue is embroiled in that tempest of chance, into which it has been drawn,"[19] and the "fourth book or act" of the *Old Arcadia* is indeed full of intrigues and tempests. Dametas, searching for the missing Pamela, discovers Pyrocles in bed with Philoclea and bars the door so that they cannot escape. Dametas runs to tell the Duke what he has seen but instead meets another group of shepherds who inform him that the Duke is dead and that Gynecia has confessed to the murder. Philanax happens along in time to discover the Duke's death, and he takes control of the situation, sending out a group of horsemen to search for the missing Pamela. Against all probability, the soldiers run into Pamela and Musidorus led by the remnants of the Phagonian rebels. In a modification of Scaliger's *catastasis*, however, Sidney has transformed these seeming acts of chance into the carefully planned proceedings of God's providence.[20] Even the evil that is so rampant throughout the third and fourth books is given a new dimension as Sidney, reaffirming Boulon's counsel in the Second Eclogues, reveals it too to be a means by which God calls us back to Him.

Although providence may be behind the revelations of the nobles' activities and although the "everlasting justice" may be responsible for the captures of the princes and princess and the "death" of the duke, the fourth book begins and ends with a "picture of rude discord" (p. 270). During the course of the book, however, the narrator's tone changes from amused contempt to sympathetic concern. While we cannot ignore this change in tone, we must also ask ourselves if anything has changed. Is there any difference between the discord pictured so rudely in Dametas, Miso, and Mopsa at the beginning of the book and the political discords which the sun is so weary of seeing at the end of the fourth book (see p. 326)? In both cases the action is instigated by the maneuverings of the princes; in both cases greed, lust for power, and envious hatred are the motivating causes.

Given the pastoral setting, we might indeed think that Sidney was merely adopting a perspective which would let us see these

Alexanders and Dariuses striving to be "cock of this world's dung-hill" (*MP*, p. 95) properly. Such a perspective would be akin to that adopted by de Mornay in showing that "all the evill which is doone, or seemeth to be doone, in the world, is subiect to the prouidence of God" (sig. M_6):

When a Tragedie is playd afore thee, thou are not offended at any thing which thou hearst. Why so? Because that in two howres space: thou hast shewed vnto thee the dooings of a ten or twelve yeres, as the rauishing of Helen, and the punishment of Paris, or the miserable end of Herod vpon his murdering of Iohn Baptist. Insomuch that although thou bee not acquainted with the storie, yet the arte which thou perceiuest, and the end which thou expectest, make thee both to beare with the matter, and to commend the thing which other-wise thou wouldst thinke to be both vniust, and also cruell in the gouerner of the Stage. How much more oughtest thou then to refreine thy mislyking, if thou considerest that the world is a kind of Stageplay conueied to a certeine end by a most excellent maker: And what an excellent order wouldest thou see there, if thou mightest behold all the ages and alterations thereof as in a Comedie, all in one day. [Sig. N_3 –$N_3{}^V$]

Yet, in a sense, it is precisely because we perceive that "art" and expect the "end" signaled at the beginning of book 4 by the narrator that we find ourselves for the first time seriously at variance with his perceptions. Looking to see the "everlasting justice" make the nobles' "actions the beginning of . . . [their] chastisement, that . . . [their] shame may be the more manifest, and . . . [their] repentance follow the sooner" (p. 265), we are looking at the fourth book as a comedy.

The narrator, however, seems to be viewing it as a tragedy, his sense of detachment from the world he is recreating through telling his story having been shattered by the relative disparity of the persons who people it. Thus, next to Dametas' selfish and panic-stricken fear for his life (pp. 271–72), Pyrocles' "unshaked magnaminity" (p. 294) as he prepares for suicide seems to demonstrate "true fortitude" (p. 296). But as the presentation of Pyrocles' attempt to kill himself approaches farce, we may recall that it is not "the confidence in oneself which is the chief nurse of true magnaminity" but "fayth in Christ, through the new birth, by which the mind is renewed & made free."[21] We, at least, remember that those who seek fortitude through confidence in themselves, who "endeuour by their owne naturall powers, and faculties of the minde, through humane courage to become valiant, run in the wrong way, and although they attaine to an exceeding hardinesse, yet is it no vertue, but a resolute or rather a desparate boldness, beeing in deede a vice vnder the shewe or resemblance of vertue."[22] As we are reminded that this is a pagan conception of magnaminity by the narrator's use of Achilles, whom "Homer doth ever make . . . the best armed" (p. 289), as an exemplification of fortitude, so we become aware that the narrator seems to have forgotten for the first time that, although he is dealing with pagans, he must judge them according to his standards, not theirs. The point of the episode, at least for us, remains that Pyrocles, feeling no shame (p. 296), does not repent his actions (p. 291).

This sudden relativism may be seen, I think, in each of the episodes of the fourth book where the narrator's tone is at odds with our expectations. The "every way enraged Musidorus . . . enraged betwixt a repentant shame of his promise-breaking attempt and the tyrannical fire of lust" (p. 306) is quickly transmogrified into "the valorous Musidorus" (p. 308) only because he is defending Pamela against the "scummy remnant of those Phagonian rebels" (p. 306). Yet we are again aware, even though the narrator speaks as if he were not, that that "scummy remnant" have been "guided by the everlasting justice to be chastisers of Musidorus's broken vow" (p. 307), that his defense, though valiant, is also a failure, although his enemies seem to be armed only with "darts and stones" (p. 307). So, too, Philanax, in the midst of the "tumult upon tumult" that marks the end of the fourth book seems to the narrator to be exercising "a constant but reverent behaviour" (p. 324) as he prepares to "remove the prisoners [Pyrocles and Musidorus] secretly, and (if need were) rather without form of justice to kill them than against justice (as he thought) to have them usurp the state" (p. 326). Yet the narrator's parenthetical observation—"as he thought"—reminds us that the "everlasting justice" is far from Philanax's conception of what "justice" is.

The fourth book, then, represents a turning point. For the first time our sense of the design we are observing seems surer than the narrator's. Having established a perspective from which we may see the action clearly, he seems to have lost it, at least for the moment. From the standpoint of Sidney's "fore-conceit," this development is a daring but structurally sound tactical move. By establishing through the first three books and the first three Eclogues a relationship of dependency between reader and narrator which he then breaks in the fourth book, Sidney forces us to put our faith not in men—even one whom we might expect to be able to trust unerringly—but in the providential design of the "everlasting justice." By teaching us to perceive the art by which the "most excellent maker" of this world's "Stage play" has designed his work, by instructing us on the means by which it is performed, and by showing us the "certeine end" to which it is "conueied," we are moved to look for a providential solution to the drama and to have faith it will occur no matter how strongly all appearances may argue against it.

Meanwhile, although the agents of the evils that have troubled Arcadia have been rendered harmless by death or imprisonment, the consequences of their actions have thrown the state into what seems like chaos. When the noble lovers gave way to the evil within themselves they also introduced disorder into the state. With Basilius dead, and Gynecia, Philoclea, and Pamela—the only other possible sources of order—all apparently implicated in his death, there is no one who may legitimately reestablish harmony within Arcadia.

Arcadia, without a ruler, torn by conflicting factions, and ripe for civil war, has thus again become an emblem for the inner state of the characters, disabled by the unequal struggle between wisdom and will, acting irrationally, and given over to sin. In the struggle which develops, Philanax becomes the symbol for the old order and Timantus, "a man of middle age but of extreme ambition, as one that had placed his uttermost good in greatness . . . of commendable wit, if he had not made it a servant to unbridled desires" (p. 321), represents the willful disorder which has destroyed it.[23] As the fourth book ends, neither of them has been able to gain the ascendency, and the state is teetering upon the brink of civil war.

In the Fourth Eclogues, Sidney recapitulates his argument by again showing us how giving way to desire leads ultimately to turning away from God and "heavenly rules." In a time of national disaster, the foreign-born shepherds can think of nothing but their own selfish concerns. Not only has their idolatrous, cupidinous love led them away from God; it has also excluded them from the society of men. They are locked in a total involvement with themselves. Even the Arcadian shepherds are unable to remain secure in their faith, as Agelastus attributes the credit for God's accomplishments to the "dead" Basilius and questions the ways of providence, condemning them because he cannot understand them. The Fourth Eclogues and the fourth book can be considered to be a single structural unit. In it, Sidney shows us how much harm evil, once unleashed by the actions of men, can do and how unable man is to withstand either the lure of sin or the firestorm of passions that accompanies it without God's aid. Although the forces of disorder seem to be triumphing, Sidney tries to move us to adopt a perspective from which we can see that the restoration of order is as inevitable as its destruction had been. The fourth book begins by informing us that the events are not random happenings controlled by chance and ends with the arrival of Euarchus, with the strong implication that he too has not come by chance, but is rather the agent that providence has sent to restore Arcadia to the state of "harmony" and "peace" in which we first saw it.

V

Just as it appears that Arcadia, like her princes, is about to be overwhelmed by "the dangerous division of men's minds [and] the ruinous renting of all estates" (p. 351), peace is restored. Instead of civil war, Euarchus is persuaded to become Protector, and the Arcadian estates are persuaded to accept his leadership and judgments as the basis for the reestablishment of order. When Timantus, "still blinded with his own ambitious haste . . . would needs strive against the stream" (p. 354), the people turn upon him and blind him, making him physically as well as spiritually sightless. He is finally forced to seek protection at the feet of Philanax, "giving a true lesson that vice itself is forced to seek the sanctuary of virtue" (p. 355).

Through Euarchus order is reestablished, and Sidney insists that it is not based upon the overconfident exaltation of wisdom and virtue that has led to the chaos which we have seen throughout the *Old Arcadia*. The new stability promised by the elevation of Euarchus is founded upon a very Christian kind of humility. Although it is Euarchus' transparent goodness which quiets the assembly ("Neptune had not more force to appease the rebellious wind than the admiration of an extraordinary virtue hath to temper a disordered multitude" [p. 364]), his first words to them are a warning that they must not expect perfection from a mortal being: "remember I am a man; that is to say, a creature whose reason is often darkened with error" (p. 365). His implication is clear—the Arcadians must not put their trust in him but in his Creator. Just as a "wise providence" (p. 7) had been responsible for the peace and happiness of Arcadia before Basilius, by turning away from God, initiated the chain of actions that led to the disorders of the third and fourth books, so through Euarchus, the agent of providence, peace is finally restored.[24] Now, however, Euarchus must make the Arcadians (and the reader) aware that their true contentment can only come from God, not from their ruler. To do this, he must make them aware of the meaning of obedience to "heavenly rules." To this end, Sidney fashioned the trials, both private and public, which occupy most of the fifth book. Although their announced purpose is to see "the past evils duly punished" (p. 365), what is really on trial is not so much the characters as the doctrines by which they have attempted to guide their actions.

Essentially the noble lovers fall into four groups: those who put their trust in their wisdom, like Pyrocles and Musidorus, and think it sufficient to guide them through the temptations and confusions of life; those who put their faith in their own virtue, like Pamela and Gynecia, and believe it strong enough to withstand any evils they may be forced to confront; those who depend upon their own innocence, like Philoclea, and think that their unfamiliarity with evil will prevent its attack; and those who seek only their own happiness and pleasure, like Basilius, for whom there are no evils except discomfort and unhappiness, and who drift from experience to experience without learning anything at all. Despite the different doctrines they follow, all of these characters are alike in one crucial aspect.

All of them feel that the source of their strength lies within them. This, of course, is their great error. As de Mornay writes, "What may man himself doe: Surely an acceptable Sacrifice should man be to God . . . if he were such a one as he ought to be. But what should the best of all men offer vp in sacrifising himself? Soothly nothing but enuy, hatred, rayling, backebyting, vaine thoughts, vntrue words, wrongfull dealing, and (to go yet further) faynt thanks, with cold and counterfet praiers" (A *Woorke*, sig. Zᵛ).[25] As the characters discover in Arcadia, they have no strength except to evil. Pyrocles and Musidorus with their faith in reason fare no better than Philanax and Pamela do by putting their trust in virtue; Philoclea's dependence on her innocence has led her to the same judge who is to confront her guilt-obsessed mother.[26] Although Basilius is not, strictly speaking, on trial like the rest of the noble lovers, Euarchus has already rendered judgment upon him, for he had come to Arcadia "to see whether by his authority he might withdraw Basilius from this burying himself alive, and to return again to employ his old years in doing good" (p. 359).

In the judicial proceedings which take up the bulk of the fifth book, the characters are judged by a most impartial judge and condemned. Suddenly the tables are turned and the judge himself is put on trial. As the last of the defendants, Pyrocles and Musidorus, are being led away to death, a messenger rushes in to announce that the prisoners are actually Euarchus' son and nephew. The general expectation is that they will be pardoned. Euarchus finds himself torn between his love for Pyrocles and Musidorus and his sense of duty to God. In this work full of tests we have one more to watch. For the first time, however, we are not to see another failure of obedience enacted. Mindful of the task that has been imposed upon him to bring order and harmony to Arcadia, Euarchus chooses to put obedience to what he thinks are the laws of God and man above his own feelings and declares that the sentence still stands.

Although Sidney does not explicitly make Euarchus into a figure for Abraham, the parallel is almost inescapable. Like Abraham, Euarchus is called from his native country; like Abraham, he is chosen as an instrument by which other lands may be restored to righteousness; like Abraham, he is called to sacrifice his son; and like Abraham, he proves his faith and is spared the necessity of actually killing his son. Even more meaningful, however, is the functional similarity between the two as exemplars. Through Euarchus' successful resistance to his temptation to spare his son and nephew, we may learn again the lessons of obedience and faith which Abraham first taught us:

Let this then be a good aduertisement vnto vs that when God shal proue vs, that we yeeld our necks to the yoke, & suffer him to make tryall of vs. And this is the most principall point of oure lyfe, so to yeeld our selues that God may dispose of vs as pleaseth hym. . . . Abraham was euen so weake a man as wee are, yet he still strove and ouercame whatsoeuer was contrary vnto his faith, and that through the onely assistance of God.[27]

Sidney uses Euarchus as he uses the Eclogues, as a foil to the noble lovers by which the beauty of goodness may be made to stand out against a backdrop of evil.

From his first appearance, "taking his rest under a tree with no more affected pomps than as a man that knew, howsoever he was exalted, the beginning and end of his body was earth" (pp. 355, 357), Euarchus stands out from the rest of the princely characters. Although, like his son and his nephew, he strives to be virtuous, he lacks their foolish confidence in their ability to fulfill their goals on their own, for he is aware of the corruption in his nature and of the mutability or "continual change" in "the very constitution of our lives" (p. 362). In this context, we can contemplate Euarchus' attempts to act virtuously with the knowledge that his works can please God "by faythe onelye, whereby a man is assured in his conscience, that God will not straitlye examine hys workes, nor trye them by the sharpe rigoure of hys Justice: but that he wyll hyde the unperfeatnesse, and the vncleane spottes that be in them, with the purenesse of oure saviour Christe, and so accoumpt them as perfect."[28] Besides obedience and faith, Euarchus, with his hatred of evil (pp. 382–83) and his love of justice (p. 411), also teaches us the meaning of repentance, which *The catechisme* defines as "the hatred of synne, and loue of Justice, procedying of the feare of God, whyche bryngeth vs to the forsaking of our selues, and to the mortifiynge of oure fleshe, that we may geue oure selues to be gouerned by the spirite, in the seruice of God" (sig. $C_8{}^v$). The sequence is complete: from faith comes repentance and from repentance comes obedience to "heavenly rules."

Sidney's initial emblematic image of Euarchus sitting under a tree resonates with significance. His position, according well with his knowledge that the "beginning and end of his body was earth," suggests his humility and stands in contrast with the pride of those who "exalt" their "height . . . aboue all the trees of the field" (Ezek. 31:5). But the tree itself forms a significant part of the image, "for the tre of the field is mans life" (Deut. 20:19). Sidney's presentation of Euarchus as a whole is foreshadowed in this description, and his use of Euarchus is clearly figurative: "Blessed *is* the man that doeth not walke in the counsel of the wicked, nor stand in the way of sinners, nor sit in the seat of the scorneful. But his delite *is* the Law of the Lord, & in his Law doeth he meditate day and night. For he shal be like a tre planted by the riuers of waters, that wil bring forthe her fruite in due season: whose leafe shal not fade: so whatsoeuer he shal do, shal prosper" (Ps. 1:1-3). Besides his love of justice, Euarchus is notable for his wisdom, which he knows is "an essential and not an opinionate thing" (pp. 361–63). His wisdom, too, is suggested by this initial figure, for wisdom "is a tre of life to them that laie holde on her, and blessed *is* he that reteineth her" (Prov. 3:18). It is part of his wisdom to know, as those he is judging do not, that "what is evil in itself no respect can make good" (p. 358). Finally, the image serves to remind us that "the frute of the righteous *is as* a tre of life, and he that winneth soules [or as the marginal note in the Geneva Bible glosses the phrase, "that is, bringeth them to the knowledge of God"] is wise." (Prov. 11:30).

Herein lies the crux of the fifth book, for, from all appearances, the book ends with no souls won. It is this appearance, I think, which makes the narrator so despairing as he considers the princes' attempt to prevent their "kinfolk" from learning of their disgrace, "wherein the chief man they considered was Euarchus, whom the strange and secret working of justice had brought to be the judge over them—in such a shadow or rather pit of darkness the wormish mankind lives that neither they know how to forsee nor what to fear, and are but like tennis balls tossed by the racket of the higher powers" (pp. 385–86). While some of Sidney's critics have accused Euarchus of executing an "unjust justice,"[29] the narrator, like Plangus in the Second Eclogues (see *OA 30*.11-25, p. 147), is here accusing providence itself. And yet, as in Plangus' case, providence's reasons for bringing Euarchus onstage as judge illustrate precisely the "strange and secret workings of justice."

The end of justice, we recall from the beginning of the fourth book, is our shame and repentance. To all appearances, however, Pyrocles and Musidorus throughout the fifth book have felt little shame and no repentance whatsoever. They hear their sentence of death almost without emotion, "reason and resolution" overruling Pyrocles' "bashfulness" and Musidorus' "anger" (p. 408). Thus far, the justice we have seen is natural justice, for, as de Mornay points out, "By nature then we can looke for none other than the wages of sinne, which is death; neither can wee haue any other inheritance than our fathers, who hath left vs nothing els to inherit but damnation" (*A Woorke*, sig. G_g^8). Were the work to end here, the "everlasting justice" would be frustrated, God's "power and mercy neuer comprehended."[30] Instead, a messenger enters and reveals the identities of both judge and judged. Pyrocles and Musidorus take turns pleading with and reviling Euarchus, each begging for the life of the other.

The effects of this new turn, however, prove indeed that mankind "neither know[s] how to forsee nor what to fear." Pyrocles, listening to his cousin curse his father, is moved, if only by filial piety, to recognize finally that he and Musidorus, not justice, are the causers of their impending deaths as he wills Musidorus to "consider it was their own fault and not . . . [Euarchus'] injustice." Although he still does not understand justice, and begs his father to spare Musidorus since "A father to have executed his only son will leave a sufficient example for a greater crime than this" (p. 413), Pyrocles' repentance, however halting, reminds us that repentance is possible only because a "father . . . executed his only son." Because "God himself . . . step[ped] in betweene his Justice and his mercie" (*A Woorke*, sig. H_h), our repentance, however halting, is acceptable, since "the case here standeth not vpon merit, but vpon mercy" (*A Woorke*, sig. K_k^v).[31]

Although according to the laws of natural justice, nothing has changed, Basilius suddenly revives and pardons everyone, declaring himself chiefly at fault and all to have "fallen out by the highest providence" (p. 416). Even Musidorus is now willing to acknowledge his fault (p. 417), and the *Old Arcadia* ends with a round of marriages. Basilius' "resurrection" is thus not completely void of meaning. Although his "return" to consciousness should not transform him into a figure for Christ, he can be seen rather as an ironic parody of Christ, a bad shepherd who may provide "a great foil to perceive the beauty" (*MP*, 96) of the missing "Shepherd of shepherds" (*OA* 74.128, p. 343) so mistakenly identified by Agelastus with Basilius.[32] While he himself cannot truly forgive anyone because he still does not understand what has happened, his actions figure forth, albeit grotesquely, the mercy which *is* the "everlasting justice." All has indeed "fallen out by the highest providence," and as de Mornay says, "let not euen sinne it selfe, which is the very euill in deede, cause any grudge of mynd in vs; for God created Nature good, but euill is sproong thereof. He created freedome, and it is degenerated into Loosenesse. But let vs prayse God for giuing vs powers, and let us condemne our selues for abusing them. Let vs glorifie him for chastising vs by our owne Loosenesse, for executing his Justice by our vniust Dealings, and for performing the ordinaunce of his rightfull will by our inordinate passions" (*A Woorke*, sig. O$_8$^{v}).

There remains only the narrator, distressed at the injustice of "mortal judgements" (p. 416). While his complaint is valid,[33] it is beside the point. Although his story has demonstrated, as the "Histories of all ages" do, "that man is straungely infected with vyce,"[34] it has also demonstrated that the "everlasting justice" views men not as tennis balls to be tossed about in a cosmic game, but as something precious. If he has shown us that human reason is to be humbled, he has also shown us that we lose nothing if we "willingly give place to divine providence" (p. 265, textual notes). Despite the narrator's pessimism about man's ability to live by "heavenly rules," heaven's rule is supreme and man cannot impede the workings of the "everlasting justice."

Elizabeth Dipple, noting that "Whenever Sidney's voice intrudes into the text . . . the reader must make a decision about the nature of the authorial interruption. The very diversity of voices—condescending, comic, ironic, explosive, sententious, morally absolute—forces a pause in the narrative flow while the decision is being made," sees the ending of the work as flawed by Sidney's "pettish, impatient, and negative" response to his characters.[35] However, if we substitute the narrator for Sidney, this quotation seems to me to describe very nicely the function of the narrator and to answer Dipple's objection to the conclusion. The narrator begins with a rather scornful attitude toward his subject matter and a rather condescending attitude toward anyone in his audience who might be inclined to romanticize his story and characters. As his tale continues, however, he moves from ridicule to sympathy for the dilemmas of his characters and admiration for their relative virtue. In the final moments of the work, as Euarchus becomes the ideal by which he judges and again condemns his characters, he once again loses sympathy with them, replacing his feelings of pity with a universal scorn for the uncertainness of "mortal judgments" (p. 416). As our stand-in, so to speak, Sidney's narrator functions to make us stop, evaluate *his* response, and compare it to our own. It also forces us to consider the reasons for those differences, and to try to reconcile both our diverse responses and our shared, fallible humanity not with "absolute moral abstractions" but with the absolute providence which unfailingly directs the play which we watch while we simultaneously play our own roles.

As we have seen, the structure of the *Old Arcadia* is designed to strip from us any possibility of dependence upon the merely human. In the first two books, with the aid of Sidney's sardonic narrator, the claims of the various classical philosophies to lead us to wisdom, virtue, and happiness are tested and found wanting. By contrast, the first two Eclogues enunciate a set of values that seem both far more attractive and far more Christian. The split between the princely characters and the Arcadian shepherds grows widest in the third book and the Third Eclogues, where, following a series of rampant failures by the main characters, we are brought to our closest point of identification with the shepherds only then to witness their own failure to stand by their principles in the Fourth Eclogues. Moreover, as the "everlasting justice" intervenes more and more directly into the events of books 4 and 5, we find that the narrator is no more immune than the Arcadian shepherds from getting so involved with his sympathies for the characters—sympathies at least in his case that do not really develop until almost the moment of their refusal to bow to the "everlasting justice" and repent—that we can no longer depend completely upon him to guide us through the labyrinthine ways of Arcadia. Finally we are left only with Euarchus, the man who remembers that he is only a man, "a creature whose reason is often darkened with error" (p. 365), and who knows as well that "howsoever he was exalted, the beginning and end of his body was earth" (p. 357). Although even Euarchus, true to his warning, cannot receive an accurate picture of why what has happened did happen—he is forced to depend upon the narrations of Philanax, Gynecia, Pyrocles, and Musidorus, each of whom feels no compunction about distorting the facts or lying outright any time they feel that their idea of justice will be so served—his decision does render strict justice. If that is so abhorrent to us, we should perhaps be grateful that Sidney's fore-conceit has shown us that Euarchus' belief that "what is evil in itself no respect can make good" (p. 358), however valid it may be for his world, is fortunately not true in ours, where the "everlasting justice" has as its end not punishment but repentance, so that the workings of justice become, as Boulon proclaimed, God's "kindly way to beat us on to bliss" (*OA 30.76*, p. 149). And although the narrator's final disgruntlement at the "uncertain state of mortal judgements" (p. 416) reminds us still again that to be human is to err, we are also reminded by the manner in which "all had fallen out by the highest providence" (p. 416) that to be divine is to forgive.

In a sense, then, we might say that the structure of the *Old Arcadia* develops in us a trust that all may be well despite any efforts man may make in his own behalf. If part of Sidney's fore-conceit is that "by reason of our fall, we find our selues astonished here by loue lyke folke falne out of the Clouds, and moreouer benighted with very deepe darknesse in a place that leadeth many sondrie waies cleane contrarie one from another . . . [so that] wee knowe not in this perplexitie which way to take, and yet euery of vs thinks himselfe wise enough to direct his companion,"[36] the other —and more important—part of his fore-conceit is that we "pray God to bring the freedome of our wills ["to follow our owne Nature; and our Nature is become euill through sinne"] in bondage to his will, and free our soules from this hard and damnable kind of freedome, and to graunt vs by his grace, not as the wicked, to doe his will in being vnwilling to do it; but as to his Children, at least wise to be willing to doe it euen in not doing it."[37] Sidney may be creating imaginary gardens but he has stocked them with real toads, for it is only by starting off with man as he really is that a reader may gain the self-knowledge necessary to conceive of man as he should have been and could yet perhaps become. If for no other reason, the *Old Arcadia* succeeds in moving us to "take that goodness in hand" and in teaching us to know "that goodness whereunto . . . [we] are moved" (*MP*, 81) by making us see that we have no other options open. For Sidney, God's game may be a hard one, but it is the only one in town.

NOTES

NOTES

Preface

1. Edwin C. Rozwenc, "Captain John Smith's Image of America," *William and Mary Quarterly*, 3d ser. 16 (1957): 28; cited by Norman S. Grabo, "The Veiled Vision: The Role of Aesthetics in Early American Intellectual History," in *The American Puritan Imagination: Essays in Revaluation*, ed. Sacvan Bercovitch (London: Cambridge University Press, 1974), p. 23.

2. Erasmus-Luther, *Discourse on Free Will* (1524), trans. Ernst F. Winter (New York: Frederick Ungar Publishing, 1961), pp. 86-87. Future citations to the two treatises in this volume will be given parenthetically.

3. Erasmus, *Christian Humanism and the Reformation: Selected Writings*, ed. John C. Olin (New York: Harper & Row, 1965), p. 93.

4. Sir Thomas Wyatt, *Collected Poems*, ed. Kenneth Muir and Patricia Thomson (Liverpool: Liverpool University Press, 1969), poem 106, lines 70-74, 97-112. Despite its flaws, I have cited this edition, rather than Joost Daalder's recent edition of the poems (London: Oxford University Press, 1975), for its commentary. I have, however, checked the text against the corrections printed in H. A. Mason, *Editing Wyatt: An Examination of Collected Poems of Sir Thomas Wyatt* (Cambridge: Cambridge Quarterly Publications, 1972).

5. Sir Philip Sidney, *Miscellaneous Prose*, ed. Katherine Duncan-Jones and Jan van Dorsten (Oxford: Clarendon Press, 1973), p. 92. All citations to *The Defence of Poesie* (although I have refused to follow van Dorsten in modernizing the title) and Sidney's "Letter . . . to Queen Elizabeth" are to this edition and will be given parenthetically wherever possible, with the abbreviation *MP* followed by page number.

6. For Wyatt as a convert to Protestantism and the Psalms as offering a specifically Protestant argument for justification by faith alone, see H. A. Mason, *Humanism and Poetry in the Early Tudor Period* (London: Routledge & Kegan Paul, 1959), pp. 204-21, and *Editing Wyatt*, pp. 178-98. See also Robert G. Twombly, "Thomas Wyatt's Paraphrase of the Penitential Psalms of David," *Texas Studies in Language and Literature* 12 (1970): 345-80. I find Mason's arguments (*Humanism and Poetry*, pp. 203-6, 222) in favor of an early date for the Psalms (ca. 1536) and a later one for the Satires (1536-41) convincing. For Googe, see Frank B. Fieler's introduction to his facsimile reproduction of Googe's *Eglogs Epytaphes, and Sonettes* (1563; reprint ed., Gainesville, Fla.: Scholars' Facsimiles & Reprints, 1968), pp. v-vii, xiii-xiv. I discuss Gascoigne in more detail in chap. 1.

7. *A Hundreth Sundrie Flowres* (1573; facsimile reprint ed., Menston: Scolar Press, 1970), sigs. U^v-U$_2$.

8. For Sidney's usefulness to Shakespeare, see my "'Multiformitie uniforme': *A Midsummer Night's Dream*," *ELH* 38 (1971): 329–49; for Milton's response to Sidney, see my article, "Sir Philip Sidney," in the *Milton Encyclopedia*, s.v. "Sidney."

9. *The Poetry of The Faerie Queene* (Princeton: Princeton University Press, 1967), p. 293.

Chapter 1

1. James M. Osborn, *Young Philip Sidney, 1572–1577* (New Haven: Yale University Press, 1972), pp. 537–40, gives the text of the letter; I quote from p. 538.

2. Useful studies of the *Old Arcadia* include Richard A. Lanham, *The Old Arcadia*, in Walter R. Davis and Lanham, *Sidney's Arcadia* (New Haven: Yale University Press, 1965); Neil L. Rudenstine, *Sidney's Poetic Development* (Cambridge, Mass.: Harvard University Press, 1967); Elizabeth Dipple, "Harmony and Pastoral in the *Old Arcadia*," *ELH* 35 (1968): 309–28, "The 'Fore Conceit' of Sidney's Eclogues," *Literary Monographs* 1 (1967): 3–47, and "'Unjust Justice' in the *Old Arcadia*," *Studies in English Literature* 10 (1970): 83–101; Clifford Davidson, "Nature and Judgment in the *Old Arcadia*," *Papers in Language and Literature* 6 (1970): 348–65; Franco Marenco, "Double Plot in Sidney's Old 'Arcadia,'" *Modern Language Review* 64 (1969): 248–63, and "Per una nuova interpretazione dell' 'Arcadia' di Sidney," *English Miscellany* 17 (1966): 9–48. Walter Davis, "Actaeon in Arcadia," *Studies in English Literature* 2 (1962): 95–110, and *A Map of Arcadia: Sidney's Romance in Its Tradition* in Davis and Lanham, *Sidney's Arcadia*, discusses a number of episodes in books 3–5 in their 1593 incarnation as well as suggesting some useful contexts. David Kalstone, *Sidney's Poetry: Contexts and Interpretations* (Cambridge, Mass.: Harvard University Press, 1965), serves a similar function. Jon S. Lawry, *Sidney's Two Arcadias: Pattern and Proceeding* (Ithaca: Cornell University Press, 1972), appeared after most of chapters 2 and 3 had taken their final shape, but I am grateful for the support of his occasionally similar readings, especially since he reaches them from a fairly different perspective than mine. Anyone toiling in the vineyards of the *Old Arcadia* needs all the help he can get, and I owe a large debt to all who have written on Sidney before me.

3. *The Life of Sir Philip Sidney*, ed. Nowell Smith (Oxford: Clarendon Press, 1907), p. 40.

4. See *ibid.*, pp. 29–38.

5. *The Correspondence of Sir Philip Sidney and Hubert Languet*, trans. Steuart A. Pears (London, 1845), pp. 23–24. I have quoted the Sidney-Languet letters from Pears, but have elsewhere used the letters printed in Albert Feuillerat, ed., *Prose Works of Sir Philip Sidney*, 4 vols. (Cambridge: Cambridge University Press, 1962), 3:73–184. Citations from Feuillerat, where possible, are given parenthetically in my text to *Prose Works*, vol. 3.

6. Pears, *Correspondence*, pp. 47–48.

7. *Ibid.*, p. 152.

8. The situation has not been helped by the general critical tendency to use such terms as "Calvinist" or "Puritan" as if everyone were agreed on what they meant and as if what they meant were something clearly different from what is meant by such terms as "Anglican" or "Church of England." In the 1570s such was not the case. Archbishop Grindal, for instance, was arguably both a Calvinist and a Puritan at the same time that he was the spiritual leader of the Church of England. One might also mention his successor, Arch-

bishop Whitgift, whose ecclesiastical career was devoted to putting down the Puritans but whose theology was clearly in line with Calvin's. I have preferred the usage "Reformed Protestant" throughout to denote that group theologically distinct from the other two major Christian Churches of the period, the Catholics and the Lutherans.

9. *An Apology for Poetry* (London: Thomas Nelson & Sons, 1965), p. 26.

10. See Patrick Collinson, *The Elizabethan Puritan Movement* (Berkeley: University of California Press, 1967), p. 295. Leicester's patronage of the Puritans is detailed by Collinson and also by Wallace MacCaffrey, *The Shaping of the Elizabethan Regime* (Princeton: Princeton University Press, 1968).

11. See Paul S. Seaver, *The Puritan Lectureships: The Politics of Religious Dissent, 1560-1662* (Stanford: Stanford University Press, 1970), p. 150. A year after Sidney's death, Stiles became chaplain to Sir Francis Walsingham, Sidney's father-in-law and Elizabeth's first secretary—the most principle-bound member of the privy council.

12. See Jean Robertson, "Sir Philip Sidney and Penelope Rich," *Review of English Studies* 15 (1968): 296-97; and *Dictionary of National Biography*, s.v. "Gifford." Whitgift and Aylmer considered Gifford to be a "ringleader" of a group of nonconforming Essex ministers who had formed a Puritan synod in London and deprived him of his living.

13. *Letters of Thomas Wood, Puritan, 1566-1577*, ed. Patrick Collinson, *Bulletin of the Institute of Historical Research*, Special Supplement no. 5 (London: University of London, Athlone Press, 1960), p. 15 (19 August 1576).

14. *Ibid.*, p. 16 (20 August 1576).

15. A convenient genealogical table indicating the relationships among Elizabeth's privy councillors may be found in Michael Barraclough Pulman, *The Elizabethan Privy Council in the Fifteen-Seventies* (Berkeley: University of California Press, 1971), p. 41.

16. See John Field's dedicatory epistle to his translation of a treatise by Sidney's friend, Philip de Mornay, *A Notable Treatise of the Church* (1579), to the Earl of Leicester: "and as by your Honour I dedicate it to the Church of England, so I humbly craue that it may be defended: for hereunto is your Honour called of God, and therefore hath he giuen you aucthoritie, that you should maintaine his Church, loue his religion, set your selfe against Poperie, and liue and die to his glorie. He hath honored you, that you shoulde honor him, and hath set you vp, that you shoulde maintaine him" (sigs. A^{iiv}-A^{iii}). For Field's role as organizer of the London presbyterian movement, see Patrick Collinson, "John Field and Elizabethan Puritanism," in *Elizabethan Government and Society: Essays Presented to Sir John Neale*, ed. S. T. Bindoff, Joel Hurstfield, and C. H. Williams (London: Athlone Press, 1961), pp. 127–62.

17. Collinson, *Elizabethan Puritan Movement*, p. 23.

18. *Ibid.*, p. 55.

19. *Ibid.*, p. 25.

20. See Field's epistle to Leicester: "seeing therefore that they [the Catholics] will not be satisfied with trueth, but abuse the mercifull lenitie of their gratious Souereigne, it is more then high time (my Lord) that y^e Lords discipline be restored, & that their spreading poyson be restrained . . ." (*A Notable Treatise of the Church*, sig. A$_{iii}$^{v}).

21. See Leicester's letter to Wood of 19 August 1576: "I take Almighty God to my record, I never altered my mind or thought from my youth touching my religion, and yow knowe I was ever from my cradle brought up in it . . ." (*Letters of Thomas Wood*, p. 13).

22. For Ashton, see Roger Howell, *Sir Philip Sidney: The Shepherd Knight* (London: Hutchinson, 1968), pp. 128–30. The purchase of Calvin's *Catechism* is noted in the accounts of his servant, Thomas Marshall, whose account book is reprinted in Malcolm W.

Wallace, *The Life of Sir Philip Sidney* (Cambridge: Cambridge University Press, 1915), pp. 406–23. The purchase of "Caluines chatachisme" is recorded for February 1565/66 on p. 410.

23. See, e.g., Conyers Read, *Mr. Secretary Walsingham and the Policy of Queen Elizabeth*, 3 vols. (Oxford: Clarendon Press, 1925), 2:10, for Casimir. For de Mornay, see Lucy Crump, trans., *A Huguenot Family in the XVI Century: The Memoirs of Philippe de Mornay, Sieur du Plessis Marly, Written by his Wife* (London: George Routledge, n.d.), esp. pp. 82–110, 170–73, and 205–17; and Raoul Patry, *Philippe du Plessis-Mornay: Un huguenot homme d'Etat* (Paris: Librairie Fischbacher, 1933). For Greville, see Ronald A. Rebholz, *The Life of Fulke Greville, First Lord Brooke* (Oxford: Clarendon Press, 1971), esp. pp. 23–28. For Languet, see Henri Chevreul, *Hubert Languet* (Paris: L. Potier, 1856), pp. 6–17, 118–38. The common note in the various discussions is not so much the concern over doctrinal questions in dispute between various Protestant theologians but rather dedication to the common cause of the Reformed Protestant religion *contra* both Catholics and Lutherans.

24. See Philip Schaff, *The Creeds of Christendom*, 3 vols. (New York: Harper & Bro., 1905), 1:392–94. The *Second Helvetic Confession*, issued at the request of Frederick III, Elector Palatine, "who was being threatened by the Lutherans with exclusion from the treaty of peace on account of his secession to the Reformed Church" pp. 392–93, was composed by Henry Bullinger, Zwingli's successor at Zurich, and consented to by, among others, Peter Martyr, Calvin (before his death in 1562), and Beza, Calvin's more dogmatic successor at Geneva, whose French translation was published at 1566. One of the projects Sidney's friend John Casimir, second son of Frederick III, was most interested in discussing with Sidney in 1577 was a conference of Reformed Protestant churches to produce a common formulary for defence against—again—attacks from the Lutherans and the Catholics (see *Calendar of State Papers* [*CSP*], *Foreign, 1575–77*, item 1425, 8 May 1577, p. 575). Given the international bent of the Sidney circle, especially in the late 1570s, the *Second Helvetic Confession* seems a particularly apt doctrinal formulation for our discussion of the impact of Reformed Protestantism as an intellectual system in the Sidney circle.

25. Bullinger offers as one of the advantages of *A Confession of Fayth, made by common consent of divers reformed Churches beyonde the Seas* (London, n.d. [1568?]) that "Men shall easely gather this also, that we doo not by any wicked Schisme sever or cut of our selves from Christ his holie Churches of Germany, France, Englande, and other Christian Nations, but that we well agree with all and every one of them in the truthe of Christe" (sigs. A$_2$–A$_2$^{v}). The *Confession* was published with Beza's *Exhortation to the Reformation of the Churche*, but each work was printed separately before they were bound together. Where possible, references will be given parenthetically in my text. Although there is some doubt about the extent to which the translation of de Mornay, published in 1587 as *A Woorke concerning the trewnesse of the Christian Religion*, "Begunne to be translated into English by Sir *Philip Sidney* Knight, and at his request finished by *Arthur Golding*" (London, 1587), preserves untouched any of Sidney's actual language, there is none that, as Madame de Mornay puts it, Sidney "did M. du Plessis the honour to translate into English his book" (*A Huguenot Family*, p. 169). Whether the translation we have is Sidney's, Sidney's completed by Golding, Golding's revision of Sidney's, or completely Golding's work is, for our purposes, irrelevant. What is important is Sidney's close relationship with de Mornay, who was in England for eighteen months during 1577 and 1578, during which time de Mornay worked on his book, fathered a child for which Sidney stood as godfather, and argued heartily against Elizabeth's marriage to Monsieur (pp. 170–71). De Mornay's *A Woorke* must have struck a resonant chord in

Sidney for him to agree to translate what is by no means a short book. Feuillerat prints the first six chapters in *Prose Works*, vol. 3, and I have parenthetically cited his edition as well as 1587 where possible.

26. H. C. Porter, *Reformation and Reaction in Tudor Cambridge* (Cambridge: Cambridge University Press, 1958), p. 277.

27. *Hamlet*, ed. Willard Farnham, in *The Complete Works*, ed. Alfred Harbage (Baltimore: Penguin, 1969), 2.2.300-304.

28. See John Calvin, *Institutes of the Christian Religion*, trans. Henry Beveridge, 2 vols. (1845; reprint ed., Grand Rapids, Mich.: Wm. B. Eerdmans, 1970), p. 165, bk. 1, chap. 15, sec. 4: "The image of God constitutes the entire excellence of human nature, as it shone in Adam before his fall, but was afterwards vitiated and almost destroyed, nothing remaining but a ruin, confused, mutilated, and tainted with impurity." Like Bullinger, Calvin sees fallen man "drowned in wicked concupiscence": "For our nature is not only utterly devoid of goodness, but so prolific in all kinds of evil, that it can never be idle. Those who term it *concupiscence* use a word not very inappropriate, provided it were added . . . that everything which is in man, from the intellect to the will, from the soul even to the flesh, is defiled and pervaded with this concupiscence; or, to express it more briefly, that the whole man is in himself nothing else than concupiscence" (bk. 2, chap. 1, sec. 8). All citations to the *Institutes* are to this edition and will be given by book, chapter, and section number. See also article 9 of the Thirty-Nine Articles of the Church of England.

29. Calvin, *Institutes*, 2.1.12.

30. See de Mornay, *A Woorke*, sig. N$_8$: "God therefore created man good, howbeit chaungeably good; free from euill, howbeit so as he might choose the euill; and he Created him rightly mynded, howbeit in such sort as he myght also go a stray. And this man by turning away from the Wellspryng of goodnesse, did thereby fall away from his owne goodnesse; and by following his owne will instead of God's Will, he left his freedome and became a bondseruant vnto euill."

31. From this, de Mornay concludes (like Sidney in his letter to the Queen [*MP*, 47-48]) that "the true Religion can be but one; namely euen that only one which sheweth vs the onely one meane of saluation: and that all other Religions, if they abate any whit of mans debt vnto God, are traiterous to his maiestie; and if they set not downe a sufficient meane of discharge, they be but vayne and vnauaylable ceremonies: and so as well the one sort as the other, vtterly vnworthy of the name of Religion. . . . And so shal those other Religions be, but either Idolatrie or Atheisme, that is to say, vtter Godlesness" (*A Woorke*, sigs. Z^v-Z_2).

32. Erasmus, *Concerning the Immense Mercy of God* (1524), in *The Essential Erasmus*, trans. John P. Dolan (New York: New American Library, 1964), p. 265.

33. "The Author's Preface to the Commentary on the Book of Psalms," trans. James Anderson, in John Dillenberger, ed., *John Calvin: Selections from His Writings* (Garden City: Anchor, 1971), p. 26. All citations to Wyatt's Psalms will be to *The Collected Poems of Sir Thomas Wyatt*, ed. Kenneth Muir and Patricia Thomson (Liverpool: Liverpool University Press, 1969), and will be identified by poem and line numbers.

34. Dillenberger, *Selections*, p. 23.

35. Faith is freely given by grace, yet it is freely given only to those whom God has chosen to receive it. As the *Confession* puts it, "God hath from the beginninge predestinated or chosen freely, and of his mere grace, for no respecte that is in men, the Sainctes, whom he will haue saued, for Christes sake. . . . Wherefore not without a meanes, although not for our merites, but in Christe for Christ God hath chosen vs, so that they whiche are nowe ingraffed in Christe by faithe, be also elected, and they be reprobate or caste awaies whiche are without Christe" (sigs. C_7-$C_7{}^v$).

36. For the futility of attempting to work out one's salvation by doing good works, see article 13 of the Thirty-Nine Articles of the Church of England, "of works before Justification": "Works done before the grace of Christ, and the inspiration of his Spirit, (1) are not pleasant to God, forasmuch as they spring not of faith in Jesus Christ, (2) neither do they make man meet to receive grace, or (as the school-authors say) deserve grace of congruity: yea rather, (3) for that they are not done as God hath willed and commanded them to be done, we doubt not but they have the nature of sin." I cite the Articles from the texts printed in Thomas Rogers, *The Catholic Doctrine of the Church of England: An Exposition of the Thirty-Nine Articles* ed. J. J. S. Perowne (1579, rev. ed. 1607; reprint ed., Cambridge: Cambridge University Press, 1854), p. 125. Any references to the Articles are to this edition.

37. See *Confession*, sigs. D8–D8V: "We teache also, that this Lawe is not geuen to man, to the ende he should iustified, by the keepyng and obseruyng it, but rather, that by the knowledge of the lawe, he might acknowledge his infirmitie, sinne and condemnation, and dispaire of any helpe by his own strength might be conuerted to Christ, through faith. . . . Neither could, nor yet any flesh is able, to satisfie the law of God, and to fulfill it, for the weaknes that is in our fleshe, and still remaineth in vs, euen to our laste gaspe. . . . Therefore Christe is the perfection of the Lawe, and hath fulfilled it for vs: who, as he did beare the cursse of the lawe, while he was made accursed for our sakes, so he maketh vs by faithe, partakers of his fulfillying the Lawe, his rightuousnes and obedience beyng accepted, as though it were ours. In this respect therefore, the lawe of God is abolished, in that it dooeth no more condemne vs, nor cause wrathe to fall vpon vs: For we are vnder grace, not vnder the lawe."

38. It is to this combination of knowledge and incapacity, of desire to act and of frustration in acting that Sidney points in the *Defence* as an argument "to the credulous of that first accursed fall of Adam, since our erected wit maketh us know what perfection is, and yet our infected will keepeth us from reaching into it" (*MP*, 79).

39. See 2 Cor. 12:7–10: "And lest I should be exalted out of measure through the abundance of reuelations, there are giuen vnto me a pricke in the flesh, yᵉ messenger of Satan to buffet me, because I shoulde not be exalted out of measure. For this thing I besought the Lord thrice, that it might departe from me: And he said vnto me, My grace is sufficient for thee: for my power is made perfite through weakenes. Verie gladly therefore wil I reioyce rather in mine infirmities, that the power of Christ may dwell in me. Therefore I take pleasure in infirmities, in reproches, in necessities, in persecutions, in anguish for Christs sake: for when I am weake, then am I strong." See also Calvin's commentary on this passage, stressing the necessity for us to rejoice in our weakness, *Calvin's Commentaries: The Second Epistle of Paul the Apostle to the Corinthians and the Epistles to Timothy, Titus and Philemon*, ed. David W. Torrance and Thomas F. Torrance, trans. T. A. Smail (Grand Rapids, Mich.: Wm. B. Eerdmans, 1964), pp. 158–62.

40. See *Confession*, sig. C3V: "Neither are we ignorant that those things whiche are done, are not euell, in respecte of Gods Providence, will, and power, but in respect of Sathan, & our will, whiche rebelleth against Gods will."

41. State Papers, Domestic, 131, no. 54, cited by Read (*Mr. Secretary Walsingham*, 2:19).

42. *Prose Works*, 3:130–31.

43. Read (*Mr. Secretary Walsingham*, 2:1–117) offers the most sustained exposition of the episode, but see also Stanford E. Lehmberg, *Sir Walter Mildmay and Tudor Government* (Austin: University of Texas Press, 1964), pp. 156–64, and Raymond B. Waddington, *The Mind's Empire: Myth and Form in George Chapman's Narrative Poems* (Baltimore: Johns Hopkins University Press, 1974), pp. 72–91.

44. Lloyd E. Berry, ed., *John Stubbs' Gaping Gulf with Letters and Other Relevant Documents* (Charlottesville: University Press of Virginia, 1968), pp. 3-4.

45. Paul L. Hughes and James F. Larkin, c.s.v., eds., *Tudor Royal Proclamations: The Later Tudors, 1553-1587*, 3 vols. (New Haven: Yale University Press), 2:446.

46. William Camden, *The Historie of the Moste Renowned and Victorious Princesse Elizabeth* . . . (London, 1630), p. 10.

47. Read, *Mr. Secretary Walsingham*, 2:20.

48. Osborn (*Young Philip Sidney*, p. 504) follows tradition when he calls the affair the occasion for the composition of the *Old Arcadia* as Sidney, rusticated by the Queen's displeasure at his letter to her against the marriage, was freed from the business of politics to an "enforced inactivity" in which to engage in the sport of his "toyfull booke," whose conclusion, he wrote to his brother Robert on 18 October 1580, he hoped to accomplish by the following February (*Prose Works*, 3:132). I shall argue for a stronger connection than the simple provision of enforced leisure.

49. *Shaping of the Elizabethan Regime*, p. 398.

50. Pears, *Correspondence*, p. 187.

51. *CSP, Spanish, 1568-1579*, Bernardino de Mendoza to the King, 25 August 1579: "Leicester, who is in great grief, came hither recently, and when he came from his interview with the Queen, his emotion was remarked. A meeting was held on the same night at the Earl of Pembroke's house, there being present Lord Sydney [i.e., Sir Henry, Philip's father] and other friends and relatives. They no doubt discussed the matter and some of them afterwards remarked that Parliament would have something to say as to whether the Queen married or not" (pp. 702-3). Greville (*Life*, p. 60) gives a more restrained picture of Leicester, reacting to the "aspersions" cast upon him by "the French faction reigning," by deciding "like a wise man (under colour of taking physick) voluntarily [to] become prisoner in his chamber"—thus leaving Sidney to fight alone.

52. *CSP, Venetian, 1558-1580*, Hieronimo Lippoman, Venetian Ambassador in France, to the Signory, 27 October 1579: "It is reported that another English Lord is coming to Monsieur to give him account of the Queen's regret at the publication of the book against their marriage, and that the Queen, having heard that Secretary Walsingham had knowledge of this affair, had dismissed him from the Court" (p. 621).

53. *CSP, Spanish, 1568-1579*, Mendoza to Zayas, 16 October, 1579: "The Queen is greatly irritated with anyone who opposes the marriage, saying not once but many times that she had never broken her word yet and she will keep it now [and marry Monsieur]. Speaking to Walsingham about it she told him begone and that the only thing he was good for was a protector of heretics. Knollys who is a great heretic and the treasurer of the household, married to her first cousin, asked her how she could think of marrying a Catholic, she having forbidden Protestants to do so. To this she replied that he might pay dearly for the zeal he was displaying in the cause of religion, and it was a fine way to show his attachment to her, who might desire, like others, to have children. She had another squabble about it with Hatton, and he was a week without seeing her" (p. 704).

54. See Read, *Mr. Secretary Walsingham*, 2:1-18, and Greville, *Life*, pp. 42-60.

55. Osborn (*Young Philip Sidney*, pp. 525-28) prints Elizabeth's instructions to Sidney; he also prints the text of Sidney's letter of 13 May 1577 to the Landgrave of Hesse (pp. 476-78), in which Sidney writes of the need to "repulse the designs of the Bishop of Rome who seeks with all his might to destroy those who have cast off the yoke he had laid upon the necks of our forefathers, and who now maintain themselves in such liberty as enables them rightly and devoutly to worship God and to work out their own salvation. To achieve these ends, however, the Pope is attempting to join such Kings and Princes as are still bound to his tyranny in alliances that are to destroy us in concert.

This, in their view, will be easy unless we also join together, to repel the harm they will try to inflict on us" (p. 477).

56. *Ibid.*, p. 478.

57. *CSP, Spanish, 1568-1579*, pp. 575-76.

58. Osborn (*Young Philip Sidney*, p. 496) prints Elizabeth's response to William's proposals, both for the marriage and for an alliance between Elizabeth and himself: "We have in all our former actions . . . sought by all meanes to bringe the provinces of the Lowe-Countrye . . . to an unitye [with Philip, their legitimate Prince] . Yf nowe, after such a coorse taken, we should, without further offence geven, seeke to dismember the body and plucke th'one parte thereof from the other, by withdrawing the subject from the Soveraigne, we should enter a matter which should much towche us in honnour and might be an evill precedent for us even in our owne case. For we could not like that any forreyn prince should enter into any such secreat combination with our President of Wales or Deputye of Ireland or any other governor under us, which might in any waye estraunge him from th'obedience he oweth us." Since Sir Henry Sidney was both President of Wales and Deputy of Ireland at the time, Elizabeth's choice of examples was fairly pointed. Whether or not, as Osborn suggests, she saw the offer of Governorship of Holland and Zeeland as a first step toward setting Sidney up as a "Dudley candidate for Elizabeth's own throne" (p. 497), she certainly saw it as an unwelcome intervention into her sphere of influence and one which could clearly endanger her own course in the Netherlands.

59. See Read, *Mr. Secretary Walsingham*, 2:9-10.

60. *Ibid.*, 2:10.

61. Osborn, *Young Philip Sidney*, p. 499.

62. Harleian MSS 1582, f. 46, cited by Read, *Mr. Secretary Walsingham*, 2:16 (citation given 2:18). Read dates the MSS "with confidence to the spring of 1579" (2:18). This memorandum was produced as part of the Privy Council's deliberations over the desirability of a marriage with Monsieur.

63. *Mr. Secretary Walsingham*, 2:18.

64. *CSP, Spanish, 1568-1579*, Mendoza to Zayas, 16 October 1579, p. 704.

65. See Read, *Mr. Secretary Walsingham*, 2:4.

66. Although this comment would fit the revised *Arcadia* as well, Greville seems to have the *Old* in mind here, as his discussion of the trial scene, lacking in the 1590 *Arcadia* that he edited, suggests, and as does his insistence that he is discussing "the infancie of these *Ideas*, determining in the first generation" (*Life*, p. 14) and "the first project of these workes" (p. 16).

67. Sir Philip Sidney, *The Countess of Pembroke's Arcadia (The Old Arcadia)*, ed. Jean Robertson (Oxford: Clarendon Press, 1973), pp. 358-59. All citations to the *Old Arcadia* are to Robertson's edition and will be given parenthetically in the text. When the citation is clear, I have just indicated a page number; when it is not and in extended quotations I have indicated the text by the abbreviation *OA* followed by the page number (i.e., *OA*, 359).

68. *Tudor Drama and Politics: A Critical Approach to Topical Meaning* (Cambridge, Mass.: Harvard University Press, 1968), p. 25. For Greek translations of many of the other characters' names, see William Ringler, ed., *The Poems of Sir Philip Sidney* (Oxford: Clarendon Press, 1964), p. 382.

69. Sidney's "dedicatory" letter to his sister, first printed by Greville in the 1590 edition of the revised *Arcadia*, is usually taken to have been written for the *Old Arcadia*. Ringler's comment (*Poems*, p. 383) is worth remembering: "Even in the intimacy of his own family Sidney assumed a mask and maintained the pose of graceful negligence that

was expected of a renaissance gentleman. His 'idle worke' had consumed most of his leisure for some three years; the 'trifle, and that triflinglie handled' ran to some 180,000 words, and was a composition more carefully structured and more artfully executed than anything in English of its time." The sixteenth-century reader who could have taken this letter as anything more than the conventional disclaimer attached to such works as Petrarch's *On His Own Ignorance and That of Many Others*, Erasmus' *Praise of Folly*, More's *Utopia*, or legions of others must have been naive indeed. Greville clearly did not intend it to signal readers to expect nothing serious in the *Arcadia*.

70. Critical opinion seems to be swinging back to an early date for the *Defence*. Jan van Dorsten argues well (*MP*, 59–63) for a date of 1579–80, supported by Arthur F. Kinney, "Parody and Its Implications in Sidney's *Defense of Poesie*," *Studies in English Literature* 12 (1972): 1–19. Shepherd, in his richly annotated edition of the *Apology for Poetry* (p. 4), suggests that the *Defence* was written "after 1580," with 1581–83 being the likeliest years, linking it to Sidney's revision of the *Old Arcadia*. Van Dorsten's arguments appear far more convincing to me, especially since Shepherd's later arguments for the genesis of certain of Sidney's positions in "some current reading, and some reports of others' reading, of much literary conversation, and of personal thought and argument" (p. 83) point to precisely the milieu that Spenser speaks of in his letter of 16 October 1579 to Gabriel Harvey: "Master *Sidney*, and Master *Dyer* . . . haue me . . . in some vse of familiarity. . . . And now they have proclaimed in their ἀρείω παγω, a generall surceasing and silence of balde Rymers. . . . New Bookes I heare of none, but only of one, that writing a certaine Booke, called *The Schoole of Abuse*, and dedicating it to Maister *Sidney*, was for hys labor scorned" (*Poetical Works*, ed. J. C. Smith and E. de Selincourt [London: Oxford University Press, 1912], p. 635).

71. See Sidney's discussion of contemporary plays in the *Defence of Poesie* (*MP*, 112 ff.) and Lodge's *Defence of Poetry* in *Elizabethan Critical Essays*, ed. G. Gregory Smith, 2 vols. (London: Oxford University Press, 1904), 1:76. All citations from Elizabethan critical works are to this edition wherever possible.

72. All citations from Gascoigne's introductory epistles to *The Posies* are to *The Complete Works of George Gascoigne*, ed. John W. Cunliffe, (Cambridge: Cambridge University Press, 1907), vol. 1, and will be indicated in my text by volume and page number.

73. See the epistle "To the yong Gentlemen . . .": "There are also certain others, who (having no skill at all) will yet be verie busie in reading all that may bee read, and thinke it sufficient if (Parrot like) they can rehearse things without booke: when within booke they understande neyther the meaning of the Author, nor the sense of the figurative speeches" (1:11).

74. For the spider/poison-bee/honey simile as an explanation of the dangers of poetry or as an excuse for the poet's failures, see Lodge (*Elizabethan Critical Essays*, 1:79), and Stephen Gosson's rather nastier variants in *The Schoole of Abuse*, in *English Reprints*, ed. Edward Arber (London, 1868), 1:19–20. Lyly uses the simile in a different context though to the same general end in *Euphues*, in *Elizabethan Prose Fiction*, ed. Merritt Lawlis (New York: Odyssey, 1967), p. 129.

75. Arber, *English Reprints*, 1:41. After *The Posies*, Gascoigne, as if aware of the futility of trying to wield the "two edged swoorde" of poetry, switches to explicity didactic satire, entertainments urging the fortunes of the Earl of Leicester, and political and homiletic works written under the patronage of Leicester revealing "an increasing tendency toward Puritanism" (see Eleanor Rosenberg, *Leicester: Patron of Letters* [New York: Columbia University Press, 1955], pp. 166–72).

76. See Don Cameron Allen, *Mysteriously Meant* (Baltimore: Johns Hopkins Press, 1970).

77. *Boccaccio on Poetry*, trans. Charles G. Osgood (1930; reprint ed., Indianapolis: Bobbs-Merrill, 1956), p. 39. For a more complete discussion of medieval aesthetics, see D. W. Robertson, Jr., *A Preface to Chaucer: Studies in Medieval Perspective* (Princeton: Princeton University Press, 1963), pp. 52–137.

78. Robertson, p. 56. Boccaccio comments that what is true of "obscurities in sacred literature addressed to all nations" is true of poetry "which is addressed to the few" in "far greater measure" (Osgood, p. 61).

79. Osgood, pp. 61–62. See Robertson, p. 56: "The incoherence of the surface materials is almost essential to the formation of the abstract pattern, for if the surface materials —the concrete elements in the figures—were consistent or spontaneously satisfying in an emotional way, there would be no stimulus to seek for something beyond them."

80. Petrarch, *On His Own Ignorance and That of Many Others*, trans. Hans Nachod, in *The Renaissance Philosophy of Man*, ed. Ernst Cassirer, Paul Oskar Kristeller, and John Herman Randall, Jr. (1948; reprint ed., Chicago: University of Chicago Press, 1963), p. 105.

81. Shepherd is most helpful on Sidney's reading and his use of it in the *Defence*; see, esp. pp. 9–11, 37–39, 43–45, 64–66, 83, and his commentary throughout. Cornell March Dowlin ("Sidney and Other Men's Thought," *Review of English Studies* 20 [1944] : 257–71) and A. C. Hamilton ("Sidney's Idea of the 'Right Poet,'" *Comparative Literature* 9 [1957] : 51–59) both argue that Sidney's transformations of his sources are crucial to an understanding of what he is attempting in the *Defence*; as Hamilton puts it (p. 51), "what he takes from others he makes his own."

82. Lewis Soens, ed., *Sir Philip Sidney's Defense of Poetry* (Lincoln: University of Nebraska Press, 1970), p. xxxvi. S. K. Heninger, *Touches of Sweet Harmony: Pythagorean Cosmology and Renaissance Poetics* (San Marino: Huntington Library, 1974), argues that Sidney's great contribution lies in his enunciation of a "new poetic credo, eclectic and syncretic in its intention but distinctly English" (p. 288), centering upon his definition of the poet as maker. Although much in Heninger's chapter on the "Poet as Maker" strikes me as important for understanding how the *Defence* differs from contemporary Italian criticism, I disagree with his explanation of why it differs. I find myself at odds with him in the emphasis he places on the teaching function of literature and on the poet's ability to push "the limit of human experience" and approach "the infinitude of the godhead" (p. 304). I also wish that his discussion of the poet as maker had included some consideration of the poet as mover as well, since, as Sidney notes (*MP*, 91), "moving is of a higher degree than teaching."

83. In fact, when Sidney talks about the Oracles' prophecies, he implies that the only reason they could have been thought holy is because "that same exquisite observing of number and measure in the words, and that high flying liberty of conceit proper to the poet, did seem to have some divine force in it" (*MP*, 77).

84. Theodore Beza, *The Psalmes of David Truely Opened and Explained*, trans. Anthony Gilbie (London, 1580), fol. ¶ 2ᵛ, cited by Soens, *Sir Philip Sidney's Defense of Poetry*, p. xii, n. 4. For the Psalms as the result of David's inspiration by the Holy Spirit, see Sidney, *Apology for Poetry* (ed. Shepherd, pp. 151–52).

85. See Golding's discussion (in the epistle to the Earl of Leicester) of Ovid's Golden Age as "Adams tyme in Paradyse" and of the "brazen age" as the time when "malice first in peoples harts did breede," *Ovid's Metamorphoses*, ed. John Frederick Nims (New York: Macmillan, 1965), p. 418.

86. Soens, p. xxii.

87. In his translation of de Mornay's *Of the trewnes of Christian Religion*, Sidney says of the Holy Spirit "that the very benefite which we receyve by his love, is a secrete and

insensible throughbreathing which worketh in us, & yet we cannot well perceyve from whence it commeth" (*Prose Works*, 3:272; *A Woorke*, sig. D$_8$^{v}). See also John Jewel, *An Apology of the Church of England* (1564), ed. J. E. Booty (Ithaca: Cornell University Press, 1963), pp. 23–24. Although Sidney's comment that Plato "attributeth unto poesy more than myself do, namely, to be a very inspiring of a divine force, far above man's wit" (*MP*, 109) is usually interpreted to be a denial of any supernatural aid, it would seem more likely that Sidney is merely distinguishing between the ordinary processes of grace and the kind of divine possession Plato suggests happens in the *furor poeticus*.

88. Virginia Riley Hyman, "Sidney's Definition of Poetry," *Studies in English Literature* 10 (1970): 51–52, suggests that Sidney's first "opening" is an overzealous appeal which, recognizing the "impertinence of such claims," he drops in favor of a more narrowly reasonable definition of the poet's role (p. 58). To say this is to neglect both the continuity of the argument and the rhetorical strategy by which audience and speaker are drawn into "solidarity." See Catherine Barnes, "The Hidden Persuader," *PMLA* 86 (1971): 423–24.

89. For reasons to be explained below in note 107, I have chosen to follow the punctuation in Ponsonby's 1595 edition of *The Defence of Poesie*, sig. C$_2$, rather than that in *MP*, 79–80.

90. Although he does remind us that against the first ("they that did imitate the inconceivable excellencies of God," a phrase that reverberates back to the description of the "maker" at work as well), "none will speak that hath the Holy Ghost in due holy reverence" (*MP*, 80).

91. *The Poetry of The Faerie Queene* (Princeton: Princeton University Press, 1967), p. 282.

92. Calvin continues: "Though these things are true, or at least plausible, still, as I fear they are more fitted to entangle, by their obscurity, than to assist us, I think it best to omit them. Let us therefore hold . . . that the soul consists of two parts, the intellect and the will." Despite Calvin's warning, Elizabethan psychological treatises usually continue to insist upon the more complex "philosophical" description cited above. Typical of these is book 2 of Peter de la Primaudaye's *The French Academie*, trans. T. B[owes] (London, 1594). All citations from this work are to the 1618 edition. For a more general treatment, see Williams Rossky, "Imagination in the English Renaissance: Psychology and Poetic," *Studies in the Renaissance* 5 (1958): 49–73.

93. See Sidney, *Prose Works*, 3:269; *A Woorke*, sig. D$_7$: "Men also doe runne with all their harts after the thing which they suppose to bee good for them, whether it bee honor, riches or pleasure. And the more they knowe it or thinke themselves to knowe it, the more doe they yeeld their will unto it: and the more they hold and possesse thereof, the more is their hart settled thereupon. Only their understanding being bewitched by vanitie, is decytfully driven to choose the evill for the good; by meanes wherof, the will which ought to be discreete and full of wit and understanding, is forced of necessitie to degenerate into fleshly and beastly lust."

94. George Puttenham, *The Arte of English Poesie* (London, 1589), sig. D$_4$. See also Sidney, *Defence* (*MP*, 78).

95. *French Academie*, p. 415. See also Rossky, "Imagination in the English Renaissance," p. 62.

96. For Sidney's conception of "*Energia*" or "forcibleness," see Rudenstine, *Sidney's Poetic Development*, pp. 149–71.

97. Whitaker (1548–95) was the master of St. John's College and the protege of Archbishop Whitgift. In 1580 he was appointed by Elizabeth to the Regius professorship of divinity at Cambridge and shortly after to the chancellorship of St. Paul's in London.

"From this time his position as the champion of the teaching of the Church of England, interpreted in its most Calvinistic sense, appears to have been definitely taken up" *Dictionary of National Biography*, s.v. "Whitaker."

98. *The Enchiridion of Erasmus*, trans. Raymond Himelick (Bloomington: Indiana University Press, 1963), p. 105. Although Erasmus' later writings move much closer to the kind of historical commentary that Colet had begun, this statement seems useful as an indicator of later medieval/early Renaissance Catholic opinion.

99. William Whitaker, *A Disputation on Holy Scripture, Against the Papists* (1588), trans. and ed. William Fitzgerald, The Parker Society (Cambridge: Cambridge University Press, 1849), p. 406.

100. See William Tyndale, *The Obedience of a Christian Man* (1528) in *Doctrinal Treatises and Introductions to Different Portions of the Holy Scriptures*, ed. Henry Walter, The Parker Society (Cambridge: Cambridge University Press, 1848), pp. 304–5.

101. *Ibid.*, pp. 307–8.

102. *Ibid.*, p. 343.

103. *Ibid.*, p. 306. See also Sidney, *Defence* (*MP*, 118). The impracticality of trying to teach through allegories is suggested by Sir John Harington's discussion of the myth of Perseus (translated, as Paul Alpers [*The Poetry of The Faerie Queene*, p. 165, n. 6] reminds us, from Leone Ebreo's *Dialoghi di Amore*). To "pike" out "infinite Allegories" (Smith, *Elizabethan Critical Essays*, 2:202–3) may be an interesting way for the reader to spend his time, but it is hardly a way that would recommend itself to poets interested in retaining control over what they are trying to teach their readers.

104. Whitaker, *A Disputation*, p. 470.

105. See *Certaine Sermons or Homilies*, ed. Mary Ellen Rickey and Thomas B. Stroup (1623; facsimile reprint, Gainesville, Fla.: Scholars' Facsimiles & Reprints, 1968), sig. Rr₃ ("An Homilie of the worthy receiuing and reuerend esteeming of the Sacrament of the body and blood of Christ").

106. *The Decades of Henry Bullinger*, trans. H. I. (1577), ed. Thomas Harding, The Parker Society, 4 vols. (Cambridge: Cambridge University Press, 1849–52), 4:242.

107. Modern editions customarily attach "metaphorically" to the phrase following it: "Poesy therefore is an art of imitation, for so Aristotle termeth it in the word μίμησις — that is to say, a representing, counterfeiting, or figuring forth—to speak metaphorically, a speaking picture" (pp. 79–80). Although I elsewhere follow van Dorsten's readings, in this case I must demur. Ponsonby's 1595 text, which van Dorsten regards as authoritative (along with Robert Sidney's copy, the De L'Isle MS) gives the reading I prefer: "a representing counterfeiting, or figuring forth to speake Metaphorically. A speaking *Picture*, with this end to teach and delight" (sig. Cᵛ). Although one would not like to place too much weight on the vagaries of Elizabethan punctuation, as Heninger has pointed out to me, to define poetry as a "speaking picture" is hardly metaphorical in the sixteenth century when the term is a commonplace; to define poetry as a "figuring forth" more aptly qualifies for the modifier (see his discussion in *Touches of Sweet Harmony*, p. 323, n. 45).

108. *Thesaurus Linguae Romanae & Britannicae* (London, 1565), s.v. "Idea," cited in Forrest G. Robinson, *The Shape of Things Known: Sidney's Apology in Its Philosophical Tradition* (Cambridge, Mass.: Harvard University Press, 1972), p. 108.

109. Robinson, *Shape of Things Known*, p. 6.

110. *Ibid.*, p. 118.

111. *Ibid.*, p. 126.

112. See Sidney's discussion of *energia* or "forcibleness," *MP*, pp. 116–17. The best discussion of *energia* is still Rudenstine, *Sidney's Poetic Development*, pp. 149–71.

113. *A Commentarie vpon S. Paules Epistles to the Corinthians*, trans. Thomas Timme (London, 1577), sigs. D_2–D_2^v.

114. "*Icones Symbolicae*: Philosophies of Symbolism and Their Bearing on Art," in his *Symbolic Images: Studies in the Art of the Renaissance* (London: Phaidon Press, 1972), pp. 123–95.

115. *Ibid.*, p. 165; but see de Mornay, *A Woorke*, sig. T_6: "Some in deede doo life up y^e eye of their mynd aloft; but how farre or what see they? Surely (as saith Aristotle) euen as much as an Owle in the bright sunne."

116. See de Mornay, *A Woorke*, sigs. Q_7^v–Q_8. For the mind's inability to follow the neoplatonic upward movement via analogies, see de Mornay, sigs. F_8^v–G.

117. *Decades*, 1:77–78.

118. "Renaissance Problems in Calvin's Theology," *Studies in the Renaissance* 1 (1954): 74.

119. Comedy and tragedy Sidney describes as genres to be viewed, lyric and iambic as apt to be heard; I have therefore grouped them together, adding, somewhat dubiously, pastoral on the analogue of the public pastorals of the *Old Arcadia*. The other genres seem clearly to be composed of works more suited for personal reading than public performance and I will consider them next accordingly. Like pastoral, the elegiac has the potential for being either publicly performed ("compassionate accompanying just causes of lamentations" [*MP*, 95]) or privately experienced, but the later strikes me as perhaps the more important and I will reserve comment accordingly.

Chapter 2

1. *Works*, ed. G. Bullough, 2 vols. (Edinburgh: Oliver & Boyd, 1939), 1:131.

2. For a fuller discussion of this crisis, see chap. 1 above.

3. Sidney, *The Countess of Pembroke's Arcadia (The Old Arcadia)*, ed. Jean Robertson (Oxford: Clarendon Press, 1973), p. 49.

4. Ringler and Robertson following him both call the *Old Arcadia* a tragicomedy, largely because they feel its inclusion of events bringing the characters near to death seems to disqualify it from comedy. This Fletcherian definition of tragicomedy seems to me unnecessary given Sidney's comments on mixed genres in the *Defence*. For a discussion of Sidneyan tragicomedy, see my "Structure and 'Fore Conceit' in *Astrophil and Stella*," *Texas Studies in Language and Literature* 16 (1974): 1–25, esp. 23–24. In his recent *Sir Philip Sidney* (New York: Twayne, 1971), Robert Kimbrough calls the work a comedy, but his use of the term (see pp. 68–69, 88) is far different from mine. Richard A. Lanham, *The Old Arcadia*, in Walter R. Davis and Lanham, *Sidney's Arcadia* (New Haven: Yale University Press, 1965), calls for the work to be read, "as much as possible as would a comic novel" (p. 367), but this causes him problems when he comes to discussing the structure, especially in the last book. Clark L. Chalifour, "Sir Philip Sidney's *Old Arcadia* as Terentian Comedy," *Studies in English Literature* 16 (1976): 51–63, argues that the *Old Arcadia's* "use of humor . . . helps to temper adverse moral judgment of the characters" (p. 53), so that although "Pyrocles and Musidorus commit what might have been treated as serious crimes, the seduction of Philoclea and the near-rape of Pamela . . . except for the judgment by Euarchus, attention is directed not to these actions but rather to the youthful rashness and imprudence of which such acts are manifestations" (p. 55). This argument seems to me to turn Sidney into Terence in despite of Sidney's testimony in the *Defence*. It also seems to me a misreading of the *Old Arcadia*, as I shall argue in this chapter.

5. Also included within this discussion of heroic poetry are works which we would normally think of as epics. Alan D. Isler, "Heroic Poetry and Sidney's Two *Arcadias*," *PMLA* 83 (1968): 369 ff., argues that the Elizabethan genre of heroic poetry was used not only for what we would call epics and romances, but also for historical poems like Warner's *Albion's England*, geographical poems like Drayton's *Poly-Olbion*, and even such works as Sir Thomas More's *Utopia*. Whatever one thinks about the way Isler tries to prove his theory—and I think he makes a very suggestive case—there is no doubt that the Elizabethan critic would have described both conventional epics and romances as heroical poems.

6. See Virgil B. Heltzel, "The Arcadian Hero," *Philological Quarterly* 41 (1962): 173-80.

7. See Walter R. Davis, *A Map of Arcadia*, in Davis and Lanham, *Sidney's Arcadia*, pp. 59–83.

8. Elizabeth Dipple, "Harmony and Pastoral in the *Old Arcadia*," *ELH* 35 (1968): 311, argues for a different set of distinctions from the "historical" Arcadia of Polybius. She contrasts Sidney's treatment of the element of music (that the Muses came to Arcadia because it was so pleasant a place) with that of Polybius, who said that the constant singing of the Arcadians was established by their wise ancestors as an antidote to the uncivilized and uncivilizing conditions of the land: "for that they see that the continuell toile of the people in manuring the land, with a rudenesse and brutishnesse of life, and moreouer with an austeere kinde of liuing which proceede from the coldnesse and roughnesse of the Ayre, to the which of necessity we growe like." Miss Dipple suggests that Sidney's description, which mentions the "sweetnes of ye Aire and other naturall benefittes," would be instantly recognized as a departure from historical reality and taken as an indication that his Arcadia is a "prototype of the perfectly imaged pastoral land" (p. 312). However, since the audience would have been equally familiar with Virgil, they would have accepted without question Sidney's use of the alternate Virgilian tradition of Arcadia as a *locus amoenus*. The one element which is not to be found in either Polybius or Virgil is the stress Sidney gives to the political harmony of his Arcadia. I think it is more likely, therefore, that we accept Arcadia as a prototype of the ideal political state, conceived along the lines of such theorists as Sir Thomas Elyot, who defined his public weal as "a body living, compact or made of Sundry estates and degrees of men, which is disposed by the order of equity and governed by the rule and moderation of reason" (*The Book named The Governor*, ed. S. E. Lehmberg [London: J. M. Dent, 1962], p. 1).

9. Like Milton after him, Sidney, following de Mornay, regards the pagan oracles (including that of Apollo) as "the confessions of the very Devilles" (*Prose Works*, 3:305-6; de Mornay, *A Woorke*, sigs. F_8–F_8^v).

10. The marginal gloss in the 1560 Geneva Bible defines "the lust of the flesh" as "to live in pleasure."

11. *Book named The Governor*, p. 95.

12. In Basilius' visit to Delphi, there is a dual perspective operative of which we must be aware. While we know that the Oracle, "that Impiety," is for Sidney and his readers the voice of the Devil whose intent is to entrap the unwary in sin, Basilius thinks it is the voice of God. Thus he sins both in going to the Oracle (from our point of view), and in rejecting the prophecy, which is (from his point of view) a preview of God's providential order.

13. The significance of the comparison would not be lost to an Elizabethan reader; see Calvin's *Commentaries on the First Book of Moses Called Genesis*, trans. John King, 2 vols. (Edinburgh: Calvin Translation Society, 1897), 1:164: "A lively picture of cor-

rupt nature is presented to us in Adam from the moment of his revolt. 'Every one,' says James, 'is tempted by his own concupiscence,' (James 1:14) and even Adam, not otherwise than knowingly and willingly, had set himself, as a rebel, against God." Jon S. Lawry, *Sidney's Two Arcadia's: Pattern and Proceeding* (Ithaca: Cornell University Press, 1972), p. 36, denies, somewhat paradoxically, that Sidney wants us to recognize in Basilius' fall an echo of everyman's repetition of Adam's fall at the same time that he insists that we are to recognize it as a fall: "The Arcadian representative of all men who exchange reason for passion is Basilius (*the king*). Although Sidney does not propose an Adam and a garden but only a Basilius and others in Arcadia, a fall from the golden world nevertheless occurs. Thus, although the name 'Basilius' is not translatable into Everyman, it may still be legion." As I shall try to show, although Basilius is not everyman and every man may not fall precisely as he does, all of the major characters in the *Old Arcadia* do fall.

14. Peter de la Primaudaye, *The French Academie* (1577), trans. T. B. (London, 1618), p. 272. Hereafter cited as *French Academie*.

15. Although Philanax's Stoicism is preferable to Basilius' Epicureanism, his insistence on man's self-sufficiency is still considerably wide of the mark so far as Sidney would be concerned. The proper response, which Philanax in part approaches, would be something on the order of Calvin's comment in the *Institutes*: "Hence it is obvious that, in seeking God, the most direct path and the fittest method is, not to attempt with presumptuous curiosity to pry into his essence, which is rather to be adored than minutely discussed, but to contemplate him in his works, by which he draws near, becomes familiar, and in a manner communicates himself to us" (1.5.9).

16. *Certaine Sermons or Homilies*, ed. Mary Ellen Rickey and Thomas B. Stroup (1623; facsimile reprint, Gainesville, Fla.: Scholar's Facsimiles & Reprints, 1968), sig. C₅.

17. See Colucio Salutati, *De Laboribus Herculis*, ed. B. L. Ullman, 2 vols. (Zurich: Thesaurus Mundi, n.d.), 2:364, cited by D. W. Robertson, Jr., *A Preface to Chaucer* (Princeton: Princeton University Press, 1963), p. 264.

18. The absurdity of his follies may be seen in his behavior on the night he is to sneak off to Cleophila's cave (where Gynecia is already waiting for him). The narrator's description is high comedy: "Having borne out the limit of a reasonable time with as much pain as might be, he came darkling into his chamber, forcing himself to tread as softly as he could. But the more curious he was, the more he thought everything creaked under him; and his mind being out of the way with another thought, and his eyes not serving his turn in that dark place, each coffer or cupboard he met, one saluted his shins, another his elbows; sometimes ready in revenge to strike them again with his face. Till at length, fearing his wife were not fully asleep, he came lifting up the clothes as gently as I think poor Pan did, when instead of Iole's bed, he came into the rough embracings of Hercules, and laying himself down as tenderly as a new bride, rested awhile with a very open ear to mark each breath of his supposed wife" (p. 225).

19. See *French Academie*, pp. 96–97.

20. *Certaine Sermons*, sig. Bb₅ᵛ.

21. *Ibid.*, sig. Eeʳ.

22. *French Academie*, p. 294, warns rulers about just this kind of disruption in the poorly governed state which Arcadia has become: "Negligence likewise breedeth the change & overthrow of a politike estate. There are two sorts of negligence, the one in those that call, choose: or receiue into any great office such men as are vnworthy, and care not for their charges: or that suffer such persons to ascend to the chiefest places of the Magistracy, that are enemies to that forme of Commonwealth. . . . The other kinde

of negligence, which is more common, is in them that are called to a dignity, office, or Magistracy, and shew themselues retchlesse in that administration and exercise: as we see that most Bishops and Prelates neglect the duty of their charges, to imploy or bestow their time in wordly affaires, for which cause they grow into misliking and contempt."

23. Plutarch, *The Education or bringinge up of Children* (1533), trans. Sir Thomas Elyot, in *Four Tudor Books on Education*, ed. Robert D. Pepper (Gainesville, Fla.: Scholars' Facsimiles & Reprints, 1966), sig. A^r (p. 8).

24. The debate has figured prominently in several studies of Sidney, particularly those of Lanham (*Old Arcadia*, pp. 244 ff.), Rudenstine (*Sidney's Poetic Development*, [Cambridge, Mass.: Harvard University Press, 1967], pp. 16–22), and Lawry (*Sidney's Two Arcadias*, pp. 43–49), but since the points which seem to me to be especially important have not been adequately covered, I feel obliged to bring up the whole question once again.

25. Trans. Martin Ostwald (Indianapolis: Bobbs-Merrill, 1962), p. 169, 1144a 6–8.

26. See *Nicomachean Ethics*, p. 25, 1100b 9–10. Reformed Protestantism, of course, denied any role in the providential universe to fortune; see Calvin, *Institutes*, 1.5.11.

27. *Nicomachean Ethics*, p. 25, 1100b 11–22; see also p. 26, 1101a 1–2.

28. *Ibid.*, p. 5, 1094b 8–10.

29. *Ibid.*, p. 289, 1177a 25.

30. *Ibid.*, p. 290, 1177b 24–27.

31. *Ibid.*, p. 292, 1178b 5–7. De Mornay, after noting Aristotle's two blessednesses, turns to reject both kinds of "blessedness" (*A Woorke*, sig. Y$_2$^{v}).

32. *Sidney's Poetic Development*, p. 19.

33. *Ibid.*, p. 20.

34. *OED* sb2b, the only meaning of desert which could possibly apply here, is an uninhabited wooded area. Pyrocles' conclusion negates his definition, while clarifying our understanding of the passage.

35. Lanham, *Old Arcadia*, p. 248.

36. *Ibid.*, p. 248.

37. See Castiglione, *The Book of the Courtier*, trans. Sir Thomas Hoby (1561; reprint ed., London: J. M. Dent, 1928), pp. 318 ff.

38. Sears Jayne, ed. and trans., "Ficino's Commentary on Plato's *Symposium*," *University of Missouri Studies* 19 (1944):130.

39. Lawry (*Sidney's Two Arcadias*, p. 47) sees not a similar fall on the part of Musidorus, but "charity" aiding "reason" in his response to Pyrocles. Although he argues that this "prophetic act of restorative friendship" (p. 47) plays "out in minature something of the *Old Arcadia's* total design" in which "mercy, friendship, and images of true virtue . . . point . . . [a] way back to a golden world" (p. 48), Lawry undercuts his argument immediately by noting that both princes meet the challenge of love by redefining themselves as "new, transformed, Basilian" princes (p. 48).

40. *The Decades of Henry Bullinger*, trans. H. I. (1577), ed. Thomas Harding, The Parker Society, 4 vols. (Cambridge: Cambridge University Press, 1849–52), 2:404–5.

41. *Old Arcadia*, p. 204.

42. This name change elicits the narrator's first address to the "ladies" to whom he occasionally refers after this point, always in an ironic way. His comment here—"and thus did Pyrocles become Cleophila—which name for a time hereafter I will use, for I myself feel such compassion of his passion that I find even part of his fear lest his name should be uttered before fit time were for it; which you, fair ladies that vouchsafe to read this, I doubt not will account excusable" (p. 27)—marks the adoption of a kind of

Ariostan pose, since, in the context of the debate, only someone "womanized" by "this effeminate love" (p. 20) could account Pyrocles/Cleophila excusable. Another example of this ironic pose may be found on p. 39.

43. Compare the narrator's description of the psychological progress of love in Pyrocles with *The Decades of Bullinger*, 3:404.

44. See Bullinger, *ibid.*, 3:385: "Original sin is neither a deed, nor a word, nor a thought; but a disease, a vice, a deprivation, I say, of judgment and concupiscence; or a corruption of the whole man, that is of the understanding, will, and all the power of man."

45. The great exemplar of love as madness for the Renaissance is Ariosto's *Orlando Furioso*; see esp. 24.1, where Ariosto states this theme.

46. John Calvin, *Commentaries on the Epistles of Paul to the Galatians and Ephesians*, trans. William Pringle (Edinburgh: Calvin Translation Society, 1854), p. 147.

47. The two yokes play a part in the first and last poems of Sidney's *Certain Sonnets*. In *CS 1*, the speaker likewise gives way to his passion and cries "I yeeld, o Love, unto thy loathed yoke" (*CS 1.9*). At the end of the sequence, having rejected desire (*CS 31*), he exhorts his mind to seek another yoke:

> Draw in thy beames, and humble all thy might,
> To that sweet yoke, where lasting freedomes be:
> Which breakes the clowdes and opens forth the light,
> That doth both shine and give us sight to see.
>
> [*CS 32.5-8*]

The sweet yoke, of course, is the yoke of "Eternal Love" (*CS 32.14*).

48. See Mark Rose, "Sidney's Womanish Man," (*Review of English Studies*) n.s. 15 (1964): 353-63, for the way an Elizabethan audience would react to Pyrocles' new womanish dress and habits. Lucas Cranach the Elder apparently popularized the depiction of Hercules dressed in Omphale's clothes, spinning, of the kind to which we have seen Sidney allude in the *Defence* (*MP*, 115-16). In one version painted for Cardinal Albrecht of Brandenburg in 1535 and presently in the Statens Museum for Kunst, København (see fig. 1; the painting is reproduced in E. Ruhmer, *Cranach* [London: Phaidon Press, 1963], fig. 2C), one of Omphale's attendants is coyly adjusting Hercules' bonnet while another looks on amusedly and Omphale leers at the viewer. In another, listed as "School of Lucas Cranach" in the catalog to sale 3891 (New York: Sotheby Parke Bernet, 1976; see fig. 2), item 99, Omphale's daughter stands with her hand negligently resting on the bebonneted Hercules' head, grinning at the viewer, while Omphale keeps Hercules spinning. Both pictures bear the same inscription:

> Hercvleis manibus dant lidae pensa pvellae
> Imperivm dominae fert deus ille suae
> Sic etiam ingentes animos insana volvptas
> Et domito mollis pectore frangit amor.

49. *French Academie*, p. 481.

50. See Jayne, "Ficino's Commentary" p. 230.

51. As Sidney's narrator will comment later, it is "a barbarous opinion, to thinke with vice to do honour, or with activity in beastliness to show abundance of love" (p. 126). Lanham comments that Cleophila's role as hunter "is not altogether metaphorical" but, "a graphic illustration of precisely what the noble prince does throughout the first three books" (*Old Arcadia*, p. 208) and notes (p. 216) that Gynecia explicitly makes the con-

nection between wild ravenous beasts and passions. Lawry remarks (*Sidney's Two Arcadias*, p. 58) that "Musidorus has all but duplicated the bear."

52. *Nichomachean Ethics*, pp. 294–95, 1179a 22–32.

53. For a different interpretation of the lion-bear episode, see Isler, "The Allegory of the Hero and Sidney's Two *Arcadias*," *Studies in Philology* 65 (1968): 182–83.

54. *French Academie*, p. 97.

55. Lanham (*Old Arcadia*, 268–69) also calls attention to the dramatic ironies of the scene.

56. See 1 Cor. 1:27: "But God hathe chosen the foolish things of the worlde to confounde the wise, and God hathe chosen the weake things of the worlde, to confounde the mightie things."

57. Davis, "Actaeon in Arcadia," *Studies in English Literature* 2 (1962): 110.

58. *Ibid.*

59. See Seneca, epistle 24, *Epistulae Morales*, trans. R. M. Gummere, 3 vols. (London: William Heinemann, 1928–35), 1:164 ff., and epistle 77, 2:168 ff.

60. The narrator emphasizes the workings of providence in the death of the rebels: "such an unlooked-for end did the life of justice work for the mighty-minded wretches, by subjects to be executed that would have executed princes, and to suffer that without law which by law they deserved" (p. 317). In view of this design, the rebels' end becomes threateningly prophetic of the fate of the princes, now both "made prisoners for love as before they had been prisoners to love" (pp. 288–89), since they too have operated outside the law.

61. *Nicomachean Ethics*, p. 5, 1094b 8–10.

62. *The Ancient Theology: Studies in Christian Platonism from the Fifteenth to the Eighteenth Century* (London: Duckworth, 1972), p. 146.

63. Seneca, *Epistulae Morales*, 3:185.

64. Davis (*A Map of Arcadia*) sees the scene as based on the Christianized Macrobian scheme of the four levels of virtue (pp. 65–66), and as indicating that "It is *love* that draws a man from the life of action to the life of contemplation in Arcadia; and it is love, which operates with unusual freedom in the pastoral world, that makes a man know himself to such an extent that he wishes to contemplate pure divinity" (p. 67).

65. *Certaine Sermons*, sig. C3^r.

66. The princes may be lifting up their eyes to the heavens in this scene, but how much and how well they might see is open to question even from their Aristotelian starting point. As de Mornay suggests, "some in deede doo lift vp ye eye of their mynd aloft; but how farre or what see they? Surely (as saith Aristotle) euen as much as an Owle in the bright sunne" (*A Woorke*, sig. T$_6$). As the prayer immediately following suggests, much of their speculation is simply whistling in the dark, however valiant the posture may be.

67. For a sixteenth-century English audience, the only laws which "fold us within assured bounds" are God's commandments, and ignorance of them is no excuse. As William Perkins says, "even the Heathen which knew not God, are inexcusable, because they were bound to have knowne him. For Adam had the perfect knowledge of God imprinted in his nature, and lost the same through his owne default, for himselfe and his posteritie. And it is the commandement of God, whereunto every man is bound to performe obedience: that man should *know him*, that is, his will and word" (Thomas F. Merrill, ed., *William Perkins, . . . "A Discourse on Conscience" and "The Whole Treatise of Cases of Conscience"* [Nieuwkoop: B. De Graff, 1966], p. 93).

68. Davis, *A Map of Arcadia*, p. 79. As the "Sermon against Whoredom and Uncleanness" reminds us: "yet aboue other vices, the outragious seas of adulterie (or breaking of

wedlocke), whoredome, fornication and uncleannesse, haue not only burst in, but also ouerflowed almost the whole world, unto the great dishonour of GOD, the exceeding infamie of the name of Christ, the notable decay of true Religion, and the vtter destruction of the publike wealth, and so abundantly, that through the customable vse thereof, this vice is growne into such an height that in a manner among many it is counted no sinne at all, but rather a pastime, a dalliance, and but a touch of youth" (*Certaine Sermons*, sig. G₃ᵛ).

69. See *French Academie*, p. 489: "We put a difference between Loue and the Desire that is in Loue, because when we loue a thing, we desire therewithal the fruition and possession thereof. And if there be delay made, so we cannot enjoy the thing so soone as we would, this delay tormenteth vs by reason of the desire, which presseth and pricketh us forward to get the possession of it."

70. *Certaine Sermons*, sig. A₄ᵛ; see also Rom. 3:9–10.

71. Were Gynecia a Christian, rather than a devout pagan, her condition would be described in the homily "of the true, liuely, and Christian faith": "There is one fayth, which in Scripture is called a dead fayth, which bringeth foorth no good workes, but is idle, barren, and vnfruitfull. And this faith, by the holy Apostle St. James [James 2], is compared to the fayth of Diuels, which beleeve GOD to bee true and iust, and tremble for feare, yet they doe nothing well, but all euill. . . . This dead faith therefore is not the sure and substantiall faith, which saueth sinners. Another faith there is in scripture, which is not (as the foresaid faith) idle, vnfruitful, and dead, but worketh by charity. . . . Which as the other vaine faith is called a dead faith, so may this be called a quick or liuely faith. And this is not onely the common beleefe of the Articles of our faith, but it is also a true trust and confidence of the mercy of GOD through our Lord Jesus Christ, and a stedfast hope of all good things to be receiued at GODS hand: and that although wee, through infirmitie or temptation of our ghostly enimie, doe fall from him by sin, yet if we returne againe vnto him by true repentance, that he will forgiue, and forget our offenses for his Sonnes sake . . . and that in the meane time vntil that kindgome come, he will be our protectour and defendour in all perils and dangers, whatsoeuer do chance: and that though sometime he doeth send vs aduersitie, yet that euermore hee will be a louing Father vnto us, correcting us for our sinne, but now withdrawing his mercie finally from vs, if we wil trust in him . . ." (*Certaine Sermons*, sigs. B₅ʳ⁻ᵛ). As a pagan, her despair is perhaps more valid since she lacks a knowledge of the faith which could save her.

72. Cf. *Certaine Sermons*, sig. B₆, which reminds us we are to be moved "through continuall assistance of the Spirit of GOD, to serue and please him, to keep his fauer, to feare his displeasure, to continue his obedient children, shewing thankefulnesse againe by obseruing or keeping his commandments, and that freely, for true love chiefly, and not for dread of punishment."

73. See Christopher Marlowe, *Doctor Faustus*, ed. John D. Jump (Cambridge, Mass.: Harvard University Press, 1962), pp. 100–101 (scene 19, lines 146–63).

74. See Greville's *Chorus Sacerdotum* at the end of *Mustapha* (*Poems and Dramas*, 2:136–37:

> "Oh wearisome Condition of Humanity!
> "Borne vnder one Law, to another bound:
> "Vainely begot, and yet forbidden vanity,
> "Created sicke, commanded to be sound:
> What meaneth Nature by these diuerse Lawes?
> Passion and Reason, selfe-diuision cause . . .

In both cases, however, we must remember that the speakers are pagans and not confuse them with their makers.

75. See Rudenstine (*Sidney's Poetic Development*, pp. 149-71) for Sidney's concept of *energia*.

76. Besides the oft-repeated biblical injunctions and such repositories for common-places as the *French Academie*, pp. 221 ff., see the letters from Sir Henry Sidney and his wife to Philip in Malcolm W. Wallace, *A Life of Sir Philip Sidney* (Cambridge: Cambridge University Press, 1915).

77. Lanham (*Old Arcadia*, p. 206) notes the connection established by the descriptions of the dress of Pyrocles and Philoclea.

78. Pamela's resolution and her successful prosecution of it are somewhat in accord with the commonplaces of sixteenth-century thought; see *French Academie*, p. 485: "As at the entry of a forrest some one path may seeme to bee broad and beaten enough, yet afterward when a travailer is well entred into it, he beginneth to loose it by little and lit-tle, and being amazed, the farther he walketh on, the more he wandereth out of his way: euen so when as sensuality inuiteth us to the fruition of some object, we thinke it an easie matter to attaine therunto, and hope to get some great good thereby: but the further we enter into and follow that path, which our concupiscence doth shew unto vs, the worse we finde the way to bee and can see nothing before vs but a large fielde full of thornes and thistles, which not withstanding seeme for a time unto sore eyes to bee faire flowers of very goodly fruit. But the tasting of them alwaies bringeth with it a long and late re-pentance in the end. Now as the body of the sun when he first riseth may be easily looked vpon, but after being mounted vp certaine degrees in the Zodiake, dazeleth the eyes of them that behold it: so we may in some sort know our euill when it beginneth first; but when it hath gathered full force it wholly dimmeth our reason, and yeeldeth to no coun-saile. Therefore before any passion grow to be strong, we must labour, that whatsoeuer shall be rashly desired, may be suppressed by a prudent and advised discourse." Ironical-ly, only vanity supplies a sufficient spur to "prudent and advised" self-discourse in the *Old Arcadia*.

79. This, of course, is an opinion Milton shares with Sidney; see *Areopagitica* in *The Prose of John Milton*, ed. J. Max Patrick (Garden City: Anchor Books, 1967), pp. 287–88.

80. The traditional interpretation of Pygmalion as the example *par excellence* of the idolatrous lover controls our reading of the passage. See Marston's "Metamorphosis of Pigmalions Image," in *The Poems of John Marston*, ed. Arnold Davenport (Liverpool: Li-verpool University Press, 1961), stanza 14:

> Looke how the peeuish Papists crouch, and kneele
> To some dum Idoll with their offering.
> As if a senceles carued stone could feele
> The ardor of his bootles chattering,
>> So fond he was, and earnest in his sute
>> To his remorsles Image, dum and mute.

See also Golding's translation of Ovid's *Metamorphosis*, 10.261 ff., and the epistle to Leicester, p. 411 (ed. John Frederick Nims [New York: Macmillan, 1965]).

81. For a child's obligations to its parents, see *French Academie*, p. 222.

82. Although filial disobedience is something to which we have become accustomed, it was still capable of arousing many writers of the sixteenth century. La Primaudaye complains (*French Academie*, p. 222), for example, that the biblical injunction to "hon-or thy father and mother" is "very badly put to use at this day, when the sonne dothe not onely not honour his father, but euen dishonoureth him, and is ashamed of him. Hee is so farre from louing him, that hee rather hateth him, so farre from fearing him, that

contrariwise hee mocketh and contemneth him: and in stead of serving and obeying him, hee riseth up and conspireth against him." Pamela is ashamed of her father's retreat from duty in pastoral games, mocks his commands, and is even willing actively to conspire against him and disobey him by running away with Musidorus. That her flight from Arcadia is also a flight from her own responsibilities as heir to the dukedom does not occur to her, so strong is the power of her slighted pride.

Chapter 3

1. I have distinguished the four Eclogues that follow each of the first four books from the individual poems they contain through the use of capital and lower-case "e," respectively.

2. I quote the Eclogues from Robertson's text throughout; I have, however, supplied the poem number (italicized to avoid confusion with page number) from Ringler's edition of the poems for convenience of cross-referencing.

3. *Elizabethan Poetry* (Cambridge, Mass.: Harvard University Press, 1952), p. 52. David Kalstone's assessment is basically similar: "To the eclogues, Sidney allots a special function. . . . The action of the romance halts; the Arcadian shepherds, who play virtually no role in the prose narrative, gather together; and the reader is suddenly transported into that timeless world in which sports, dancing, and poetic performance are the only valuable kinds of action" (*Sidney's Poetry: Contexts and Interpretations* [Cambridge, Mass.: Harvard University Press, 1965], p. 60). See also William Ringler, ed., *The Poems of Sir Philip Sidney* (Oxford: Clarendon Press, 1964), p. xxxvii; Richard Lanham, *The Old Arcadia*, in Walter R. Davis and Lanham, *Sidney's Arcadia* (New Haven: Yale University Press, 1965), pp. 210–36; Elizabeth Dipple, "The 'Fore Conceit' of Sidney's Eclogues," *Literary Monographs* 1 (1967): 17–18; and Jon S. Lawry, *Sidney's Two Arcadias* (Ithaca: Cornell University Press, 1972), pp. 24, 60, and passim; all discuss the structure of the Eclogues and their relationship or lack of one with the prose. For discussions of the formal aspects of Sidney's Arcadian poetry, see Robert L. Montgomery, Jr., *Symmetry and Sense: The Poetry of Sir Philip Sidney* (Austin: University of Texas Press, 1961); Kalstone; and Neil L. Rudenstine, *Sidney's Poetic Development* (Cambridge, Mass.: Harvard University Press, 1967).

4. Edward William Tayler, *Nature and Art in Renaissance Literature* (New York: Columbia University Press, 1964), p. 7.

5. "The Renaissance Perversion of Pastoral," *Journal of the History of Ideas* 22 (1961): 255.

6. Smith, *Elizabethan Poetry*, p. 17.

7. *Ibid.*, p. 17.

8. *Spenser, Marvell, and Renaissance Pastoral* (Cambridge, Mass.: Harvard University Press, 1970), p. 2.

9. See *ibid.*, pp. 2–3, and Heninger, "Renaissance Perversion," pp. 257–59. The poems of Mantuan and Aeneas Sylvius, besides being used in the schools, were also translated, in whole or in part, by Alexander Barclay (1515; reprint ed. 1548 [?]) and George Turbervile (1567). Cullen's discussion (pp. 1–26) provides a balanced view of the competing perspectives offered by the two kinds of pastoral he distinguishes.

10. *The Arte of English Poesie*, in G. Gregory Smith, ed., *Elizabethan Critical Essays*, 2 vols. (London: Oxford University Press, 1904), 2:40. In E. K.'s "Epistle" to Gabriel Harvey prefacing Spenser's *Shepheardes Calendar*, the two traditions, merged, flow naturally together as an inevitable development: Theocritus, Virgil, Mantuan, Petrarch, Boccace, Marot, Sannazaro, "diuers other excellent both Italian and French Poetes," and

Spenser form the line of the AEglogue. See *Spenser's Minor Poems*, ed. Ernest de Selincourt (1910; reprint ed. Oxford: Clarendon Press, 1970), p. 7. Sidney, in rebuking Spenser's "old rustic language," gives a shorter version of this chain: "Theocritus in Greek, Virgil in Latin . . . Sannazzaro in Italian" (*MP*, 112).

11. William Webbe, *A Discourse of English Poetrie*, in Smith, *Elizabethan Critical Essays*, 1:264.

12. *Minor Poems*, p. 8: "Now as touching the generall dryft and purpose of his AEglogues, I mind not to say much, him selfe labouring to conceale it. Onely this appeareth, that his vnstayed yougth had long wandred in the common Labyrinth of Loue, in which time to mitigate and allay the heate of his passion, or els to warne (as he sayth) the young shepheards .s. his equalls and companions of his vnfortunate folly, he compiled these xij. AEglogues." As Spenser's final epilogue insists, however, love is only the occasion for the *Calender*, whose purposes are far broader than a simple condemnation of unstayed youth's wanderings in the labyrinth of love.

13. I do not wish to give the impression that I believe that the pastoral genre underwent a total transformation in the 1590s. While there may have been some attempts to write exclusively "Arcadian" pastorals in the decades after Sidney wrote, as late as 1619 Drayton could still write "To the reader of his pastorals" that "The subject of Pastorals, as the Language of it ought to be poor, silly, & of the coursest Woofe in appearance. Nevertheless, the most High, and most Noble Matters of the World may bee shaddowed in them, and for certaine sometimes are" (*The Works of Michael Drayton*, ed. J. William Hebel, 5 vols. [1932; reprint ed., Oxford: Basil Blackwell, 1961], 2:517).

14. For a corresponding visual equivalent to Sidney's diminution of mundane success *sub specie aeternitatis*, see Albrecht Altdorfer's "Battle of Issus" (painted ca. 1529 for Duke Wilhelm IV of Bavaria; for a color reproduction see Wolf-Dieter Dube, ed. *Great Museums of the World: Pinakotek, Munich* [New York: Newsweek, 1969], p. 63), where the minute figures of the human participants are dwarfed by the spectacular light-effects in the heavens and the scroll which hangs in midair memorializing the event.

15. Frederick Morgan Padelford, *Select Translations from Scaliger's Poetics* (New York: Henry Holt, 1905), p. 64. Lawry (*Sidney's Two Arcadias*, p. 60) also suggests that the Eclogues "constitute a vast responsive chorus, moving parallel with the narrative."

16. Dipple, "Harmony and Pastoral in the *Old Arcadia*," *ELH* 35 (1968): 315. John Hollander, *The Untuning of the Sky* (Princeton: Princeton University Press, 1961), pp. 24–25, provides a convenient presentation of this idea: "The primary division of music into parts for the Middle Ages, the one that remained canonical even well into the sixteenth century, was the tripartite arrangement of Boethius. . . . According to this scheme, the three branches of music . . . were *musica mundana, musica humana,* and *musica instrumentalis*. By *musica mundana* Boethius meant the harmony of the universe. . . . By human music he denoted 'that which unites the incorporeal activity of the reason with the body. . . .' This paralleled the cosmic music in causing 'a blending of the body's elements.' . . . Boethius' third category, *musica instrumentalis*, involves simply what we would call music itself." See also pp. 41–43 for a sixteenth-century application of the theory to politics.

17. *The Book named The Governor*, ed. S. E. Lehmberg (London: J. M. Dent, 1962), pp. 71–72. See also Sears Jayne, "Ficino's Commentary on Plato's *Symposium*," *University of Missouri Studies* 19 (1944): 231: "[T]he whole soul [of man in his corrupted state] is filled with discord and dissonance; therefore the first need is for the poetic madness, which through musical tones arouses what is sleeping, through harmonic sweetness calms what is in turmoil, and finally, through the blending of different things, quells dissonant discord and tempers the various parts of the soul."

18. See Jayne, p. 238, where Ficino invokes "the Holy Spirit, that Divine Love," to "enlighten our own minds and kindle our wills so that we may love Him," and p. 150, where he explains that "everything is preserved by a unity of its parts. . . . But the unity of parts is brought about by mutual love. This may be seen in the humours of our bodies, and in the elements of the world, by the harmony of which . . . both our bodies and the world hold together. . . . Hence Orpheus says, 'Thou alone, O Love, of all these things holdest the reins.'"

19. *French Academie*, p. 482.

20. *The Governor* p. 79.

21. *Ibid.*

22. *Ibid.*, pp. 79–80.

23. *Ibid.*, pp. 80–81.

24. John M. Major, "Elyot's Moralization of the Dance," *Studies in the Renaissance* 5 (1958): 29, cites Lucian's *The Dance*: "how much culture and instruction . . . [dancing] gives; how it imparts harmony into the souls of its beholders, exercising them in what is fair to see, entertaining them with what is good to hear, and displaying to them joint beauty of soul and body."

25. The only exception is Musidorus' debate with Lalus, where the prince is told he must follow the shepherds' customs or leave.

26. "The 'Fore Conceit' of Sidney's Eclogues," p. 16.

27. The identification of Pan with Christ is a tempting one for the reader of pastoral poetry to make; see E. K.'s gloss on Spenser's use of Pan in the April eclogue of *The Shepheardes Calender*: "And by that name, oftymes . . . be noted kings and mighty Potentates: And in some place Christ himselfe, who is the verye Pan and god of Shepheardes" (de Selincourt, *Spenser's Minor Poems*, p. 43). See also Patricia Merivale, *Pan the Goat-God* (Cambridge, Mass.: Harvard University Press, 1969), pp. 14–28.

28. See Jayne, "Ficino's Commentary," p. 215: "So in the present we shall love God in everything, so that in the future we may love everything in God, for so we set out from there as living beings to see God and everything in Him, and whoever in the present will devote himself with love completely to God, will finally recover himself in God."

29. See de Mornay, *A Woorke*, sigs. O6^v–O7: "God by his will and power hath created all powers, and disposes all willes. . . . God then (say I) guydeth all things to the performance of his will, the mouable by their mouings, and the unmouable by their stedfastnesse; the things indewed with sense, by their appetites, and the reasonable things by their willes; the naturall things, by their thraldome, and the things that haue will, by their freedome: And the freer that they be, the greater is his glorie, as in deede it is a more commendable thing to cause libertie to yeeld freely to obedience by gentle handling, than to hale it by force and compulsion as it were tyed in a chayne. If the willes of all men were caried by Gods will without hauing their owne peculiar mouings: the power of God could not shine forth in them so much as it doth now, when all willes inforce themselues seuerally against his will, and yet neuertheless euen in following their owne sway, doe finde themselues led (they wote not how) whether soeuer it pleaseth him. . . . But albeit that God do leade foorth and guyde the one will as well as the other; yet notwithstanding right happie is that will which indeuereth to followe, and vnhappie is that which must be haled and dragged." In *The Faerie Queene* (3.3.1–2), Spenser suggests that God's "gentle handling" of man's will is through "Loue," the "sacred fire . . . ykindled first above . . . / And thence poured into men" and that love is the means by which "The fatall purpose of diuine foresight" is effected. He is, of course, careful to distinguish "the destined descents" of this love from the love the nobles of the *Old Arcadia* have embraced, "which doth base affections moue / In brutish minds, and filthy lust inflame."

All quotations from *The Faerie Queene* are from the edition of J. C. Smith, 2 vols. (1909; reprint ed., Oxford: Clarendon Press, 1968), and will be indicated by book, canto, and stanza numbers.

30. Thomas Rogers, *The Catholic Doctrine of the Church of England: An Exposition of the Thirty-Nine Articles*, ed. J. J. S. Perowne (1579, rev. ed. 1607; reprint ed., Cambridge: Cambridge University Press, 1854), p. 96.

31. Jayne, "Ficino's Commentary," p. 230; see also Sidney's description of Musidorus on seeing Pamela, p. 41.

32. Jayne, p. 144.

33. From what follows, Sidney makes it clear that Dicus does not hate all love, but only the cupidinous love which destroys its victims and drives them away from God. It is thus not unfitting that we find him in the Third Eclogues singing an epithalamion at the marriage of Lalus and Kala.

34. For the "blind Cupid," see Erwin Panofsky, *Studies in Iconology* (New York: Harper & Row, 1962), pp. 95–128. Edgar Wind, *Pagan Mysteries in the Renaissance* (1958; reprint ed., Harmondsworth: Penguin Books, 1967), pp. 53–80, argues that "the supreme form of Neoplatonic love is blind" for Ficino, Pico, Lorenzo de' Medici, and Giordano Bruno (p. 53); if Sidney were aware of this transformation of love's traditionally negative blindness into something positive, it might have contributed to his ironic transformation. If Love were indeed blind "because he is above the intellect" (Wind, p. 54), Dicus' new iconography becomes an even more pointed rejection of the Neoplatonic claims for love. For another interesting transformation of Cupid, see fig. 3, Jacopo Pontormo's "St. Michael and St. John the Evangelist," painted ca. 1518–19 for the chapel of the Madonna in the Church of St. Michael in Pontorme and now in the Museo della Collegiata, Empoli. Saint Michael stands with his foot on a little bat-winged Cupid who is thus equated with the Saint's traditional iconographic attribute, Satan. For color reproduction and monochrome details, see Luciano Berti, *Pontormo* (Florence: Edizioni d'Arte Il Fiorino, 1964), fig. 6 and plates 60 and 61.

35. According to Ringler (*Poems*, p. 387), Dicus' genealogy of Cupid is Sidney's own invention. It is fitting that this Cupid be covered with eyes, since "Love's desire most rules the eyes" (*OA, 8.*41). Thomas P. Roche has suggested to me that by making Argus Cupid's father, Sidney is warning against allowing the watchfulness that should keep us from loving cupidinously to be perverted into the means by which we succumb to lust.

36. Sidney, following the ancient custom of pastoral poets, has enlisted himself among his cast of characters. In creating an alter ego for himself, moreover, he has ironically portrayed himself as "sick among the rest," just as in *The Defence of Poesie* he sought to "show some one or two spots of the common infection grown among the most part of writers" (*MP*, 119).

37. *Certaine Sermons*, sig. Xx3^v.

38. *French Academie*, p. 441.

39. *Ibid.*, p. 6; see also Sidney, *Prose Works*, 3:193–94; *A Woorke*, sigs. **6–6^v: "To be short, the marke that our faith looketh at, is the Author of Nature & principle of all principles. . . . And he is also the verie reason and truth it selfe. All other reason then, & all other truth dependeth upon him, & relieth upon him, neither is there, or can there be any reason or truth but in him."

40. See Sidney, *Prose Works*, 3:196–97; *A Woorke*, sigs. **7^v–8: "But wee say that Reason and Nature haue such a Rule, and that that is the common way, and yet notwithstanding, that this thing or that thing is done or spoken beyond reason and beyond nature. I say then that the worke and word of God are an extraordinarie case, & that foras-

much as they are of God, it behoueth us to beleeue them; and to beleeue is to submit our reason and vnderstanding to him. And so it is a making of reason seruant to faith by reason, and a making of reason to stoope to the hignesse of faith: and not an abasing of faith to the measure of reason."

41. It seems clear that Sidney would agree with Spenser's assessment of human nature and human capabilities:

> What man is he, that boasts of fleshly might,
> And vaine assurance of mortality,
> Which all so soone, as it doth come to fight,
> Against spirituall foes, yeelds by and by,
> Or from the field, most cowardly doth fly?
> Ne let the man ascribe it to his skill,
> That thorough grace hath gained victory.
> If any strength we haue, it is to ill,
> But all the good is Gods, both power and eke will.
>
> [*The Faerie Queene*, 1.10.1]

42. It is also, as Ringler points out (*Poems*, p. 399), a parody of Virgil's Third Eclogue.

43. See *The Histories of Gargantua and Pantagruel*, trans. J. M. Cohen (Harmondsworth: Penguin Books, 1955), p. 46 (1.3). Ringler (*Poems*, p. 402) classes the riddles as "of the simple nursery variety. The answer to Sidney's first may be a man on crutches wearing spectacles; I give up on the second." Lawry (*Sidney's Two Arcadias*, p. 91) also recognizes the Rabelaisan nature of the riddles.

44. "Boulon," as Ringler notes (*Poems*, p. 382), is Greek for "Counsel."

45. Ironically, his complaints themselves are the means by which the "high justice" proves their unjustness, since as a result of his earlier recitation of woes, Plangus, "though unwittingly, had now done his errand" (p. 71).

46. See Sidney, *Prose Works*, 3:254; *A Woorke*, sig. C$_8$^{v}: "Therefore it behoveth vs to conceiue [God] a most single singlenesse, which neuerthelesse in one perfection comprehendeth al perfections, as the roote of them; which seemeth a thing contrarie to mans understanding: that is to wit, that his Providence is no more Providence than Justice, nor his Justice more Justice than mercie."

47. Ringler (*Poems*, p. 401) suggests Prov. 3:11-12 and Wisd. of Sol. 3:4-6 as "proof texts for the sweet uses of adversity."

48. See "Congruity," *OED*, sb. 1 and 2, and "grammar," *OED*, sb. 6a.

49. See Henry Bullinger, *The Decades of Henry Bullinger*, trans. H. I. (1577), ed. Thomas Harding, The Parker Society, 4 vols. (Cambridge: Cambridge University Press, 1849-52), 3:381: "For when the Lord calleth man and he resisteth, making himself unworthy of the kingdom of heaven, he doth then permit him unto himself: that is, he leaveth man unto his own corrupt nature, according unto which the heart of man is stony, which is mollified and made tractable by the only grace of God: therefore the withdrawing of God's grace is the hardening of man's heart; and when we are left unto ourselves, then are we hardened."

50. Interestingly enough, Pyrocles and Musidorus condemn the Palestinian lady for allowing the Arabian prince to seduce her upon promise of marriage: "they knew she should have done well to have been sure of the church before he had been sure of the bed" (p. 154).

51. Sidney has prepared us to see the "death" which is the "all" of their love as figurative, rather than the hyperbolic death of Petrarchan love convention, through Gynecia's

dream: "The dream was this: it seemed unto her to be in a place full of thorns which so molested her as she could neither abide standing still nor tread safely going forward. In this case she thought Cleophila, being upon a fair hill, delightful to the eye and easy in appearance, called her thither; but thither with much anguish being come, Cleophila was vanished, and she found nothing but a dead body which seeming at the first with a strange smell so to infect her as she was ready to die like wise, within a while the dead body (she thought) took her in his arms and said: 'Gynecia, here is thy only rest.' With that she awaked, crying very loud, 'Cleophila, Cleophila!'" (p. 117).

52. For fuller discussions of Protestant attitudes about marriage, see William and Malleville Haller, "The Puritan Art of Love," *Huntington Library Quarterly* 5 (1942): 235–72, and Charles and Katherine George, *The Protestant Mind of the English Reformation* (Princeton: Princeton University Press, 1961), pp. 257–305.

53. *Liturgies and Occasional Forms of Prayer set forth in the Reign of Queen Elizabeth*, ed. William Keatinge Clay (Cambridge: Cambridge University Press, 1847), p. 217.

54. *French Academie*, p. 199.

55. *Ibid.*, p. 197.

56. See *ibid.*, p. 202: "The marriage of loue, is that which is betweene an honest man and a vertuous woman, linked together by God. . . . It may bee called a charitable conjunction, vnity, and society of them that are good, being made by grace, peace and concord." See also Henry Smith, *A Preparative to Marriage* (1591), in *The Works of Henry Smith*, ed. Thomas Smith, 2 vols. (Edinburgh: James Nichol, 1866), 1:8: "Houses and riches are given of God, and all things else, and yet he saith, houses and riches are given of parents, but a good wife is given of God, as though a good wife were such a gift as we should account comes from God alone, and accept it as if he should send us a present from heaven, with this name written on it, *the gift of God*." For figurative meanings of marriage, see Smith, *ibid.*, 1:24; John Ayre, ed. *The Sermons of Edwin Sandys* (Cambridge: Cambridge University Press, 1842), p. 317; and Andrew D. Weiner, "'Multiformitie Uniforme': *A Midsummer Night's Dream*," *ELH* 38 (1971): 345–47. It is perhaps worth noting that the *Old Arcadia's* two explicit references to "church" both occur in the context of marriage, either achieved (Kala and Lalus, p. 244) or lacking (the lady of Palestina, p. 154).

57. In the "Homilie of the state of Matrimonie," the bride and groom are reminded of those who do not share their inclination to marriage: "you, as all other which enter the state, must acknowledge this benefit of GOD, with pure and thankfull minds, for that he hath so ruled your hearts, that yee follow not the example of the wicked world" (*Certaine Sermons*, sig. Vu$_6$).

58. Various critics have tried to mine a consistent political philosophy from the poem, including William Dinsmore Briggs ("Political Ideas in Sidney's *Arcadia*," *Studies in Philology* 28 [1931]: 137–61), Irving Ribner ("Sir Philip Sidney on Civil Insurrection," *Journal of the History of Ideas* 13 [1952]: 257–65), and E. W. Talbert (*The Problem of Order* [Chapel Hill: University of North Carolina Press, 1962], pp. 97 ff.). Ringler (*Poems*, p. 412) justifies its inclusion in the Third Eclogues on the grounds that "it discusses the best kind of government for a state, just as the other marriage poems in the Third Eclogues discuss the best kind of government for the family." Lawry (*Sidney's Two Arcadias*, p. 114) sees the poem "as a painful alteration of the Genesis story" guaranteeing "arrogant passions in the governor and slavery for the governed."

59. *Commentary on the Book of the Prophet Isaiah*, trans. William Pringle, 4 vols. (Edinburgh: Calvin Translation Society, 1850–53), 1:383.

60. See *Ovid's Metamorphoses*, trans. Arthur Golding, ed. John Frederick Nims (New York: Macmillan, 1965), p. 418 (from the epistle to Leicester).

61. *Commentary on Isaiah*, 1.383.

62. *Ibid.*, 1:385.

63. *Ibid.*

64. See *Certaine Sermons*, sig. Vu$_6$r.

65. Geron's conception of marriage is neatly contained in his tribute to his wife: "We bear our double yoke with such consent, / There never passed foul word" (*OA* 67.92, p. 262). As Henry Smith wrote in *A Preparative to Marriage* (1591), "A wife is called a yoke-fellow . . . to shew that she should help her husband to bear his yoke, that is, his grief must be her grief, and whether it be the yoke of poverty, or the yoke of envy, or the yoke of sickness, or the yoke of imprisonment, she must submit her neck to bear it patiently with him, or else she is not his yoke-fellow, but his yoke." (*Works*, 1:28).

66. See p. 245: "as for Strephon and Klaius, they had lost their mistress, which put them into such extreme sorrows as they could scarcely abide the light of day, much less the eyes of men."

67. Richard Hamilton Greene, "Alan of Lille's *De Planctu Naturae*," *Speculum* 31 (1956): 668, cites Bernard Silverstris, *Comm . . . in Eneid*, p. 9 for a further conflation of the celestial Venus with Astrea and "natural justice," "Legitiman Venerem dicimus esse mundianuum musicam i.e. aequalem mundanorum proportionem, quam alii Astream, alii naturalem iustitiam vocat. Haec enim est in elementis, in sideribus, in temporibus, in animantibus." Dipple, "The 'Fore Conceit' of Sidney's Eclogues," pp. 42–43, follows Strephon and Klaius in their evaluation of Urania, and adds some new identifications: "The traditional Urania, identified with knowledge and the Holy Ghost, is the chief of the Muses and comprises in her own voice that of all her sisters: hence she controls all music. Because of her divine nature she is, by extension, a symbol of divinity and a partaker of it. In Sidney's context, she is tuner of the Spheres and the sustaining power of harmony . . . she functions for the *Old Arcadia* as a real symbol of the loss suffered by the error of one man which then contaminates the world and draws all men into its sphere."

68. 2 Tim. 4:8. Were their obedience to God not to Urania, they might be able to use their present adversity more profitably by turning away from her commandments to his. As de Mornay puts it, "Unto the ordinarie complaynt concerning the prosperitie of the wicked, and the adversitie of the vertuous; he [Plotinus] answereth that the prosperitie of the wicked is but as a Stageplay, and the aduersitie of the godly is as a gaining of exercise, wherein they bee tyed to a streight dyet, that they may win the prize for which they contend" (*A Woorke*, sig. O$_3$).

69. The situation in the revised *Arcadia* is far less clear. Even there, however, despite the far different tone of the opening and despite the far more positive effects love has had upon Strephon and Klaius, Kalendar (the renamed Kerxenus) gently ridicules their pretensions to be the servants and devotees of a divinity.

70. Sidney's use of the elegaic mode to show us the folly of overzealous mourning is consistent with his discussion of the genre in *The Defence of Poesie*, where he does not limit the use of elegy to "compassionate accompanying just causes of lamentations," but also stresses its capabilities for "rightly painting out how weak be the passions of woefulness" and bewailing "the weakness of mankind and the wretchedness of the world" (*MP*, 95).

71. *Poetry and Dogma* (New Brunswick, N.J.: Rutgers University Press, 1954), p. 10.

Chapter 4

1. *The Poems of Sir Walter Ralegh*, ed. Agnes Latham (Cambridge, Mass.: Harvard University Press, 1962), pp. 51–52.

2. See Elizabeth Dipple, "Harmony and Pastoral in the *Old Arcadia*," *ELH* 35 (1968): 310. By the late 1560s there was more or less common agreement with J. C. Scaliger's formulation of the structure necessary for comedies, a formulation that had grown out of the earlier work of Melanchthon, Wagnerius, and Willichius. According to Scaliger, *Poetice libri septem* (1:5), cited in T. W. Baldwin, *Shakspere's Five-Act Structure* (Urbana: University of Illinois Press, 1947), p. 295, there were four necessary parts in a comedy: "The legitimate parts are those without which the play can not exist, and which must be included. The protasis is [the part] in which the sum of the business is propounded and narrated without a declaration of the conclusion, for so it is more cunning, holding the mind of the auditor suspended in expectation. For if the conclusion were told beforehand, it would become rather pointless. Although you should get the whole business from the argument; yet the information is so expeditious and short, that it does not so much satiate the mind as fire it. The epitasis, in which turbulences are either begun or made tense. Catastasis is the full vigor and crisis of the play, in which the intrigue is embroiled in that tempest of chance, into which it has been drawn. Many do not mention this part, but it is necessary. The catastrophe, the conversion of the debated trouble into unexpected tranquility. To these parts is added, as we said, the prologue which some attribute to the Latins only." These parts were normally distributed so that the first two acts contained the protasis, the third began the epitasis, the fourth presented the catastasis, and the fifth act presented the catastrophe. For discussions of the development of the five-act comic structure in the sixteenth century, see Baldwin, pp. 160–311, and Marvin T. Herrick, *Comic Theory in the Sixteenth Century* (Urbana: University of Illinois Press, 1964), pp. 73–122. For an application of the comic theory to the *Old Arcadia*, see Robert W. Parker, "Terentian Structure and Sidney's Original *Arcadia*," *English Literary Renaissance* 2 (1972): 61–78.

3. See my "Structure and 'Fore Conceit' in *Astrophil and Stella*," *Texas Studies in Language and Literature* 16 (1974): 1–25.

4. See *A Midsummer Night's Dream*, ed. Madeleine Doran (Baltimore: Penguin 1959), 5.1.208–12. See also my discussion in "'Multiformite Uniforme': *A Midsummer Night's Dream*," *ELH* 38 (1971): 329–35.

5. This formulation perhaps holds only for a writer as explicit as Sidney is about what he is saying; for a poet such as Spenser who is far less explicit, the emotional component takes on an even greater importance in the reader's attempts to reach the fore conceit. For a discussion of book 1 of *The Faerie Queene* that suggests that the pattern of responses *is* the fore conceit of the poem, see my "'Fierce warres and faithfull loues': Rhetorical Pattern as Structure in Book I of *The Faerie Queene*," *Huntington Library Quarterly* 37 (1973): 33–57.

6. Musidorus is not given the chance to actually state these arguments to Pyrocles. Although he had "framed" them in his mind, Pyrocles' change of subject forces him to respond differently in an attempt to put the physical beauties of Arcadia into proper perspective (see p. 16).

7. See St. Augustine, *The City of God*, trans. John Healey (1610), ed. R. V. G. Tasker, 2 vols. (London: Dent, 1945), 2:265: "For though there be a seeming of these things [i.e., that the soul rules the body and reason the passions], yet if the soul and the reason serve not God, as He has taught them how to serve Him, they can never have true dominion over the body, nor over the passions. . . . No, those things which she seems to

account virtues, and thereby to sway her affections, if they be not all referred unto God, are indeed rather vices than virtues. For although some hold them to be real virtues, when they are desired only for their own account, and nothing else; yet even so they incur vainglory, and so lose their true goodness." For Musidorus' remark about the transforming power of love according to the nature of the thing loved, see St. Augustine, *Enchiridion*, cap. 117. For a commentary on the fundamental importance of this concept everywhere in Augustine's works, see Etienne Gilson, *The Christian Philosophy of St. Augustine*, trans. L. E. M. Lynch (1960; reprint ed., New York: Random House, 1967), pp. 135 ff.

8. See *A Woorke*, sigs. Z_7^v–Z_8: "Some tell us that Religion is nothing els but charitie; that is to say, the performing of a mannes duetie towards his neighbour: and those men would tell vs if they durst, that Religion is but an instrument of ciuil gouernment. . . . But the godly or Religious man vttereth his Religion, (that is to say, that God hath touched him truely in his hart,) in that he performeth all the dewties of vnfeyned freendship and godly affection towards his neybor who is the Image of God. Charitie therefore is nothing els but a rebounding of godlynes or of the loue of God, backe vnto our neybour, or a reflecion or sign vpon this Image. . . . Now this charitie which they speake of, is but a linking of Man vnto Man. It is not that which maketh a man happie, neither doth the fault which hath destroyed vs all, consist in want of charitie, (I meane that Charitie which they pretend); but in rebelling against God. Therefore it booteth vs not to be at one with our neybour, except we be at one with God."

9. As de Mornay observes in his chapter on God's governance of "the World and all things therein by his Prouidence," "Thou complaynest of the wilde Beastes; And who hath made them wild but thy selfe? Nay rather, thou shouldest wonder at the prouidence of God, who . . . hath printed such an awe of man in them, that they hurt him not vnlesse they bee assaulted or pinched with extreme hunger. And therein what do they more than man would do in like extremitie?" (*A Woorke*, sigs. M^v–M_2).

10. Robert Kimbrough, *Sir Philip Sidney* (New York: Twayne Publishers, 1971), identifies the *Old Arcadia*'s audience as Sidney's sister and her "fair-lady friends" (p. 69) and the narrator as Sidney (p. 71). Kimbrough sees the tone of book 1 as defined by "the voice of the delightfully ironic, highly urbane narrator" (p. 69); like him, his audience knows that "the princes were being 'bad boys'" but sees that shared knowledge merely as "the simple key to the sophisticated, courtly fun" (p. 76). Given the development and use of the concept of "womanish" in the first book, the "ladies" spoken to, without regard to sex, might be more usefully considered to be anyone "romantic" enough to believe such of his observations as, e.g., his comments on the reactions of Gynecia and Pamela to Pyrocles' dumbstruck admiration of Philoclea and his subsequent praise of her: "You ladies know best whether sometimes you feel impression of that passion; for my part, I would hardly think that the affection of a mother and the noble mind of Pamela could be overthrown with so base a thing as envy is" (*Old Arcadia*, p. 39). The irony is clear since the narrator, who knows in advance the things we shall "after hear" (p. 48), knows that Gynecia will quickly "fall" into a "jealous envy against her daughter Philoclea" (p. 49) and will soon vow that unless Pyrocles rejects Philoclea and turns to herself instead, "I will end my miseries with a notable example of revenge; and that accursed cradle of mine shall feel the smart of my wound, thou of thy tyranny, and lastly, I confess, myself of my own work!" (p. 184). This is hardly "sophisticated, courtly fun" and the narrator's irony is teasing (Kimbrough, p. 72) only to those who do not recognize the murderous envy and the poisonous anguish love can and will cause.

11. See Calvin, *Institutes*, 1.57.

12. Baldwin, *Shakspere's Five-Act Structure*, p. 295.

13. *French Academie*, p. 448.

14. "Lastly she [Cleophila] determined thus: that there was no way but to yield to the violence of their [hers and Gynecia's] desires, since striving did the more chafe them; and that following their own current, at length of itself it would bring her to the other side of her burning desires" (p. 185).

15. See *French Academie*, pp. 493–94: "Now desire & joy, they commonly accompany the perishing goods of the body. For they are of that nature, that they inflame the soule with an insatiable lust, insomuch that the obtaining of any one thing is the beginning of a new and vehement desire of having another. And the enjoying of them besotteth the spirite with a sugred poison of fained delight and pleasure, vnder the yoke of which it easily suffereth it selfe to bee ouercome, to be bound and gouerned."

16. See Thomas F. Merrill, ed., *William Perkins, . . . "A Discourse on Conscience" and "The Whole Treatise of Cases of Conscience"* (Nieuwkoop: B. DeGraff, 1966), p. 127: "The forme and life of an oath . . . [is] that in things doubtfull, we call God as a witnesse of truth, and a just revenger of the contrairie." Perkins adds that although "an oath by false gods . . . be not a lawful oath, yet it is in value and effect an oath. For though that thing be a false god indeed, by which it is taken, yet it is the true God in the opinion of him that sweareth" (p. 128).

17. We must note the narrator's description of Pyrocles rushing in to excuse himself for the wrongs he has overheard Philoclea complaining he has done her, "blown up and down with as many contrary passions as Aeolus sent out winds upon the Trojan relics guided upon the sea by the valiant Aeneas" (p. 262). The narrator's simile here serves two functions. By its oblique comparison of Pyrocles' state not with Aeneas but with Aeolus' winds, the figure provides a standard of heroic behavior, *pius* Aeneas, who put the gods' commands above love, against which Pyrocles' actions can be measured. It also reminds us of the fate of Troy and of the consequences of the Trojans' approval of Paris' rape of Helen (which both Pyrocles and Musidorus seem in their different ways to be emulating) and prepares us to see the narrator pointing in his description of Pyrocles' seduction of Philoclea to Chaucer's description of Troilus' "seduction" of Criseyde (see *Troilus and Criseyde*, 3:940–1365). Like Troilus, Pyrocles faints at Philoclea's bedside. Like Criseyde, Philoclea finally arouses him with kisses. Like Chaucer's ill-fated lovers, they immediately forgive each other and go to bed. The analogy lends an air of black comedy to the whole affair, which the narrator reinforces by having a 146-line *blazon* of Philoclea flit through Pyrocles' mind at the moment of consummation.

18. J. C. A. Rathmell, ed., *The Psalms of Sir Philip Sidney and the Countess of Pembroke* (New York: Anchor Books, 1963), has suggested that Sidney (and his sister) "took their bearings . . . from the work of . . . Sir Thomas Wyatt and Clement Marot" (p. xvi), and it is Wyatt's versions of the penitential Psalms (especially Psalms 6, 32, and 38) which offer the same kind of distinctly Protestant insistence on man's inability to repent without God's grace to first pardon him; see Psalm 51:

> But off thi selff, o god, this operation
> It must proced, by purging me from blood,
> Among the just that I may have relation

(*Collected Poems of Sir Thomas Wyatt*, ed. Kenneth Muir and Patricia Thomson [Liverpool: Liverpool University Press, 1969], p. 115, poem 108, lines 490–92).

19. Baldwin, *Shakspere's Five-Act Structure*, p. 295.

20. The narrator's comment on the slaughter of the Phagonians by Philanax's men again points to the role providence is playing: "such an unlooked-for end did the life of

justice work for the mighty-minded wretches, by subjects to be executed that would have executed princes, and to suffer that without law which by law they had deserved" (p. 317).

21. George Gifford, *A Treatise of True Fortitude* (London: 1594), sigs. A_5-A_5^v.

22. *Ibid.*, sig. A_5^v.

23. Davis (*A Map of Arcadia*, pp. 154-55, in Walter R. Davis and Richard A. Lanham, *Sidney's Arcadia* [New Haven: Yale University Press, 1965]) sees the episode as a fictionalization of Platonic political theory, with Timantus being Plato's Tymocratic man.

24. Philanax presents his plan for making Euarchus "Protector" of Arcadia to the assembled nobles as "a blessed mean the heavens have sent unto you, if you list embrace it" (p. 353), emphasizing that Euarchus has been "bestowed" upon Arcadia by the "heavenly powers" (pp. 353-54). Later, the narrator too characterizes the situation by which Euarchus must judge his son and nephew all unknown to each other as the "extraordinary . . . course . . . the order of the heavens [had] produced at this time" (p. 376) and later still emphasizes that "the strange and secret working of justice had brought [Euarchus] to be the judge" (p. 385) over Pyrocles and Musidorus. Clearly we are to accept Euarchus' arrival as providential and his judgments as definitive within the limitations he himself has put upon himself.

25. The idea, of course, is one of the essential commonplaces of Reformed Protestantism. As Calvin writes in his *Catchisme or maner to teache children the Christian religion* [London, 1563], sig. C_6^r), "all suche workes as wee doe of our selues, by oure nature, are utterlye corrupte: whereof it followeth necessarilye, that they cannot please GOD, but rather doe prouoke his wrathe, and he condempneth them every one." It is also embodied in article 13 of the Thirty-Nine Articles of the Church of England.

26. De Mornay, again, is a useful guide to commonplace Protestant attitudes towards such subjects as reason and virtue: "Seeing that reason is so much more excellent than passion or affection . . . whence commeth this infection in vs, that . . . putteth reason in subiection to affection, & to the impressions which affection yeeldeth, contrary to the order which is observed in all the world beside? For what els is this Intemperance of ours, but reason (such as it now remayneth) imprinted with lust and concupiscence? And what els is anger, but reason atteynted with choler, and so foorth of the rest? . . . Soothly then, the motions of anger and lust against reason in man, are not naturall nor originall, that is to say, they proceede not of his first creation; but are come in afterward by corruption" (*A Woorke*, sigs. T_4^v-T_5). "Al the vertues which we make account of, as Hardiness, Wisdome, Justice, and Temperance, are nothing if they be not referred vnto God, and used in respect of him" (*A Woorke*, sig. Y_8^v). Thus we can see, for instance, that since for Pamela her virtues are "used" simply to define her essence, her "desire of honor" signified in her impresa ("a perfect white lamb" [p. 37]) is "but a self loue" (*A Woorke*, sig. Z_8).

27. *Sermon of Maister Iohn Caluin, on the historie of Melchisedech*, trans. T. Stocker (London: 1592), pp. 245, 277. See also the conclusion to Theodore Beza's *Tragedie of Abrahams Sacrifice*, trans. Arthur Golding (1577), ed. Malcolm W. Wallace (Toronto: University of Toronto Press, 1906), pp. 62-63.

> The faithful hart so stedfastly is grownde
> As it abideth euer unconfounded
> Contrariwise the man that trusteth too
> His own self wit, thereafter for to doe,
> And standeth in his own conceyt shall find,
> The more he goes, the more he comes behind.
> And euery litle puffe and sudein blast

From his right course shal quite & cleane him cast
Agein, his owne self willed nature will
Him ouerthrowe and all his dooings spill.

In the preface, Beza finds Abraham to be one of the three persons in the Old Testament "in whome . . . the Lorde meant to set forth his greatest wonders . . . in the lives of whome if men would nowe a dayes looke uppon them selues, they should knowe them selues better then they doe" (p. 4). To Beza, the story of Abraham is one of a "multitude of examples, whereof euen the least are able enough, not only to encourage and harten the weakest & fayntest harted in the worlde, but also to make them inuincible" (pp. 3-4).

28. Calvin, *The catechisme*, sig. C_7^v.

29. See Elizabeth Dipple, "'Unjust Justice' in the *Old Arcadia*," *Studies in English Literature* 10 (1970): 83-101; Jon S. Lawry, *Sidney's Two Arcadias* (Ithaca: Cornell University Press, 1972), pp. 142-53; and Margaret D. Dana, "The Providential Plot of the *Old Arcadia*," *Studies in English Literature* 17 (1977): 39-57.

30. See Fulke Greville, *Caelica* 98, *Poems and Dramas*, 1:143.

31. As de Mornay rather laconically comments (sig. L^v), "the very repentance of the best men, is but a sorynesse that they cannot be sorry enough."

32. Lawry (*Sidney's Two Arcadias*) sees Basilius as "not quite Immanuel" (p. 120) and the Fourth Eclogues as intimating "an Easter" (p. 129) in their "somber Good Friday lamentations" (p. 136) since "a resurrection is to be treated no more lightly than a true judgment" (p. 136). As Dipple has remarked, however, the "verbal and rhythmic biblical overtones" are undercut by "the narrator's parenthetical insertions of the imperfections of the world and very strongly through the ironic distance between Christ's office as prince of peace and Basilius' inept, escape-ridden rule" ("'Unjust Justice' in the *Old Arcadia*," p. 89).

33. See de Mornay, *A Woorke*, sig. T_7: "O how many doe we esteeme to be good men, whom we should see to be wicked men if their thoughts lay open, or if we had eyes to see into them? O what sort of wild beasts should wee see harbered in a mans heart as in a Forest? . . . Moreouer, what is all our inforcing of our selues to vanquish our vices, but a laboring to out ronne our owne shadowe, which (doe what we can) will alwayes accompany vs whether wee will or no?"

34. *Ibid*., sig. U_2^v.

35. "'Unjust Justice' in the *Old Arcadia*," p. 85. Dana ("Providential Plot," p. 57) sees "the flexible narrator himself, whose mellow tact and ironic compassion for all the characters finally seem the most humane response to life's riddling text," as a model "for our emulation."

36. De Mornay, *A Woorke*, sig. Y^v.

37. *Ibid*., sig. O_8^v.

INDEX

INDEX